MAYBE YOU'RE THE PROBLEM

It's Time To Take Control Of Your Life

JACK WILLIAMSON

DISCLAIMERS

MAYBE YOU'RE THE PROBLEM. Copyright © 2024 by Jack Williamson. All Rights Reserved. Printed in the United Kingdom. No part of this book may be used or reproduced in any manner whatsoever without written permission except in the case of brief quotations embodied in academic work, critical articles and reviews.

Every effort has been made by the author and publishing house to ensure that the information contained in this book was correct as of press time. The author and publishing house hereby disclaim and do not assume liability for any injury, loss, damage, or disruption caused by errors or omissions, regardless of whether any error or omissions result from negligence, accident, or any other cause. Readers are encouraged to verify any information contained in this book prior to taking any action on the information.

The advice, tools and techniques shared in this book are there to help support and enhance your mental health, and not intended to replace professional help should it be required. If you require professional help around your own mental health please contact your GP, or if in crisis please contact the Samaritans on 116 123

MAYBE YOU'RE THE PROBLEM may be purchased for education, business, sales or promotional use. For information, please email hello@musicandyou.co.uk

Published by Jackal Entertainment

First Edition

Edited by Emily Lewis

Cover Design by Two Suns

ISBN 9798876757661

USEFUL DISCLAIMERS

To protect the identities of client names in the stories throughout this book, pseudonyms have been used instead. Any similarities to anyone you may know or think of, are merely coincidental.

This book is written through the lens of a white male, who identifies as gay, living in a western world society. Whilst every effort has been made to be as objective as possible with the stories, teachings and action points, to help support you, some may not align with your own unique set of circumstances. As such, I ask you to approach these areas with curiosity, rather than furiosity, to understand what comes up for you.

Not everything that is written in this book will apply to you. Take what works for you, leave what doesn't.

If you need additional help or support in any of the areas listed in this book, feel free to reach out to me on enquiries@jackwilliamson.co.uk

I would like to dedicate this book to the friends, family members, partners, colleagues, acquaintances, therapists, and adversaries, who, over the years, have helped me realise, knowingly or unknowingly, when I am the problem.

CONTENTS

Chapter 1 - Anti-Hero - Page 1

Chapter 2 - Wave After Wave - Page 11

Chapter 3 - Don't Leave Me This Way - Page 29

Chapter 4 - When Two Tribes Go To War - Page 59

Chapter 5 - Mad World - Page 85

Chapter 6 - Talking About My Generation - Page 111

Chapter 7 - Please Have Mercy On Me - Page 133

Chapter 8 - Man In The Mirror - Page 151

Chapter 9 - Who Do You Think You Are - Page 169

Chapter 10 - I Don't Want To Miss A Thing - Page 197

Chapter 11 - When It All Falls Apart - Page 225

Chapter 12 - All I Do Is Win - Page 247

Chapter 13 - A Hero Lies In You - Page 273

Chapter 14 - Can I Get An Encore - Page 279

Acknowledgements - Page 291

Notes - Page 295

1
ANTI-HERO
Introduction

The sunlight beamed through a crack in the curtain, shining directly onto Taylor's face, abruptly awaking Taylor from a deep sleep. The frustration at the audacity of the sun to shine turned into rage, when, reaching for her phone, she realised that the alarm that she never set had failed to go off. Rushing to get herself together for work, Taylor berated her roommate Selena for being in the bathroom when she needed to use it. Struggling to find clean clothes in her messy room, Taylor managed to pull an outfit together, spray dry shampoo in her hair, and leave for the station.

Walking at a pace that resembled that of a power walker, Taylor entered the train station, barging past an elderly lady, knocking her to the floor. With the train about to depart, Taylor ignored calls from others about what she'd just done to catch the train. Just as she made it down the final stair, one of her heels gave way, sending her stumbling forward onto her knees as the train doors shut and set off without her. As she cursed at her heel and the fact that she would now be forced to wait another 20 minutes for the next train, the old woman, whom she had knocked over in her rush, confronted her. Looking for an apology, the elderly lady was fooled if she thought

Taylor would engage in such a conversation. For Taylor believed it was the woman that caused her to miss the train and break her heel. Waving her shoe to the woman, Taylor exclaimed, 'Look what you made me do!'

On the train and with only standing room available, Taylor, who was accustomed to using her looks and charm to secure a seat, had no choice but to stand like a sardine in a tin can, on what she referred to as the peasant wagon, for the entire journey. Pulling into her stop, with a ten-minute walk to the office ahead of her, the heavens above opened up. Already late for work, when the Uber app showed no available rides, Taylor was left with no choice but to dash to work. Arriving looking like a drowned, harassed rat, Taylor was greeted at the door by one of her clients, completely forgetting that she had an important meeting to renew their contract. Taylor signalled the receptionist to show her client and team to the meeting room, then rushed to the restroom to fix her appearance. Reaching into her bag to pull out a hairbrush, Taylor realised that in the rush to get to the office, she'd forgotten her laptop, which had all the slides on for the meeting.

Her horror turned to despair when she realised the presentation hadn't saved to the cloud, and that she could not access the slides remotely. Unable to fall back on her looks, owing to her dishevelled appearance, Taylor created an elaborate story to gain sympathy from her client. Explaining how she'd been the victim of an attack and her laptop stolen, Taylor placed her shoe complete with broken heel on the table for dramatic effect. The performance, worthy of an Oscar nomination, garnered the response Taylor hoped for, allowed her a brief reprise of what had been the morning from hell.

Whilst waiting for her lunch order, Taylor complained to her colleague Blake about her morning and the elaborate story that she'd told her client to save face. Unbeknownst to Taylor, her boss, who she was due to have a performance review with after lunch, was listening in. As Taylor's order was served, she started behaving aggressively and rudely towards the server. She caused an almighty scene when the salad included an ingredient she had asked to be removed. Her boss, who was watching this all unfold, was still within earshot.

As the afternoon brightened, so did Taylor's mood, although it wasn't to last for very long. Taylor, expecting her performance review to go glowingly, was brought down to earth with a thud, when her boss, who sat alongside a HR representative, called her out on her behaviour, her time-keeping, lying to her client to save face, and the reputational damage that her behaviour caused the company. Caught like a deer in the headlights, Taylor didn't know what to do, and when she heard the words, 'Owing to this ongoing pattern of behaviour, we've been left with no choice but to terminate your employment', Taylor's world fell apart. The day from hell had taken an unexpected turn for the worse. Taylor's colleagues had seen this train-wreck coming a mile off. For they knew Taylor was trouble from the moment she walked in, and were not surprised as she was escorted to her desk to collect her belongings.

Karma, it seemed, was playing a cruel game on Taylor. But the trouble of the day was only starting to unfold. Looking for comfort and reassurance, Taylor reached for her phone to dial Joe, her latest in a long list of partners, to complain about what had happened. With the phone going unanswered, Taylor frantically typed on her phone for Joe to call her as she made her way to the station and back home. A further three attempts to call Joe went unanswered, and as she stepped into her house, Joe's name appeared on the phone. Turning combative, Taylor expressed her disdain for being kept waiting for over an hour to hear from Joe when she was going through a crisis. Joe, unable to get a word in edgeways, finally pipped up, saying 'Enough Taylor, enough! I'm sick and tired of constantly being pulled into all of your drama. I'm done. With you. With this relationship.' And with that, Joe hung up the phone before Taylor could respond. Taylor made several further unsuccessful attempts to reach Joe through calls and texts. Feeling abandoned, she resorted to drinking wine to ease her pain.

Taylor's heart jumped when her phone pinged, hoping it was Joe. But it sank when she saw it was Selena asking about where she was, for Sophie's birthday dinner had already started. In drowning her sorrows, Taylor had completely lost track of time and forgot about her Sophie's birthday dinner. Thankfully, the celebration was at a restaurant near her home, and she could quickly pull herself together to join the squad. Arriving like a hurricane, Taylor quickly swept the group up in all her drama that had unfolded. Without breathing for air, she recalled the morning's commute, the firing from her job and that Joe had dumped her. Finally, pausing, she said to the group, 'Can you believe it?'

Looking at each other, the group all wondered whether now was the time to confront what they'd all been thinking for a while. Taking a breath, Abigail decided it was and said, 'Taylor, have you ever taken a moment to stop and think maybe you're the problem?' Taken aback, Taylor went into defensive mode. 'How can you say that? I thought you were my friend.' Before Abigail could respond, Martha, the comedian of the group, jumped in. 'Taylor, hold on. I've just received a call from NASA, and they've just confirmed to me that the world does still in fact revolve around the sun and not you.' The group all laughed as Taylor's rage bubbled up inside of her. Taylor had experienced the day from hell, but she didn't expect to not receive support from her friends. With the silence, deafening, Selena attempted to address what was unfolding. 'Taylor, we all love you, but tonight we're here to celebrate Sophie's birthday, and since you arrived, it's become all about you. Obviously, we're sorry to hear that you lost your job, and that Joe broke up with you. We are. But at some point, you've got to stop and realise that actually, maybe it isn't everyone else. You are the common theme tying all these issues together, and as Abigail said, maybe you're the problem.'

Taylor, feeling overcome with emotion, declared, 'I've come to you all looking for support on what has been the worst day of my life. Instead, all I'm met with is confrontation.' With that, Taylor grabbed her coat and bag, storming out of the restaurant, and made her way home. Collapsing into her bed, Taylor wondered how the day had continued to go from bad to worse. The question that her friends posed to her 'Maybe you're the problem?' kept circling round and round in her head. Was it true she thought? Taylor tried to dismiss the thought, but it continued to grow louder and louder, until she finally came to the realisation that actually, maybe I'm the problem.

In our lives, we've all come across someone like Taylor. Whether that's in our family, our friendship group, our work environment, someone we've watched on TV or on the big screen, or even in the mirror. We've all encountered someone who seeks to place blame and responsibility at everyone else's feet except their own. Irrespective of whether the other person is to blame in the situation. By shifting blame away from themselves and onto something or someone else, it allows the individual to move away from responsibility and accountability of their actions or interactions in the situations they find themselves in.

The issue with blame is that it leads to a giving away of one's power, placing it in the hands of another. It renders the individual powerless in the situation to the forces that come into play. Now whilst this may be true during the formative years of your life, when you depend on another human to meet your primary needs, as you grow through life, gaining a sense of agency and autonomy over your choices and decisions, so too comes a level of accountability and responsibility for those actions. Responsibility and accountability for oneself give us the power to change our lives.

Yet we cannot change. We cannot move away from what we are until we are willing and able to accept who we are. In Taylor's case, she was oblivious to many of the issues that plagued her drama filled day. Not until her friends took a collective stand and pointed out that maybe she was the problem. Much of who we are and how we operate forms during our early infancy, and dependent on your religious belief, most of us don't have a choice of what we are born into. We become shaped by all that is around us. Our primary caregivers, extended family, the environment, the generation we are born into, the cultural climate and more all play a role in how we grow into the adults we are in the here and now.

These all form and shape our values, our beliefs, and our behaviours, that can serve or hinder us, in any environment, in reaction to any stimuli. They shape the stories we tell ourselves and inform our decisions and pathways through life. Yet, in many a case, these values and beliefs often go unexamined. Until a situation, or as I more commonly refer to it, a shituation occurs, and it forces us to confront our values, beliefs and behaviours.

In the world we find ourselves in today, technology is a cornerstone in almost every aspect of our lives. Even with this book, there's a high probability you're reading it on a kindle or digital device or listening to the audiobook via your phone. With our digital devices, we periodically get notifications, alerting us to software updates that need to be installed. This is to help fix glitches or bugs in the system, allowing them to run and operate more smoothly and effectively. Some happen automatically, and some are optional. If, in the optional case, we opt out of the software, our devices run slower and, sometimes, programmes or applications, are unable to run at all. The same is true of our brains. Unfortunately, unlike tech companies and service providers, we don't have the luxury of push notifications being sent to us to address issues we experience because of our thinking.

The human body is a miraculous thing. The ability for it to regenerate itself is remarkable. Our skin cells and guts regenerate in months, our liver in three years, and our skeleton in ten years. Almost every part of our body can regenerate itself, except for a few areas. The main two areas being the neural pathways in our brain, and the retinas in our eyes. Our eyes are one of the main stimuli we use to see the world and take in information. Our brain is the fundamental processing unit of how we interpret that information.

If we rely on our eyes and our brain to operate as they are, with no input to challenge our perception and thought processes, then we will seek what we always sought, think what we always thought and feel what we always felt. Sometimes, this may serve us well, but in other cases, this may hinder us. For we don't see the world as it is, but as we are. When we face something that makes us uncomfortable, that challenges our thoughts, feelings, or our behaviours, if we are not ready, able, or even willing to confront it, we may become truth-adjacent to the reality we find ourselves in. To be truth-adjacent (a term I've invented), is to tell ourselves and others' stories that make things more comfortable. More palatable for us and/or others to digest than facing or confronting the truth.

Every day, every human in some way, shape or form, is truth-adjacent in their interactions with others. It can be through interactions with others saying 'I'm okay' when, really, you're not. Another way it can show up is in messages sent to people after they call saying 'Sorry I missed your call', when actually you didn't want to speak to them. According to research carried out by Psychology Today (2011), we hear between 10-15 lies a day and tell roughly 1-2 lies a day ourselves. However, this research doesn't account for the lies we tell ourselves. The lies that may cause us less discomfort in the short term but end up harming us more in the long-term. For there is comfort in the familiarity, and as humans we are wired to fear the unknown. This causes many of us to stay in uncomfortable situations and thinking patterns much longer than needed. The pain of staying the same feels less painful than the pain of changing who we are.

Not everyone is like this. Some embrace change with a curiosity. They realise we don't go through life; we grow through life. Given that change is the only constant, they would rather deal with a problem or change when it shows up than when it blows up. Think about yourself for a moment. Do you go to the dentist for regular check-ups, or only when there is a problem with your teeth? If you own a car, do you check your car tyres at regular intervals to ensure they have the right air pressure and no holes? Or do you rely on them to just work, in the hope they won't blow? The way we do something is the way we do everything. Examining your approach to these examples can give insight into how you may interact with your thoughts, values, and beliefs that shape your behaviours and outlook on life.

Adverse childhood experiences can shape who we become, ranging from financial difficulties and abuse in its various forms, to growing up in a broken home. In adulthood, there are also experiences that can influence our thoughts, values, and beliefs. As I write this introduction, the perpetual war has broken out between Israel and Palestine, this time brought on by an attack carried out by terrorist organisation Hamas. Not all things that happen in our lives are within our control, and the purpose of this book is not to blame or to shame. In a lot of cases, what happened to you was not your fault. What you do with what happened, however, is your responsibility.

This book explores many of the areas of your life that have shaped the person you've become today to help you gain a better understanding of yourself. To confront and challenge your thoughts, your values, your beliefs. Exploring how they serve you and how, in many cases, they may hinder you. And then to provide an opportunity to unlock and discover what makes you who you are, and to take accountability and responsibility for the changes that can be made, enabling you to live a more fulfilling life.

At various moments in your life, you may have asked yourself questions, including, why do I keep attracting the wrong partner in a relationship? Why do I always fall into the same role in friendship groups? Why do I never feel like I am enough? In the pages of this book, I hope to answer many of the questions you may have. To help address the problems you are facing in your life. Maybe you're the problem, maybe you're not. One thing is for certain, though. If you are willing and able to look within, you will find more than likely that you are the solution to most, if not all, of your problems. I often find in my private practice when clients initially come to me, they come to deal with people that won't come to therapy. They want to find ways they can change the other person/s, to live a happier and healthier life. I understand their frustrations. I hear their challenges and concerns. But I have to remind them I can only work with the person in the room. Not those outside of it. For someone forced against their will, is of the same behaviour still. An individual has to want to change and be willing to change, otherwise it becomes a futile exercise.

I am often drawn to a quote accredited to Persian poet and scholar Rumi from the thirteenth century, who said 'Yesterday I was clever, so I wanted to change the world. Today I am wise, so I am changing myself.' If you are ready, willing, and able to embark on a journey through the pages of this book. To become wiser about yourself and create the changes you need to live a more fulfilling life, then let's begin by understanding the brain more in chapter two.

2

WAVE AFTER WAVE

Brainwaves

The audience grew silent as the studio lights dimmed and a spotlight illuminated the two people on stage, building anticipation of what was to come. The woman sitting on stage had let curiosity get the better of her, when she volunteered to be hypnotised under the direction of infamous hypnotist Paul McKenna. Yet with the moment drawing closer and feeling the eyes of the studio audience watching her, nerves set in, and the woman became fidgety.

Reassured by Paul McKenna that everything would be okay and that she was safe in his hands, the woman agreed to move forward. Over the next several minutes, McKenna guided the woman into a state of hypnosis. Directing the woman to close her eyes, McKenna asked the lady to count backwards in her head from 300, joining in from time to time in a calm and directive tone. 'You are sinking deeper and deeper as you count back further from 300,' McKenna said to the woman, and as she continued to count backwards, her physical appearance changing ever so slightly. As she relaxed more into the chair, and with his trained eye, McKenna could tell she had fallen into a state of hypnosis.

Under a state of hypnosis, McKenna addressed the woman and said, 'I want you to forget the number seven'. Turning his attention to the audience both in the studio and watching on the TV, he shared, 'Now what's the point of this? If we can forget something that's as fundamental as a number that we use every day, then we can forget to overeat or we can forget to feel bad about ourselves.' Returning his attention to the woman, McKenna brought her out of the state of hypnosis to showcase both to the audience and the woman the results of the hypnosis.

'How many fingers do you have on your hands?' McKenna asked the woman. Acknowledging she had ten fingers (for those saying we have eight fingers and two thumbs right now, you are correct, but most would say ten, so let's go along with the woman's answer) McKenna asked her to count each finger out loud. 'One, two, three, four, five, six, eight, nine, ten, eleven', the woman shared. Audible gasps came from the audience. McKenna, engaging with the woman, said, 'That doesn't seem to be right. Let's try that again'. Once more, the woman counted each finger out loud, and once again upon reaching the sixth finger, she then proceeded to say eight, nine, ten, eleven.

There was conviction rather than confusion in the woman's face that what she was saying was correct, as the audience watched on. Some were in shock, others in disbelief, and a few were sceptical at what they were witnessing, believing this was all pre-planned. For how on earth had this woman forgotten something as fundamental as the number seven? Re-inducing the woman back into a state of hypnosis, McKenna then told the woman, 'The number seven is back in your memory once again' before counting to ten to bring her out of a state of hypnosis. Asking 'How many days of the week are there?' the woman confidently shared 'Seven.'

Hypnosis over the years and decades has divided audiences and people around the world. Whilst many believe in the power of hypnosis and its abilities, many also view it sceptically akin to that of tarot card reading or astrology. What often hasn't helped the case for hypnosis has been the gimmicky tricks that hypnotists sometimes use. Making people bark like a dog when they hear a certain word or carry out a certain behaviour when they hear a certain sound. Whilst these tricks make for good entertainment value, they don't help to showcase the deeper value hypnosis offers in speaking to the unconscious and reprogramming it to change or evolve behaviours or patterns of relating.

UNDERSTANDING HOW YOUR BRAIN WORKS

To understand how hypnosis works, let's get a better understanding of the brain and how it began calibrating in your formative years. In both psychology and psychotherapy, the first seven years of a human's life are viewed as the most important years of our development as humans. It is during this period that our brain downloads much of its programming, shaping our values, beliefs and behaviours that begin to form our identity. As adults, our brain has many wave lengths with which we operate on, akin to the different frequencies we can switch between to listen to different stations on the radio. Tune into one frequency and we can hear a soothing, relaxing song playing on that radio station. Tune into another frequency, and we can hear an energized song pumping out from that radio station.

These different brainwaves induce varied states within us as adults, but during childhood, we don't have access to all the different brainwaves. The brain gradually develops during this time, bringing forth new brainwaves at different age stages, enhancing both thinking and processing capabilities. There are five different brain waves that our brains operate on, as highlighted in Figure 2.1.

Wave	Age	Frequency	Type
Delta	0-2	0.5 – 4 Hz	Relaxation, restorative healing sleep and memory consolidation.
Theta	2-7	4 – 8 Hz	Creativity, intuition, daydreaming and fantasising. Repository for memories, emotions and sensations.
Alpha	7-12	8 – 12 Hz	Enhanced ability to absorb information, increase in creativity and calm feelings.
Beta	12+	12 – 35 Hz	Consciousness, logical thought processes analysis, organisation skills, productivity.
Gamma	3+	35 HZ +	States of peak performance.

Figure 2.1 - Brain Wave Frequencies

A study by Carole Peterson (2021) reveals humans can recall things from around the age of two and a half years old, where a pool of potential memories can be accessed, as opposed to a fixed beginning memory. If you take a moment to think of your earliest memory, it isn't unsurprising to think that your memory can only go back to when you were a toddler. Don't be disheartened if your earliest memories are from the ages of four and upwards. This is quite common too. The Delta brain wave is the first brain wave that occurs when we are born, causing us to be in a dreamlike state. Have you ever noticed how babies are typically relaxed during this period, except when they cry to express hunger or discomfort? As they observe the world around them, their eyesight continues to develop. Shapes, voices, and sounds form and, as time passes, they distinguish one from another.

At around the age of two years old, a fresh wave, Theta, is accessible to us. When in a Theta brain wave state, we live in the realm of imagination and daydreaming. This explains why at that age, we are so good at creating whole worlds with items such as cardboard boxes. Spend time with any child in that age range, and you'll often be amazed at the worlds they come up with. At this stage of brain development, with the other brainwaves yet to be tapped into, we are unable to show any signs of critical or rational thinking. This, in part, proves problematic. During the period between the ages of two to seven years old, we are continuously downloading information from our primary caregivers, siblings (if we have them), extended family, teachers and friends at nursery and primary school (kindergarten and elementary school for our North American readers) and the surrounding environments, straight to the theta brainwave, without the ability to decipher whether the information we are taking in is grounded in fact. Whether it is a subjective truth or belief or an objective one. As a result, our brain is left to believe everything it receives as true, thus shaping our values, beliefs, and behaviours, without the ability to analyse whether the information is serving or hindering us.

Whilst a lot of the information our brains take in during that period may be true, and continue to serve us well throughout our lives, there will be information we downloaded in those formative years that hinder us in our current and future lives, unless examined. Many times, we were led to think there is a right way and a wrong way to do things. Things that we should or shouldn't do or believe in. That there is only one way to do things, when in reality there can often be more than one way in which to do something. Yet our brain hadn't developed enough at that point in our lives to know any different. The brain became programmed to follow what it has downloaded. This is not a critique of the people that were in your lives during those formative years or the environment you grew up in. The majority were doing the best they could with the resources they had. For they themselves were shaped by their primary caregivers. Inheriting many of their values, beliefs and behaviours which have been passed on to you. Also, as we will explore in Chapter 5, Mad World, the environment at the time will have reflected the rules within which that society lived by.

Up to the age of seven, your brain is literally being taught what to think, not how to think. This is a criticism often expressed in the antiquated way many educational establishments around the world have taught children; though in many cases this is now evolving, with teachers given more freedom in how the curriculum is now delivered. You will have learned rules to live by 'Do as I say' and 'Don't disagree with me.' Or ways to behave in certain environments or situations to get your needs met 'Children should be seen and not heard', are three rules I often hear from clients. These rules that shape the way we live can often be at odds with our natural disposition as children. As discussed further in the next chapter, we are dependent at this age to get our needs met. Therefore, we adapt our behaviour to ensure we are included and not excluded from people or environments, to make sure we stay connected and to reaffirm the two core beliefs we want reaffirmed; I am loveable, and I am enough. If we don't adapt our behaviour, we can start feeling that we are unlovable or that we are not enough.

During this period of our lives until the age of seven, all the information that we download whilst in the Theta wave frequency from the people around us and our environment goes directly into our subconscious, forming the core foundations of our operating system. The subconscious brain is an extremely powerful operating system, with the ability to process up to eleven million pieces of information per second compared to forty pieces of information per second in your conscious mind. The subconscious mind also reacts up to five hundred times faster than the conscious mind. This can be extremely beneficial in certain settings, like if you are under attack, for you don't have time to think, you just need to react. However, it can be a real hindrance in other settings if your subconscious mind is in the driver's seat. In several areas, your operating system will have outdated values, beliefs, or behaviours from your childhood that you once took as fact, which, are at odds with what you face in the here and now and can have a profound impact on your interpersonal relationships (relationships with others), as well as the relationship with yourself.

Before we delve deeper into this, let's pick up on the remaining three brain waves that form our ways of thinking. As we continue to grow through life, from the ages of seven to twelve, the Alpha brain wave emerges. It is during this period that our ability to take on information increases. Our ability to question certain truths comes into form (think about the age you discovered the truth about Santa, the Tooth Fairy and the Easter Bunny). Your creativity continues to flourish during this period as you operate from the addition of the Alpha brain wave, and you have a stronger ability to induce a sense of calm within yourself.

The next brain wave to develop in the human brain is the Beta brain wave. The Beta brain wave comes into being around twelve years old. It is during this period in our lives that we become fully aware of and responsive to our surroundings. Logical thought processes and analysis are now developing to a point where we can come to our own informed rational and logical decisions. Organisation skills develop to a point where in many areas such as commuting to school, completing homework, and arranging and meeting up with friends, is carried out without the requirement or input of our primary caregivers. Productivity levels of what we can do in a given period have continued to increase.

This period coincides with what leading psychologist Erik Erikson (1998) identified in his psychosocial stages of development, as identity vs role confusion. Between the age of twelve to nineteen, Erikson identified this time as a period in which an individual needs to develop a sense of self and personal identity, separate to that of their primary caregivers. We embark on an outward exploration to find where we belong in the world. Turning to friends to explore common interests. Listening to music to find lyrics that resonate with how we feel. Relating with influential figures who symbolise what we stand for. We are drawn to characters in TV series and films whose journeys they embark on and obstacles they overcome are similar to what we are experiencing or going through. We follow sports teams to feel a sense of connection and belonging.

During this period, we look to others to reaffirm that each part of our identity is accepted by others. If we find during that exploration that they accept it in some way, shape, or form, we embed it into our identity. If a part of our identity is not accepted or perceived to be accepted by others, which could include being bullied for your taste in music/your sexuality, or in more recent times not gaining enough likes on a social media post, then one is more likely to reject that part of oneself and adopt a different part in order to fit in, to remain connected and to belong.

SELF REFLECTION TIME

Take a moment to turn your attention inwards.

- What was your favourite song during adolescence?
- What was it about the lyrics of that song that spoke to you?
- Alongside this, think of your favourite TV series at that point in your life or film. What made you resonate with the storylines and/or characters?
- What does this tell you about yourself and the problems you faced?

You can often tell a lot about a person and who they are, or at least who they were during that period of their life, by asking these two questions.

These continued adaptations we make during the period of twelve to nineteen are downloaded into our subconscious to form our identity in the here and now. Whilst in the Beta wave frequency, we have the ability to think more rationally and logically about whether something is true and aligns with our authentic self, but we are not immune to over-riding our rationality and logic. This is because, as humans, we all crave connection and to belong to something or someone. From time to time, we may relinquish a part of ourselves in order to get our needs met. But this time we are consciously doing so, whereas during the ages of two to seven when we are in the Theta brain wave, we don't have the skill set to evaluate whether what we are taking on is true to ourselves.

The final brainwave is the Gamma brainwave. The Gamma brainwave is most commonly associated with peak performance. Neuroscientists believe Gamma waves handle our learning, memory, information processing and cognitive function, and can link information from all parts of the brain, akin to a cross-referencing system. It is the wave that an individual can find themselves in when they are in peak mental and physical performance and referred to by many as the brainwave state of 'being in the zone'. Gamma brainwaves are higher in elite athletes, top musicians, and high achievers than in average individuals. Individuals who can regularly tap into the Gamma brainwave are also exceptionally intelligent, compassionate, and have a strong sense of self-control. Their IQ scores are correspondingly high, with many finding themselves in the Mensa International high-IQ society. It's worth noting here that the Gamma wave state isn't necessarily the brainwave state we should all be aiming for. Each brainwave has its own function and purpose that proves useful to us. The number of Gamma waves produced by each individual varies, with lower amounts of Gamma brainwave activity being linked to learning difficulties, poor memory, and impaired mental processing.

As adult individuals, we are most commonly found in the Beta brainwave frequency during our waking hours. During our sleeping/resting hours, we will oscillate between Alpha, Theta, and Delta brainwaves. When our brain relaxes, we tap into both the Alpha and Theta brainwaves. As our bodies relax, we move more into the Theta brainwave before moving into the Delta brainwave as we enter a deep sleep state. When we are dreaming, as our subconscious brain processes our thoughts, we oscillate between the Theta, Beta, and Gamma brainwave ranges.

One of the most famous quotes used in the Bible (Luke 32:34) is during Jesus's crucifixion. 'Forgive them, father. For they know not what they do.' Whilst this quote is in the context of the killing of Jesus, it can equally apply to how our brain operates from time to time. There will be moments in our lives where we go into autopilot, reverting to what we know, based on our programming. If triggered or activated, we are likely to move from the rational and logical brainwave Beta to our more primitive Theta brainwave, where problematic beliefs that are stored in our subconscious are available to us, potentially causing us to act out.

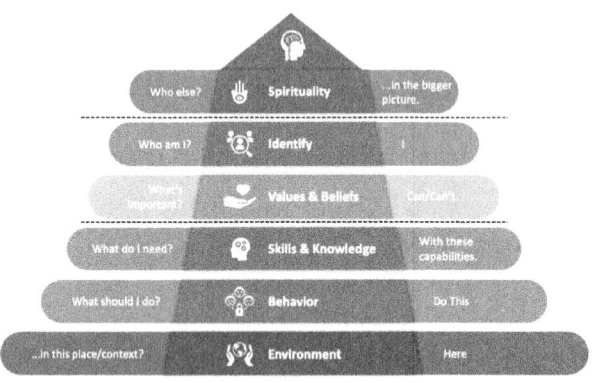

Figure 2.2 - Neurological Levels

In the 1990s, Robert Dilts, a renowned neuro-linguistic programmer (NLP), introduced the neurological levels a human operates on. As seen in Figure 2.2, there are six neurological levels. They range from Spirituality down through Identity, Values & Beliefs, Skills & Knowledge, Behaviour and, finally, Environment. These different neurological levels shape who each of us are as individuals. For our values and beliefs govern our thoughts. Our thoughts then shape our behaviours, and our behaviours, both those that serve us and those that hinder us, can be activated in different environments. Let's look at an example of where someone's rational and logical Beta brainwave shuts down, and how that can cause problems.

JUST HAVE A LITTLE PATIENCE

A group of friends were all heading off on holiday together, with the taxi making the rounds to pick people up before heading to the airport. In great spirits, the group was waiting for the last friend, Adam, to join them. As time continued to pass, Mike became more and more irate. Eventually, after several minutes, Adam emerged to cheers from many of the group, whilst Mike remained irate. Not a mile had passed, when Adam realised he'd left his passport on the side, and needed the taxi to turn around quickly so he could grab it. Whilst most of the group laughed off the friend's behaviour to their disorganised way of being, Mike lost his mind. As the taxi returned to the house; Mike laid into Adam. 'Why the hell do you never have your life together? First you run late, keeping us all waiting. And now we have to change our plans, because you can't remember something as important as your passport!' Mike's tirade continued until Adam went into his house to retrieve his passport. They sat the rest of the journey to the airport in complete silence, awkwardness permeating through the taxi, completely changing the mood of the group.

Once the group arrived at the airport and checked in, they made their way to the departure gate. By this point, Mike had calmed down, and when approached by Stuart about the situation, Mike shared, 'I don't know what came over me.' Not wanting to ruin the holiday that the group was about to embark upon, Stuart mediated between Adam and Mike to resolve the issue. Mike was raised in a military family, with an importance placed on punctuality and being organised. During childhood, he was reprimanded for running late and holding the family up. Mike would also misplace things, as children often do, but there was no space for this in his father's eyes, and so Mike learnt you must be on time and organised to avoid punishment. This belief carried forward into adulthood, and in his outlook on others. Mike acknowledged that his family belief around punctuality and organisation, whilst having merit, didn't stop the group from being able to check in or make the holiday. Stuart posed maybe Mike could relax a little with his punctuality, whilst also acknowledging that Adam could make more of an effort in realising that his time keeping skills impact others in the group.

At the tail end of the holiday, as the group made their way to the airport, Mike acknowledged that something had shifted in him. Having taken a more relaxed approach to timekeeping, Mike found he enjoyed himself more. Feeling less pressure in social settings to be on time for everything meant Mike could adjust his own schedule if he wanted to. He could spend more time doing something he was enjoying and move or reschedule plans to facilitate this. As the plane took off, and the group made its way back to England, Mike wondered, 'Has my family's strict beliefs around punctuality and organisation in every area of life held me back from properly enjoying myself?'

Whilst the example above may not be something you've experienced; we can all recall a time when our rational and logical brain shuts down, and we cannot control what comes out of our mouths, leaving us to deal with the implications of our actions afterwards. Some can be related to interpersonal relationships, which we will look at more in Chapter 4, When Two Tribes Go To War. Others can be related to issues within ourselves, which we will look at more in Chapter 9, Who Do You Think You Are. Whatever the issue, it has helped shine a spotlight on a thought process that may have proven problematic and could continue to be so if the same or a similar situation occurs.

SELF DEVELOPMENT TIME

Let's think about a time when your beliefs caused issues in your relationships. Where a belief you have shared as either a reaction or a response has caused a problem for you. Some common examples include, 'No one will help me.' and 'My needs are not as important as others.' Answer the following questions based on your problematic belief/s:

- When was this belief/position formed?
- Is this belief my own, or is it a belief I've adopted from others?
- Does this belief/view/position I hold align with my own genuine belief?
- How does this belief shape my reaction to or interaction with others?
- Is my reaction to the situation/thought proportionate to the action?
- Would a different reaction, or delivery of my position garnered a better outcome?
- Is my reaction serving or hindering me and the relationship?
- Is there an alternative belief that I could hold moving forward?

Our conscious mind is the processing unit of all our thoughts and feelings and makes up a mere 10% of our brain's capacity. The remaining 90% of our brain is the subconscious and is our memory bank, where all our files are stored. Our values, beliefs, thoughts, memories that are not needed in the here and now are stored in the subconscious, ready to be called upon if needed. Hypnotherapy works by accessing the subconscious mind through Theta brainwave. Here new thoughts, behaviours and beliefs can be programmed without the rational or logical part of your brain, the Beta brainwave, questioning these new thoughts, behaviours and beliefs. Old beliefs that were causing faulty programming in your brain and not serving you can be deleted. Other processes, including EMDR and psychedelic therapy, can also have profound effects on reprogramming your mind by removing those beliefs, thoughts and behaviours you directly downloaded whilst in your Theta brainwave years between two to seven years old, as well as those beyond that point that also no longer serve you.

Going back to the hypnosis story at the beginning of the chapter, after her hypnosis, when asked by the host if she realised that she'd forgotten/skipped the number seven, the woman shared 'It's like you think it (the number seven) but you don't say it. It's so strange.' We learn here that the woman was aware on some level of the number seven, but she wasn't able to communicate it. A new code had been entered into the brain's operating system to override the old code, creating a new way of thinking that, in this case, had resulted in the omission of one number when counting. Through accessing your subconscious programming, questioning whether beliefs you took on in your formative years serve you, and updating the faulty values or beliefs that are causing you problems in your life, you will face fewer problems, and your ability to navigate problems with relative ease will increase.

ACCESSING DIFFERENT BRAINWAVE STATES

Before we move on from brainwaves and onto attachment and dependency, one other area in the realm of brainwaves, where you may be the problem and getting in your own way, is when you are operating from a brainwave frequency that is different to the one required for you to do what you are required to do. As mentioned earlier, during most of our adult waking lives, we are operating from the Beta brainwave. This is ideal when we need to be aware of ourselves and our surroundings, using logical thought processes to analyse things, and for being organised and productive. However, sometimes we need a unique set of skills and being stuck in the Beta brainwave isn't conducive to achieving what we need.

PEAK PERFORMANCE STATE

If you need to be in a peak performance state, like an athlete about to run the 100m Olympic final or an artist about to perform a headline show at Wembley Stadium, we need to move ourselves into a Gamma wave state. To induce a Gamma wave state, you will need to:

1. Increase your energy levels whilst decreasing any tension to gain clarity and focus.
2. Embrace a pure perception of everything around you, removing any judgment from your thinking and being.
3. Enter a loving place of gratitude and compassion for yourself and everything and everyone around you.

To achieve the first point, you need to change your physiology aka your physical state. Engage your physiology through exercise and listen to music with a positive and up-tempo theme running through it, can be a good starting point. To release tension, scan your body with your mind, identifying any areas with tension and release the pressure. Using a masseuse can help here too. Gaining a pure perception of everything around you and removing judgment can be gained through relinquishing any negative thoughts or feelings. To do this, tap into mantras and affirmations such as 'I remove any judgment from my life, for I know it does not serve me.' Forgiving other people for their behaviour doesn't mean you forget what they have done, but it relinquishes the control it has over you and the judgment you hold. The last point can be achieved through the attitude of gratitude. Be grateful for whatever is in the environment where you need to be in a Gamma brainwave state, and what got you to that point. There are different meditation and breathing exercises that can aid in this process, or you can tap into this by yourself.

CREATIVITY STATE

If you are looking to generate new ideas, create new art, come up with solutions, you need to move into an Alpha state. Have you noticed that it is often when you are in the shower, getting ready to sleep, or out in nature that your best ideas come to you? That your writer's block disappears. That solutions to problems you were struggling with suddenly make themselves known. It is very rare that they come to you when you are stuck at your office desk for hours, sat your laptop responding to emails and writing reports. Sir Isaac Newton discovered the theory of gravity not by sitting at a table, but by watching an apple fall from a tree. Stephen King, author of classics such as It and The Shining, has shared that many of his book ideas have come from being in the shower. To induce an Alpha wave state, you need to:

1. Place yourself in a soothing and relaxing environment.
2. Remove any stresses and tensions that you feel.
3. Close the tabs in your head of any issues, problems, or work that you need to do.
4. Slow things down, deepen your breath, slower your heart rate to help open your mind.

What is a soothing and relaxing environment for you? It could be out in nature, the shower, your bed. Identify what works for you. Like in the Gamma brainwave state, doing a body scan can help remove any stresses and tensions you feel. To further aid this, closing the tabs in your head by telling your brain you will come back and deal with any issues, problems, or work at a later point will free your mind of any stresses associated with them. Focusing on your breath will help regulate your breathing, slowing down your heart rate and inducing the Alpha brainwave state. By doing these four points, you will significantly increase your ability to access your creative state. Why not try it out today and watch your creativity flourish and ideas flow in.

SUMMARY

During our formative years, various brainwaves develop within our minds, enabling us to think differently. To begin with, from the ages of zero to two, we are in a dreamlike state (Delta), before we move into a downloading of information state (Theta) from two to seven-years-old, where everything we take in is perceived as fact. As the Alpha brainwave emerges at around seven years of age, our creativity and intuition develop and come the age of twelve as the Beta waves form, our rational and logical brain kicks in, enabling us to assess the validity of information as it's presented to us and determine whether we choose to take it on board. The final brainwave is the Gamma brain wave, and this is a state that we enter when we look to induce a peak performance state, enabling us to operate at our best.

Problems with our thinking in correlation to our brainwaves come because of two main reasons. The first is that from birth to seven years old, our brains weren't developed enough to decipher whether the information we were taking in was an objective or subjective truth or even an outright lie. We could not tell if it was aligned with who we are or how we want to be, and at that age, we may well have been unlikely to know who we were. Therefore, we were shaped by values and beliefs that others put on us without our ability to question them. If there was a bug in your operating system on your phone, you would before long get a new software update to resolve the issue. Yet as adults, we rarely take the time to review the 'bugs' in our brain that are causing us issues in our lives because of values, beliefs, and behaviours that no longer serve us. By seeking support through hypnotherapy, psychotherapy or EMDR, we can address these 'bugs', by tapping into the Theta brainwave state to work out if the values and beliefs we downloaded between zero and seven are helping or hindering us, updating them as and where needed, and enabling us to operate more efficiently.

The second problem with our thinking in correlation to our brainwaves is that if we are experiencing an issue, it is likely that we are operating from a different brainwave frequency to the one that we need at that given moment. To be creative, we need to primarily be tapping into the Alpha brainwave. To reach peak performance, we need to tap into the Gamma brainwave. As adults during our waking hours, we are primarily in the Beta brainwave, so if we are having an issue with our thinking or our ability to perform, we need to reflect and ask ourselves, are we in the right brainwave right now, or do I need to change frequency to achieve what I need in this moment.

3

DON'T LEAVE ME THIS WAY

Attachment and Dependency

On a cold and wet autumn evening, Sarah, Kim, Cynthia, and Kristen all found themselves single for the first time since they met fifteen years ago. They gathered at a new cocktail bar on the sixty-seventh floor overlooking New York City. Ushered to a booth in the corner that looked out across the room, Kim ordered four cosmopolitans for the group as they sat down, catching up to discuss the various dates they had all been on recently. Gone were the days where they would meet potential partners in person. Dating now seemed to revolve around a variety of dating apps that ranged from ones focused solely on hook ups, through to one focused on finding your soul mate and everything in between.

Kim was the first to share her trials and tribulations with the dating apps. Kim had always been confident in life, knowing what she wanted and going out and getting it. She had the natural confidence and security within herself and her body, that attracting a suitor was never hard for her. Kim's previous relationship of ten years had ended amicably with her partner three months earlier, and after a month of untethering from her ex, she was enjoying the dating scene and all the excitement and mystique that it brought. In no rush to settle down, Kim was happy to go from date to date, with no hard feelings felt, if someone she was interested in didn't feel the same. Kim was happy to see where the wind would take her, feeling that she wasn't missing anything from her life. Kim didn't need a man to complete her, for she was already complete. She was instead looking for someone to complement and enhance what she already had inside. Kristen, shocked to hear that Kim was on a whole range of dating apps, asked, 'But don't you want to find someone to settle down with?' 'What's the rush?' Kim responded, 'Why not have fun whilst we're single, ladies?'

Fun was not a word Kristen associated with dating and finding a partner, for Kristen was the opposite of Kim. Kristen had been in a steady flow of relationships ever since the women knew her. Though she never cheated on a partner, for that went against Kristen's moral code, Kristen was rarely single. In fact, this two-week period since she'd broken up with her ex had been the longest time between relationships for Kristen since she started dating. Kristen's anxiety was palpable, to the point that Kim reached into her Birkin bag and pulled out a prescription bottle of Xanax offering Kristen one. Kristen politely declined, but Kim was insistent, 'It's not for you, it's for us.' Dating for Kristen was akin to a military operation. She had a spreadsheet, lining up all the various dates she had, with space for ratings based on attractiveness, marriage suitability and whether they were father material. As she recalled the morning coffee walks before work, the lunches near the office, and the back-to-back dinners/drinks she would have each day, the other women were left feeling exhausted. As the server passed, Sarah exclaimed, 'We're gonna need another four Cosmo's please.' There were two guys that Kristen had really liked, but her keenness to find a partner had been somewhat off-putting to them both. One ghosted her, and the other hadn't shown the same level of interest in Kristen as she had shown in them. 'Why do you think he hasn't texted back yet? Do you think I should message him again?'

Cynthia reached across the table, grabbing the bottle of Xanax prescription pills, and swallowed one down with the last of her cosmopolitan, as the next round arrived. 'God, that's enough to put me off dating for life.' Cynthia had a more dogmatic approach to men and dating. In her eyes, men were not to be trusted. They were there to fulfil a need, be that sexual or to help pro-create, but other than that, the need for a man in her life was limited. Cynthia had been in a couple of relationships over the fifteen years the women knew each other, lasting a year and two-years respectively, but there had been enormous gaps of single life in between. In one relationship, the partner ended up leaving her, because no matter how hard he tried, he felt there was an insurmountable wall, that he could never climb over to get close to her. The other partner was okay with the wall Cynthia built. For he too had a wall, and Cynthia felt she may have found someone to settle down with. But a company transfer to Europe curtailed the relationship when Cynthia was unwilling to give up her career as a lawyer to follow him to Europe so he could pursue his career. Cynthia had agreed with the other women that she would go on the dating apps too, and reluctantly did so. Yet she had avoided meeting up with anyone, always finding a reason to cancel a planned date.

Attention turned to Sarah, and the bartender returned to the table. 'Another round?' the server asked. 'I think we're going to need something stronger for this one,' as Kim pointed to Sarah. 'Make it another four cosmopolitans, and four patron silvers.' Sarah had earned the nickname Toro from the women. For like a bull, whenever she saw a red flag, she ran towards it. At one point she had seemed to settle down with John, a steady and reliable man, but true to the form the woman had come to know Sarah for, when her ex, Chris, returned to the city that never sleeps, she self-sabotaged her relationship with John, by running back to Chris. The women were all wary of Chris. He had broken Sarah's heart several times over the years. From missing her birthday because of being held up at work, to standing her up at the airport when they were due to go away on holiday together, there would always be some way in which he'd let Sarah down. They thought they'd finally seen the back of

Chris, when Sarah surprised the women by announcing she was meeting up with him the following night. Kristen and Cynthia looked at Kim, knowing that Kim was a straight shooter and best placed to address a problem called Chris. 'Sarah, darling. How many red flags must Chris wave before you finally realise, he's not the one for you?' As Kim placed her hand on Sarah's, she pulled her hand away. 'You don't understand. Chris is the love of my life. I know he has let me down in the past, but when it's great, it's great.' 'The problem is Sarah,' Kim responded, 'it's often far from great, and we are the ones left picking up all the pieces time and time again. It's almost like you want to be hurt.' An awkward silence fell upon the table as Kim's words left a sting in their delivery. Sarah, close to tears, excused herself from the table and made her way to the bathroom. As she washed her hands and looked into the mirror, she wondered, 'am I blinded by love and can't see the relationship with Chris for what it is?'

ATTACHMENT

As outlined in the story, each of the four women has a different approach to dating. Their approaches to interactions with potential partners reflect their own personal values and beliefs that shape their behaviours, stemming all the way back to their infancy. In the late 1960s, British psychologist John Bowlby developed attachment theory around humans and their interactions with a primary caregiver. According to Bowlby (1969), 'attachment is a deep emotional bond that develops between an infant and their primary caregiver, usually the mother.' Bowlby believed that attachment must occur in two directions. The primary caregiver must be bonded to their child in order to care for them and aid their survival, and the child must be bonded to the primary caregiver for safety and security. The attachment period for a child forms roughly between eighteen months and three years old. At this stage in a child's development, it is highly likely that they can walk and talk. No longer immobile, they are free to explore the spaces and places they find themselves in. With a primary caregiver there to overlook the child's exploration, the child freely roams, knowing that when they look around, they can see their primary caregiver.

Problems arise when a child separates from a primary caregiver. During this developmental stage, when a child is separated from the primary caregiver, fear is activated within the child. Sometimes, the child is quickly reconnected with the primary caregiver; the bond is restored, and the child soothed, returning the child to a state of equilibrium. In other cases, if a longer period passes and attempts by the child to connect with the primary caregiver, by searching or calling/crying-out, don't produce the desired results, the child can become quite emotional. Upon the primary caregivers' return, the child becomes clingy, fearful that they are going to be left again and not wanting to let the parent out of their sight. Further still, if the separation is prolonged and attempts to reconnect with the primary caregiver fall flat, at some point the child is likely to give up, feeling detached and abandoned. Should the primary care-giver return, it is common for the child to disengage with the primary caregiver and avoid contact. One last area that is least common is when a child looks to a primary caregiver as both a source of love but also a source of fear. This disorganised relationship with the primary caregiver will occur with children whose primary caregiver is verbally, physically, emotionally, or sexually abusive to them. They depend on the primary caregiver to meet their needs, but also fearful of the abuse that is inflicted by the primary caregiver upon them.

Bowlby first identified three types of attachment in childhood, and in 1986, Mary Main discovered a fourth type: disorganised attachment. The four types are:

1. **Secure attachment** – feeling and dealing.
2. **Avoidant attachment** – dealing, but not feeling.
3. **Anxious attachment** – feeling, but not dealing.
4. **Disorganised attachment** – the source of love is also the source of pain.

A 2023 YouGov study showed that in America, 38% of respondents have a secure attachment, 19% have an avoidant attachment, 14% have an anxious attachment, 14% have a disorganised attachment, and the remaining 15% were unclear. Statistics around attachment styles will vary from country to country, continent to continent. In the western world, it is more common to find a traditional nuclear family set-up with the raising of children primarily carried out by the parents of the child. In the eastern world, and in developing nations, it is not uncommon to find a child raised by a village/community, rather than just one individual. Added to that, the evolution of society over the centuries continues to play a contributing factor in the attachment style of the child. With women more likely to be a part of the workforce than three generations ago, the bond between child and mother is not a given. With retirement ages increasing incrementally over time, and people moving away from where their own biological families live, access to additional support to look after the child falls more into the hands of childminders and nurseries than with grandparents.

These factors, amongst others, will contribute to the developing state of a person's attachment, how they form bonds with humans and objects, and what will come up for them when experiencing separation and loss. It will play out in the interpersonal relationships, shaping how an individual interacts with another, what attracts them to one individual and what repels them from another. Looking at the four women at the start of the chapter, Kim has a secure base. She is comfortable within herself, free to explore dating men, safe in knowing that when the right person comes along, it will be right for her. Kristen has an anxious attachment style, as seen in her behaviour. From the need to be in a relationship and the extreme lengths she goes to, to make that happen, through to the fear of disconnection from a potential partner and the need to follow up messages. Kristen's anxiety of not being in a relationship is so palpable that it even affects her relationships with the other women. Cynthia has an avoidant attachment style. Used to fending for herself, having been abandoned as a child, she keeps a wall up to protect her from others, whilst also protecting others from herself. This attachment style makes it hard for her to form deep and meaningful relationships. Even the women from time to time have found hard to bond more deeply with Cynthia. Sarah, the last of the four women, has a disorganised attachment. Having grown up in an abusive family, love is complicated for her. The source of love was also the source of fear for her. In adulthood, Sarah formed what's known as repetition compulsion, repeating in the present physically or emotionally painful situations that happened in the past, hoping to create a different outcome. Red flags are familiar to Sarah. A source of both comfort and fear. Knowing no different, Sarah is drawn to what she knows and so the cycle repeats, with her being drawn back to Chris time and time again.

SELF RELFECTION TIME

Turning to you, let's take some time to understand your attachment style and your patterns of relating:

- Are you aware of your attachment style?
- Do you identify more with Kim, Kristen, Cynthia, or Sarah?
- How are you in relationships, not only in a romantic sense, but with friends and family?
- Do you engage calmly and collectively? (Secure)
- Do you enrage anxiously and aggressively? (Anxious)
- Do you disengage completely? (Avoidant)
- How has your attachment style caused problems in your relationships?
- Has your anxious attachment driven people away because you are too controlling or clingy?
- Has your avoidant attachment made you miss out on deeper connections?
- Has your disorganised state seen you always attract the wrong people?

Your attachment style is likely to be a combination of styles dependent on what situation you are in, but which is your default interaction with people? If you don't know, think for a moment. If you lose your keys, misplace your bag, or find yourself separated from an item, how do you react?

- Do you go into a panic, searching frantically for the item, retracing your steps?
- Do you reside at it being lost, and set about looking for a replacement?
- Do you stay measured in your response and rationally work out where it might be?

Give it some thought. If you don't know what your attachment style is and want to find out, check out the book Attached by Amir Levine and Rachel Heller.

SELF DEVELOPMENT TIME

Based on a 2023 YouGov survey, whilst nearly two-fifths of the US population have a secure attachment, nearly two-thirds of the US population don't. For those who don't have a secure attachment; irrespective of whether or not you live in the US, it can cause you problems in your relationships and your patterns of relating.

ANXIOUS ATTACHMENT STYLE TIPS

If you have an anxious attachment style, fear of abandonment might often cause intense feelings of jealousy or suspicion in partners. Trust is the foundation of any relationship, but the fear of abandonment stemming from childhood can block the ability to trust a partner in the present, leading an individual to become desperate, clingy, and pre-occupied with a relationship. There is a fear of being alone, which, for some, results in needing to be with or around someone all the time. It can lead to conflict in relationships, based on the other party feeling smothered. The insatiable need to be with someone stems from the fear that they are going to be abandoned at some point. Thoughts may include 'I need to get as much as I can now, because at some point it won't be there.'

If you have an anxious attachment style, here are five things that you can work on to evolve into a more secure attachment style.

1. **Learn how to utilise other people to regulate your emotions**. If you are feeling anxious or overwhelmed, it can help to increase your window of tolerance with your emotions. Having various people, including a therapist, to help you ground yourself when your anxiety is activated, to breathe, reduce your heart rate, and work through the activation triggers by talking them through can help. Sometimes it's beneficial to do this with the source of the activation if you can talk with them rather than at them, but more often than not, it is better to find a different and complimentary person to do this.
2. **Re-source yourself**. Anxious people are individuals who are emotionally under-resourced. They had big emotions as children, that weren't soothed and regulated in a way that helped temper their emotions. Tapping into breathwork, meditation, support groups, all help to learn how to feel your feelings but not become them.
3. **Work on your disappointments from the past**. Your primary caregivers were unable to show up for you in a way that you needed. That is not a judgment on them, for they were most likely doing the best they can with the resources they had at the time. If you can process what happened in the past (I always recommend using a therapist like myself for this), it can help you more accurately assess what is playing out and repeating in the present. This will enable you to distinguish if you

are projecting your past relationships onto a present relationship or not.
4. **Identify someone who is securely attached and understand what they do**. People with anxious attachment styles are usually drawn to people with an avoidant attachment style. This means that an anxiously attached individual hasn't been able to model a secure attachment with another person. By befriending or dating someone with a secure attachment, you can see how an individual communicates when they are upset in a clear and grounded way. You will see how they tap into rather than out of the relationship when stressed. They can also provide support when you feel stressed. They will be clear about when they want to see you next and if they want to be with you. That they enjoy spending time together and make it a priority.
5. **Let go of relationships where your needs for security are not being met.** If you find yourself in relationships where your needs are not being met, then it's time to let them go. Pace and grace is the name of the game here. Maybe all of your relationships fall into this category, so building healthy relationships to counter the severing of the unhealthy relationships is strongly recommended.

AVOIDANT ATTACHMENT STYLE TIPS

If you have an avoidant attachment style, there is likely to be a fear of being able to express emotions. Given your need for connection when separation occurred went on for prolonged periods of time, the emotions you felt served little purpose in garnering the desired result of reconnection. As such, these emotions are likely to have been abandoned. Closeness to others is also likely to be a problem. Physical closeness and touch may cause issues. Someone who gets too close to you may cause you to feel smothered or overly attached.

If you have an avoidant attachment style, here are 3 things you can work on your style to evolve into a more secure attachment.

1. **Understand your triggers.** When you are triggered by something or someone, it is likely that you want to build a wall up to protect yourself from getting hurt. You may want to express love, but the fear of loss can prevent you from doing this. You may fear that if someone gets too close, they will see how afraid you really are and this is scary, because you fear that might drive them away. Journal what comes up when you are triggered, or work through what comes up with a therapist, so that you can understand what comes up for you.
2. **Explore your feelings and emotions and get attuned to your body**. Many individuals with an avoidant personality avoid and detach from their feelings, thinking they should be avoided at all costs. If that is the case for you, begin by picking up on any physical sensations; tightness of the chest, change in body temperature that you feel when activated or triggered. Pick up on any thoughts that may come along with the physical sensations. Over time, feelings are likely to emerge, welcome them, and start to explore and understand what they are trying to tell you.
3. **Practice getting close to someone.** If you have an avoidant attachment style, it is likely that you have kept everyone at arm's length. It can be hard for you to trust others, through fear of being hurt again and regressing to that little child who felt abandoned. A starting point can be with a therapist who can provide you with a safe and supportive environment, free from judgment to help you navigate opening up to someone. The therapeutic relationship can be used to model a healthy relationship, and as you open up more in therapy, it will hopefully allow you to do the same in your other

relationships. Slow and steady are the name of the game here. Honour that it is likely to take time to build up closeness to others if you've spent a lifetime avoiding people.

DISORGANISED ATTACHMENT TIPS

If you have a disorganised attachment, problems are likely to manifest through an overt caution and suspicion of others and/or equally, a pull towards them. There is likely an uncertainty on how to navigate the complexities of people and interpersonal relationships. People with a disorganised attachment style are likely to struggle with mental health concerns, including anxiety, depression, social withdrawal, engaging in misconduct, and substance abuse. Someone with a disorganised attachment style will benefit from both the antidotes to the anxious and avoidant attachment styles previously listed, as well as the additional antidote below:

1. **Recognising green flags**. Having a disorganised attachment style means that red flags (such as gaslighting, the relationship being only on the others terms) in your relationships became the norm for you. Green flags that nurture and foster healthy relationships are likely to have been absent/unfamiliar to you. Equality, respect, embracing differences, sharing common interests, respecting your boundaries are just some of the many green flags that can be found in a healthy relationship. Identify when these are shown to you, or use other relationships be that in real life through friends and colleagues, or through TV and films, to help understand what this looks like, so you can incorporate collecting and giving green flags in your relationships and start the process of not being drawn to or running after and collecting red flags.

Having looked at attachment styles, let's develop our perspective further by exploring and understanding the different states of dependency and where your dependency state may cause problems.

WON'T YOU PLEASE HELP ME

Ciaran woke up in the intensive care unit (ICU) following a car crash, as a result of a head on collision with another car. Coming out of nowhere, the opposing car jumped the lights, smashing into Ciaran's car, sending it hydroplaning out of control and writing off the car. Ciaran and his friend Stephen, who was in the passenger seat, had to be cut out of the car, with both sustaining significant, but non-life-threatening, injuries. The road to recovery proved difficult for Ciaran. Although Stephen's injuries had been more severe than Ciaran's, Stephen had shown an undeterred willingness to not let his injuries define him. Stephen gave 110% when it came to the rehabilitation programme to restore his motor-neurone abilities, and within six months, he was back to full health. Ciaran, however, didn't have the same temperament.

Ciaran, until that point in his life, had lived somewhat of a sheltered life. At twenty-five, he still lived at home with his parents, where all of his responsibilities, from cooking, to cleaning, to washing his clothes, were taken care of primarily by his mother. Though used to being looked after, Ciaran became despondent that he depended on the hospital team to help nurse him back to health. Ciaran was also self-employed and, without the ability to work, had lost a steady income. This meant that he would now also depend on benefits to help cover his day-to-day living expenses. This made him more depressed and the sense of hopelessness that consumed Ciaran affected his ability to recover from his injuries.

Weeks turned into months, with little sign of any progress. The sense of dependency on others, rather than autonomy of himself to change his situation, was what set Ciaran and his friend Stephen apart. Their injuries had been similar, though Stephen had come off worse in the crash, but unlike Ciaran, Stephen hadn't lived the majority of his life stuck in dependency on others. It was Ciaran's dependent state and his subsequent learned helplessness that had stifled his ability to recover, not the injury himself.

Ciaran's story is one of the many ways in which a state of dependency can cause problems in a person's life. When we are born, we depend on others to help us meet our basic physiological needs: food, drink, shelter, sleep, safety, and security. As parents get to know their child, they learn to distinguish the cry for food, from the cry to change their diaper, to the cry because they are tired. The baby cries and the bottle/breast appears to feed them. The baby cries and the discomfort felt from the nappy is alleviated by changing it. The baby cries and is rocked to sleep to alleviate the tiredness. All babies have narcissistic traits. They are the centre of their world and when they call/cry, their primary caregiver responds.

The caveat to that is with abusive/absent caregivers who cannot show up for the infant's needs. As we grow through childhood and into adulthood, we look to move through different states of dependency. As we gain autonomy, our reliance on primary caregivers decreases, but there are different paths of dependency we can take, that will probably have been shaped by our primary caregivers.

There are four states of dependency, which are highlighted in Figure 3.1.

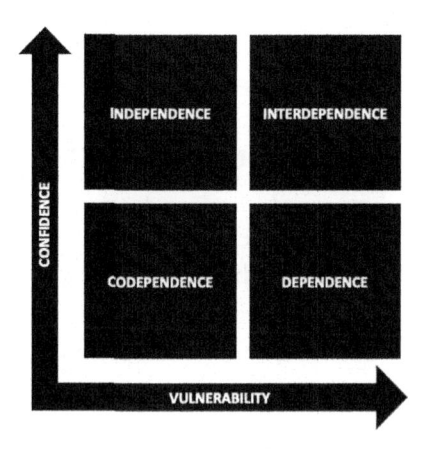

Figure 3.1 - Dependency States.

Breaking down each of the states a little further, below is a description of each state of dependency:

1. **Dependence** – An individual who is highly vulnerable and low on confidence. They rely on others to meet their needs, as they are either unable; in the case of a child, or unwilling; in the case of Ciaran, to do so themselves.
2. **Codependence** – An individual who is both low on confidence and vulnerability. There is an excessive amount of emotional or psychological reliance on another, typically one, though not exclusively, who requires help or support from an illness or addiction.
3. **Independence** – An individual who is high on confidence but low on vulnerability. An independent individual is often someone who is a go getter but feels unable to depend or rely on others to help them achieve what they want, through fear of being let down.
4. **Interdependence** – An individual who is both high in vulnerability and confidence. The opposite of co-dependency, two parties can depend on each other, but equally go off and do their own thing, without a reliance on the other.

Let's turn our attention to the co-dependent state, to understand how being stuck in this state of dependency can cause problems in an individual's life.

THE RESCUER IN ME

Amir and Sarita met on the first day of university and had an instant connection. Studying the same subject, coming from the same part of the East Midlands, and living in the same student accommodation, it felt like destiny that the two had been brought together. Amir had been raised in a single-parent household. His mum rarely having time for him unless he could help her. As such, he learned to be helpful, so as to feel loved and connected to others. Sarita, on the other hand, had been a clingy child. She was often anxious about being abandoned, owing to her parents being in hospital a lot when she was a toddler, because of her older sibling being severely ill. As Amir's helpfulness and Sarita's neediness played out, each of them were able to fall into roles that felt familiar, enabling each of them to get their needs met.

During the first year of university, their friendship was a source of comfort and support. They relied on each other for everything. From studying, to exam prep, to navigating their social lives. But as time went on, their reliance on each other became excessive. Sarita's anxiety would often flare up, and she turned to Amir for constant reassurance. Amir quickly became her sole source of validation, and she felt lost without him. Amir, on the other hand, felt responsible for Sarita's well-being and couldn't say no to her requests for help.

This pattern of behaviour resulted in Amir spending less and less time with other friends he'd made on the course, cancelling plans to hang out with them to support Sarita. He would also go home less frequently, for fear that Sarita's anxiety attacks would flare up and no one would be there to help. Amir quickly began losing himself in Sarita, their own identities becoming intertwined. Each had lost sight of their individual goals and aspirations that brought them to university, with their lives revolving around one other.

As their co-dependency deepened, they became trapped in a cycle of neediness and resentment. Sarita felt guilty for being so needy, while Amir resented always having to put Sarita's needs before his own. Yet, both were reluctant to acknowledge to the other their true feelings, for fear of causing a rupture in the relationship. It all came to a head one evening at the beginning of the second year, when Amir received a call from his mum needing his help, meaning he'd have to cancel plans he'd made with Sarita to return home. Sarita, activated by this, became resentful. She felt abandoned by Amir and tried everything she could to make him stay. From begging, to criticising, to providing ultimatums. But no matter what Sarita tried, nothing she could do would stop Amir from leaving to help his mum.

All the way back home, Amir felt guilty for abandoning Sarita when she needed him. But he needed to help his mum and couldn't understand why Sarita didn't realise this. The following week, when Amir returned, he tried to speak with Sarita, but feeling abandoned and hurt, she rejected his appeals to reconnect. At a loose end with what to do, he spoke with the student union, who pointed him to the student counsellor, to help him navigate what was going on with Sarita.

Upon encouragement from the school counsellor, Sarita agreed to meet with Amir and the counsellor to unpack and work through the fracture in their friendship, that had left them both feeling rejected and hurt. Over the course of the next couple of months, both learnt about co-dependency, and how they could work both separately and together towards creating healthier boundaries; Sarita learning how to manage her anxiety independently of Amir. Amir learning to prioritise his own needs. Each acknowledged that their co-dependent relationship had prevented them from growing as individuals and that they had to let go of their enmeshed relationship, to allow each other to grow into healthier, more balanced people. In the end, Sarita and Amir were able to salvage their friendship through establishing healthier boundaries, creating complementary and separate friendship circles and prioritising their individual growth. They learned that while having a supportive friend is important, it's also essential to maintain a sense of self and independence.

Co-dependency as can be seen in Amir and Sarita's story, often results in losing the me in the we. Co-dependency comes up regularly in the caring profession and caring roles like personal assistants, with one party in need of help and the other willing to offer it. It also comes up as previously mentioned in the realm of addiction, where the person who is addicted to a vice or several vices depends on another to help them with their needs. The problem with these types of relationships, are lines get blurred very easy, as a lack of boundaries enable the unhealthy pattern to unfold. In most cases, a person who is co-dependent wasn't shown much, if any, love as a child. As Scott Egleston (1986) notes, co-dependency is 'a way of getting needs met without getting needs met.' Co-dependents learnt often from a young age that being of help or service to another would enable them to be seen and validated. This leads to individuals mistaking love with service. Here it is important to note, that:

If you give too much too soon, people will fall in love with your hand and not your heart.

Co-dependents primarily on a subconscious level, but sometimes on a conscious level, seek individuals who need help and form relationships with them. That is where they feel most comfortable and where their needs get met, but before long, the relationship turns into a drama. In the 1960s, psychoanalyst Stephen Karpman created the drama triangle, as seen in the Figure 3.2, to highlight what played out in a co-dependent relationship.

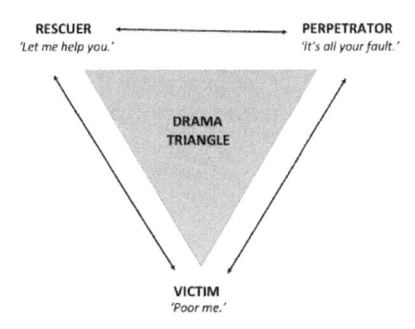

```
          RESCUER  ←————————→  PERPETRATOR
      'Let me help you.'              'It's all your fault.'

                    ╲   DRAMA   ╱
                     ╲ TRIANGLE ╱
                      ╲        ╱
                       ╲      ╱
                        ╲    ╱
                         ╲  ╱
                        VICTIM
                       'Poor me.'
```

Figure 3.2 - The Drama Triangle.

Co-dependents start off as the rescuer, finding someone who appears to be a victim and in need of help, whether or not they have explicitly asked for it, and forges a relationship. They offer help and support to the individual, giving the victim the help that they knowingly or unknowingly needed, and providing the co-dependent rescuer, fulfilment that they have been able to help someone. The drama unfolds, when either the victim no longer requires or responds to the help offered by the co-dependent rescuer, or the co-dependent rescuer is unable or unwilling to provide support to the victim. In the former, the co-dependent rescuer moves into the victim role, feeling unappreciated for all the help they have provided, with the victim then moving into the persecutor role. In the latter, the victim who is unable to get the help they want or need from the rescuer, stays in their victim role, and casts the co-dependent rescuer as a persecutor instead, blaming them for not supporting them.

The dance between roles will probably continue for some time until one or the other attempts to break away from the drama triangle. Here, the remaining party, be it the victim or the co-dependent rescuer, will resort to continue to cast the other as the perpetrator, utilising whatever tactics; name calling, emotional manipulation, withholding of finances, in an attempt to manipulate the other to return to the drama triangle, so the drama can continue. For the co-dependent, it will require a lot of strength to break away from their co-dependent tendencies and the role they've cast themselves in, but persevere one must, if wanting to break unhealthy habits that are causing problems in your life and relationships.

SELF REFLECTION TIME

Look at yourself for a moment. Do you identify as someone who may be co-dependent or have co-dependent traits? What are some of the co-dependent traits I hear you ask? Whilst there are many, here are some of the most common. See how many you identify with:

1. Home was not safe growing up.
2. Other people come first.
3. You had to become the mature child from an early age.
4. Can't (or struggle) to say no to others.
5. Nothing you do is ever good enough.
6. Crying is not okay.
7. People are unreliable.
8. No one cares.
9. Love means do as I say.

It's important to note that identifying with all or several of the nine points here does not automatically mean you are co-dependent, but that you exhibit co-dependent traits that may impact your relationships. If you identify with co-dependency:

- How do your co-dependent traits cause problems in your relationships with others?
- Do your relationships always end the same way; painfully or disastrously?
- Do you struggle to express your needs in a relationship for fear they will not be honoured or met?

When I work with clients who show co-dependent traits, to

begin the process, I ask 'Do you have a problem saying no?' In nearly every instance, the client will answer that they do. I often then challenge them with that response saying. 'I don't necessarily think you have a problem saying no. I think the problem is the person you keep saying no to.' At that moment, you see the penny drop. By saying yes to everyone else, they keep saying no to themselves and their needs.

SELF DEVELOPMENT TIME

If you struggle with co-dependency or co-dependent traits, here are five ways in which you can work through evolving your behaviours, to create a healthier relationship with yourself and others.

1. **Boundaries.** Often, someone with co-dependency has a complete lack of boundaries, so this is likely to be hard at first. Start off by putting small boundaries in place and build from there once you become more comfortable putting boundaries in place. Small boundaries can even include delaying an answer. 'Let me get back to you on that.' 'I need to check my schedule.' These responses can buy time for you to follow up at a later point where your response establishes a boundary.
2. **Work on your self-esteem and self-worth.** If you struggle with co-dependency, it is likely you also have low self-esteem and self-worth. Happiness is on the outside. Good feelings and validation are on the outside. Turn your attention inwards and look at how you can derive feelings of self-esteem and self-worth internally. It may help to work with a therapist, support group or mental health professional to navigate this.
3. **Pay attention to your intention.** It is second nature almost for a co-dependent to help others. Anytime you go to offer help, pay attention to the reason you are offering the support. Did the person ask for help? Are

you doing it to gain validation and approval, to feed your self-esteem and self-worth? Where possible, resist helping if your intention is driven purely from a place of rescuing as opposed to empowering the other person.
4. **Create new relationships.** Foster relationships, where there isn't a need for you to be the helper, the rescuer. Where you are accepted for who you are, not what you can do. The chance to break the cycle of who you are energetically drawn to, enables you to radiate on a different frequency, and over time as you strengthen this muscle, you will attract more people in your life who aren't dependents or hold a victim mindset.
5. **Find spaces where you can open up.** If you struggle with co-dependency, you've likely held the belief that your needs don't matter. You do matter. And it is important to express your needs, that are just as valid as other peoples. Again, this may initially happen with a therapist, or in a support group, but over time, once you build this muscle, it will hopefully become easier to open up to others.

Having looked at the dependent and co-dependent states, let's turn our attention to the independent state and where it may cause problems.

I DEPEND ON ME

Kali was a highly independent woman, born more out of necessity than a feminist movement or another reason. Kali's parents were very disengaged in raising her growing up. Whenever she needed help with her homework, with problems of bullying at school, they were never around to help, and so over time Kali had built a belief that she couldn't rely on other people to help her. If she wanted or needed to do something, she could only rely on herself. Kali harnessed this belief to its fullest. Powering through academia she excelled, and, realising that the corporate world was not for her, embarked on becoming a solopreneur. With a diverse array of skill sets, from marketing to communication, computing to advertising, Kali had equipped herself with everything she felt she needed to get ahead in life.

Her first three years as a solopreneur were pretty successful, especially given that 20% of all businesses fail in the first year and 60% in the first three years. But then something weird happened for Kali. Her business plateaued. To the outside world, she was the embodiment of the Destiny's Child song 'Independent Women', but inside the weight of being independent and not having others to support her growth, point out blind spots and more, was slowing her down. With Kali being a one-woman shop, the demands of the business had exponentially increased, to the point she was tied down constantly firefighting issues. Without the ability to delegate, so that she could focus on the larger company strategy and procuring new clients, Kali was struggling to keep afloat. A few months later, with the anxiety and stress piling on top of her, Kali was approached by a rival company about the opportunity to merge companies and become a joint force.

Kali was, at first, apprehensive. She was uncertain of the intention of the other party, and whether this was more of a takeover than a merger. Kali's ongoing issues with receiving help and support prevented her from seeing the opportunity that lay in front of her. The other company kept an open dialogue, whilst Kali sought therapeutic support in my private practice to work through the problems she was facing. Through exploring her independent state and working through it, Kali decided that the right decision for the long-term growth of the company was to in fact, merge with the other company. Two years on from the merger, Kali's ability to work with others has been transformational for her. Though she regresses into old beliefs that no one will help her from time to time, Kali is able to lean into the company and her partners to help drive the goals and vision for the company forward.

SELF REFLECTION TIME

Gaining independence is a pivotal moment in the developmental stages of an individual's life. Psychologist Erik Erikson (1998) discovered that this stage usually occurs between the ages of twelve to eighteen, when an individual is forming their own identity separate to that of their own primary caregivers. When they are given more freedom and autonomy to travel to and from school on their own, arrange hanging out with friends without supervision and more. Being independent is an important state for anyone to be in, but it causes problems when it is the primary or sole state you stay in. As the expression goes, 'No (hu)man is an island.' We all need help from time to time. But those who could not access support during their formative years, or worse had that need for support rejected continuously, will grow a belief, much like Kali, that other people can't be relied upon, so you can only rely on yourself to get things done. Do you resonate with this? If so;

- Has being in a state of independence caused issues or problems for you?
- Do you have trouble forming relationships or all kinds?
- Do you struggle with asking for help or communicating your needs?
- Has being independent stifled your ability to grow or expand similarly to Kali?
- Does being independent impact your ability to date or be emotionally intimate with someone?

Take a moment to think about what problems it may cause for you, and how that affects your life.

SELF DEVELOPMENT TIME

If being in an independent state has affected you, look at a few of the below ways in which you can evolve your independent mindset to better serve you in the long run.

1. **Knowing who and how to ask for help.** Having been independent as a result of not being able to rely on others, it may be hard to ask for help and knowing who to ask and how even harder. Not everyone is going to be able or willing to offer help when asked, and that can lead to a compounding of an existing belief that no one will help. By learning who is more likely to offer help; supportive, nurturing, empowering individuals, and framing the ask in a way that is clear and appreciative, you can begin unlearning the limiting belief that's held you back for years.
2. **Letting go.** People who have had to or chosen to be independent, often struggle with delegating. Sometimes delegation is giving something to someone who can't do it as well as you can, but making peace with that, so that it frees up more time to focus on other important tasks. What can you let go of/delegate to free up more of your time?
3. **Make Peace with Your Past.** Your primary caregivers were likely doing the best they could with the resources they had. Whilst sometimes it was pure neglect that led you to feel abandoned and like no one will help you, other times it may have been because of miscommunication. Taking the time to heal that part of you that was hurt and abandoned can free you from the trappings of the belief that you need to be independent. Utilising a therapist to speak to your younger self or writing a letter to those who hurt you in the past (without sending it) can help in the process of making peace.

The last state of dependence is an interdependent state. In this state, though similar to co-dependency, there is one striking difference. In an interdependent state, two individuals depend on each other, but are not reliant on each other. One does not need the other to complete them, for they are already complete themselves. They instead complement and enhance the qualities that are already there, helping each individual to become the best version of themselves. An interdependent state allows each partner the space to maintain a sense of self, the flexibility to move towards each other in times of need, and the freedom to decide without the fear of repercussions. When looking at patterns of relating to others, the interdependent state is the preferred state of dependency to be in, to foster and develop healthy relationships.

SELF DEVELOPMENT TIME

To build an interdependent relationship, there are three major components to focus on;

1. **Clear and consistent communication.** It's important to speak up for your morals, beliefs, values, and opinions with each other. There should be a forum for both parties to share without fear of being shut down. Dialogue flows smoothly, and when issues occur, an us vs the problem as opposed to a me vs them view is taken.
2. **Be supportive of the other individual.** Supporting each other's successes and challenges and showing up for one another's passions and interests helps strengthen a relationship. Through cultivating an environment where personal growth and fulfilment can thrive, a deeper bond can be built between two individuals.
3. **Maintaining quality time with relationships outside of the relationship.** Balance is key to any relationship, and though balance isn't achievable 24/7, it is important to spend time with others outside of the relationship ensuring you don't lose the me in the we. Creating space to see friends and family, separate or

alongside the relationship, creates a space for you to both grow apart and together.

Having explored both your attachment style and dependency state in this chapter, what will you do, moving forward, to address any problems, either your attachment style or dependency state is causing you?

SUMMARY

In this chapter, we have explored the areas of both attachment and dependency, and where they may cause problems in your life. UK psychotherapist and founder of attachment theory John Bowlby (1969) identified that during the period of eighteen months to three-years-old, we form our attachment styles. Initially identifying three main attachment styles, secure attachment, anxious attachment and avoidant attachment, Mary Main (1986) added a fourth, disorganised attachment. Our individual attachment style forms as the result of our ability to separate and come back to our primary caregiver, with YouGov (2023) identifying that 38% of respondents have a secure attachment, 19% have an avoidant attachment, 14% have an anxious attachment, 14% have a disorganised attachment, and the remaining 15% were unclear.

Individuals with an anxious attachment style are likely to face problems being separated from an individual or an object. There is a fear of being alone, which, for some, results in needing to be with or around someone at all times. It can lead to conflict in relationships, based on the other party feeling smothered. The insatiable need to be with someone stems from the fear that they are going to be abandoned at some point. To evolve an anxious attachment style into a healthier secure attachment, learn how to regulate your emotions. Resource yourself with techniques and support. Heal past wounds and disappointments. Identify someone with a secure attachment to model healthier patterns of relating, and let go of relationships where your needs aren't being met. Individuals with an avoidant attachment style are likely to have been abandoned. Closeness to others is also likely to be a problem. Physical closeness and touch, in some instances, may cause issues, and someone who is too close to you may result in you feeling smothered or overly attached and not separate. To help address these problems, first understand your triggers and what causes you to avoid people or situations. Second, reconnect with your physical sensations in your body, your thoughts, and, overtime your feelings. Finally, practice getting close to someone who can help you work through your avoidant attachment style in a safe and supportive environment. Individuals who have a disorganised attachment style are likely to experience uncertainty about how to navigate the complexities of people and interpersonal relationships. People with a disorganised attachment style are likely to struggle with mental health concerns, including anxiety, depression, social withdrawal, engaging in misconduct, and substance abuse. To help evolve a disorganised attachment style, work through the anxious and avoidant steps outlined in this chapter, whilst also identifying green flags in relationships and avoid running towards red flags.

Dependency has four key states: dependent (me), co-dependent (we), independent (free) and interdependent (unity). As humans, we evolve through the first state in our formative years, but an individual may find themselves stuck in this or another state, rather than alternating between states causing problems in relationships. Staying stuck in a dependent state may cause a victimhood mentality and learned helplessness. Being stuck in a co-dependent state will probably result in putting one's needs second, having a lack of boundaries, always rescuing others, and putting self-worth and self-esteem in the hands of an external force. Being stuck in an independent state may cause an inability to seek help or support, through fear of not being helped, compounding a belief no one will help me. Feelings of isolation and a lack of closeness to others may also arise. An interdependent state provides a healthy balance between partners, and is an ideal state to be in, whilst ensuring the state doesn't drift into a co-dependent state. For dependents, accepting accountability and responsibility for your life can help begin the process of moving out of a dependent state and victim mentality. For co-dependents, not getting stuck in the drama triangle of being a rescuer, by putting in boundaries, learning to say no, paying attention to your intention when helping others, seeking new healthier relationships, and finding spaces where your feelings can be honoured and nurtured will all help. To help problems that arise from being stuck in an independent state, know when and how to ask for help, learn to let go of things and make peace with your past.

4

WHEN TWO TRIBES GO TO WAR

Conflict

The night draws in as Zac, six, and his younger brother Ralph, four, are awoken by an all too familiar sound. With the noise too loud to ignore and return to sleep, they both sleepily stumble out onto the landing and perch themselves at the top of the stairs, where they witness their mother and father once more in the throes of another argument, the third in as many weeks. With the argument playing out about their father missing out on dinner with the family and Zac's five-a-side football match, the brothers witness their father complain, 'Don't you ever stop nagging? No wonder why I never want to come home to this.' The argument continues, with their father growing more and more irate, launching a tirade onto their mother, whilst their mother stands in silence, just taking it all in.

Their father threw one last insult at their mother before storming out of the house, leaving their mother crying in the aftermath. Catching her boys on the stairs, she shouts, 'Go back to your room, now!' making Zac and Ralph hurry off to their room. The next morning as the family are sitting silently around the breakfast table before getting ready for school, the boys witness their father stumble in, pour himself a cup of coffee, grabs himself a couple of paracetamol and leaves without an acknowledgement or saying a word. All too familiar with the routine by now, Zac and Ralph have the words from their mother drilled into their heads 'Don't say anything that will upset your father.' A couple of days pass, and it seems like things are back to normal again. The argument Zac and Ralph witnessed was a distant memory, never to be talked about. Their father was attentive and present to each of them, and their parents seemingly in a loving relationship.

Unsurprisingly, a few days later, conflict descends upon the household once more, as their father returns home several hours late, following the loss of his football team, Arsenal. This time the argument appears to be over something trivial, their father tripping over Zac's sports bag; that has been left in the hallway for his game the next morning. And so, it plays out once more. The familiar pattern of an argument breaking out between Zac and Ralph's parents. Their father, the instigator of the arguments. Their mother, the passive recipient. Their role is to keep their feelings to themselves and walk on eggshells around their father until his anger dissipates. An apology never witnessed or offered by their father or mother. The problem is ignored and normal service resumes, until the next time a conflict arises, and there always is a next time.

SELF REFLECTION TIME

Zac and Ralph's experience of conflict growing up is an all too familiar story experienced all around the world. Certain cultural beliefs in different parts of the world may encourage this way of navigating conflict, because of the power dynamics and roles that are expected within a relationship. Others will be down to how individuals have learned how to navigate conflict as and when it arises. Take a moment to reflect upon how you witnessed conflict growing up. The conflict may have been between two parents, between siblings, between you and another family member.

- How did that conflict play out and how was the conflict resolved, if it was resolved at all?
- How has this shaped your relationship with and to conflict?
- Is conflict something to be feared and avoided or embraced and encouraged?

Conflict is a natural occurrence between any two or more distinct entities. The entities can include people, organisations, countries, anything where there are opposing views, beliefs, or positions on a matter that arises. For no two entities hold exactly the same views, beliefs, or positions on every single matter. Healthy conflicts can help us grow as individuals, organisations, and societies. They expand our perspectives on issues, allowing us to see beyond our own subjective view by taking in other subjective views, enabling us to gain a more objective view of an issue or situation. As the conflict plays out, healthy discussions are facilitated where all parties' positions are heard and explored, an outcome can be reached and agreed upon, concessions are likely to be made by one or all parties, allowing the different parties to move forward with a healthy conflict resolution to the issue being the outcome.

In an ideal world, this is how all conflicts would play out, but unfortunately (or fortunately dependent on your perspective), we don't live in an ideal world. How you deal with conflict will depend on several factors, including your position on the conflict, how involved your ego is in the conflict, and how you approach conflict itself. When first looking at your position on a conflict, it's important to ask yourself, at which of these three levels do I hold this position?

1. Do I hold an opinion on this issue that is open to change?
2. Do I hold a belief that governs the way I approach things and is more rigid?
3. Do I hold a conviction that my position is the absolute truth and immovable?

Your position between the three options just listed will probably change dependent upon the issue you are facing conflict in and will affect how you navigate the conflict. Through their research, couples' therapist experts Julie and John Gottman (2023) identified that there are two types of problems in relationship. Perpetual problems: a recurring problem that is difficult to resolve, and situational problems: a solvable problem about an issue or topic. Their research found that in romantic relationships, 69% of all problems are perpetual, whilst 31% are situational. Perpetual problems in a relationship can include management of finances, where one person is more financially conservative and likes to be fiscally responsible, being frugal with their money and save, whilst the other person is more financially free, willing to spend frivolously, and not concerned with saving for a rainy day. Another way this can show up in a relationship is how two parents choose to raise their children. One parent may wish to be strict with their children, setting a load of rules and boundaries, where the other parent may wish to be more flexible with their children, allowing them more freedom.

Perpetual problems can also show up in business relationships and other relationships, too. Examples include how a company focuses their spending, whereby one party may wish to commit 20% to research and development to help grow the business and the other may wish to keep that in the profits to look good on annual returns and appease the stockholders. Another example may be different cultural values towards management style, where one party may wish to manage and control their team by having everything run through them, whilst the other may wish to lead and empower by giving them a high degree of freedom and autonomy. In these examples, each party feels the position they hold is the right position for their finances, children's upbringing, investment and management style and if they hold a belief or conviction that this is the right way as opposed to an opinion, then it is likely to cause a perpetual problem that can result in a stalemate. This can cause both parties continuing to stick to their approaches to the issue (unless there is a hierarchy in place where an over-riding voice dictates the outcome) and leads to a continued breakdown in communication over the issue and likely have a knock-on effect on the relationship.

Conflict is present in all our lives and all our relationships; including the relationship we have with ourselves, which we will explore later in this chapter. The problem lies within how we deal with conflict as and when it arises. According to the Gottman Institute (2023), the sign of a healthy relationship is a 5:1 ratio, where there are five positive interactions to every negative interaction. The sign of an unhealthy relationship is a 0.8:1 ratio, where for every negative interaction there is roughly one positive one.

For those of us who grew up in an environment, where rupture and repair in a relationship was healthily modelled by our parents, we are likely to approach conflict healthily, but for many of us we weren't exposed to navigating conflict and a healthy conflict resolution. This has led to our approach to conflict being problematic, and often comes because of what John Gottman (2023) identifies as The Four Horsemen of the Apocalypse showing up when conflict arises.

The Four Horsemen of the Apocalypse are:

1. Criticism
2. Defensiveness
3. Contempt   and
4. Stonewalling

Let's look at an extreme example of how the four horseman show up in a conflict.

DEBATE. DEBATE. DEBATE.

During the 2016 US Presidential election, both Donald Trump and Hillary Clinton faced off in several televised debates in the lead up to election day, allowing viewers the opportunity to better understand each candidate's viewpoints on a number of key issues they held. Given presidential debates and the respective parties they were representing, both Donald Trump and Hilary Clinton naturally held differing opinions, beliefs and convictions to the other. As with debates, the focus will always be on areas of disagreement rather than agreement, both to differentiate one candidate from another, but also because it makes for more compelling viewing.

During the debate, as the issue of Donald Trump's tax returns came up, Clinton jumped on the criticism horse, sharing 'Why won't he release his tax returns. Maybe because he's not as rich as he says he is. Maybe he's not as charitable as he says he is. Or maybe he doesn't want the American people to know…that he's paid nothing in federal taxes.' Trump, now known the world around for not being receptive to criticism, became defensive and retorted, 'I'll release my tax returns when Hilary releases the 33,000 emails that have been deleted. As soon as she releases them, I will release my tax returns, and that's against my lawyer's advice.'

As laid out by his niece Mary L Trump in her book 'Too Much and Never Enough' (2020), Trump was often exposed to significant criticism by his father Fred Trump, leading Donald to develop an exaggerated suspicion of harassment, persecution, victimhood, or unfair treatment. This hyper-sensitivity to criticism naturally affects Donald's temperament when confronted with criticism and leads him into a combative state where he becomes defensive, employing the much-used media adage of Deny, Deflect and Double Down. Deny what is being said, deflect the attention to something else, and double down on your position.

This approach became obvious when the moderator of the debate referred to Donald Trump's support of the Iraq War in 2002 before the invasion. Trump was quick to jump on the defensive horse before jumping onto the criticism horse. 'I did not support the war on Iraq. That is a mainstream media nonsense put out by her, because the best person in her campaign is mainstream media.' When challenged by the moderator, 'The record shows otherwise.' Trump once again jumped back on the defensiveness horse to state, 'The record doesn't show that. The record shows that I'm right.'

In the same presidential debate, Hillary Clinton regularly sat on the horse of contempt when comparing positions with Trump. One example was when Donald criticised her stamina to be president. Clinton responded 'Well, as soon as he travels to 112 countries and negotiates a peace deal, a cease-fire, a release of dissidents, an opening of new opportunities in nations around the world, or even testifying for eleven hours in front of a congressional committee, he can talk to me about stamina.' Contempt, of all the four horsemen of the apocalypse, has been found to be the leading cause of the breakdown of relationships. From disdain, disrespect, hostility, eye-rolling, insensitive-joking through to sarcasm and name calling, it attacks the other person's self-esteem, whilst also intentionally abusing or manipulating the other. It causes an imbalance in the power dynamics of the relationship with the person showing contempt, looking down on the other.

At the end of the debate, both wounded from blows that each of the candidates landed on the other, each jumped on the stonewalling horse. In previous debates by former presidential candidates, it had been common practice and a sign of both maturity and etiquette to shake the other candidate/s hand. Yet at the end of the debate, each candidate refused to acknowledge the other, avoiding eye contact and both giving each other the silent treatment.

Modern US presidential debates are an extreme form of conflict that plays out in real time, shining a spotlight on the best and worst characteristics of each candidate. The 2016 US presidential election was no different, producing one of the most divisive elections in modern history. Both Donald Trump and Hillary Clinton became the two most unfavourable candidates for president in modern history, with a 2016 Gallup poll showing Clinton with a 52%

unfavourable rating and Trump a 61% unfavourable rating. In the case of the 2016 election, it was Donald Trump who ended up winning the presidency, through the electoral college, though losing the popular vote by over 3 million votes.

Once the debates have passed, election votes have been cast, and a president has been elected and sworn into office, to help get the president's agenda that they were elected on in motion (unless the country is ruled through dictatorship), a president must reach across party lines in an attempt to unify the political landscape to gain the votes needed in congress/parliament on policies they are looking to implement. Now each party will not agree on everything. Sometimes, concessions will have to be made on either or both sides. In other cases, decisions may fall along partisan lines with neither side willing to take an opposing position, either leading to a stalemate if a voting threshold isn't met, or the party who holds enough votes can push through their policy securing their position.

The same logic that applies towards conflict in politics also applies in both our professional and personal relationships too. The first problem that I often see when working with individuals who are experiencing conflict in their professional relationships is a me vs them mentality as opposed to an us vs the problem mentality. When conflict arises in a relationship, the four horsemen of the apocalypse can quickly occur, leading each party to feel hurt and wounded by the other. Negative conflict is always confrontational as opposed to conversational. This leads to heightened emotions and feelings, as heart rates soar, owing to the perceived (or actual) threat our brain is picking up on. As cortisol (the stress hormone) and adrenaline (the anxiety hormone) pumps around our body, we can initially see an increase in our ability to function when our heart rate is between 115-145 bpm. However, once our heart rate goes over 145 bpm, bad things begin to happen. Complex motor skills break down and by the time we reach 175 bpm, there is a complete breakdown in cognitive processing. As author Malcolm Gladwell (2009) points out, 'arousal leaves us mind blind'.

SELF REFLECTION TIME

Do you view the conflicts you have as a me vs them, or us vs the problem? If you enter a conflict with a me vs them attitude as opposed to an us vs the problem attitude, it's likely that you will end up summoning some or all of the four horsemen of the apocalypse. That is going to lead to either a stalemate or a breaking down of the relationship. However, if you enter the conflict, with an us vs the problem approach, and an openness to work together to resolve the issue at hand, the likelihood of a healthy resolution and repair to the rupture that caused the conflict increases dramatically.

If you haven't been shown healthy conflict resolution growing up or given the opportunity to partake in healthy conflict resolution in adulthood, it is likely you will revert to what you know when it comes to conflict. You may completely avoid conflict all together, or you may adopt one of the four horsemen of the apocalypse when entering into conflict. Each approach may have served a purpose at one point in your life. To protect you from harm, to protect your ego, but at other points or maybe more frequently, your approach is causing you problems in your relationships, and you realise you need to change your approach, as maybe you're the problem.

Each of the four horsemen of the apocalypse has their own antidote, which helps prevent you from becoming aroused in conflict, allowing you to listen to understand and respond, rather than listen to react and attack. Let's look at how you can implement each antidote to help you better navigate conflict when it arises.

CRITICISM = USING GENTLE START UP

Beginning with the first of the four horsemen; criticism, the antidote to this horseman is to use a gentle start up when entering the conflict. When approaching an area of conflict, it helps to enter the discussion with curiosity rather than furiosity (anger/fury). For example, a critical engagement would be, 'You always talk about yourself. Why are you always so selfish?' Criticism will leave the other party on the back foot and likely to result in them becoming defensive or having contempt. The gentle start up offers an invitation to reflect on what is happening and allow the other party to feel involved in the decision, rather than under threat. A template that you can use to help you with gentle start ups is:

- I feel _____
- About _____
- I Need _____

There are 5 key rules to remember when engaging in a gentle start up, which are:

1. **Make statements that start with I rather than you**. This helps you focus on what you need rather than blaming the other for what is missing.
2. **Describe what is happening.** Don't judge or evaluate here.
3. **Talk clearly about what you need in a positive terms**. This will increase the likelihood of you being both heard and understood.
4. **Be polite in your approach**. After all manners cost nothing.
5. **Give appreciation**. Show gratitude for them engaging with you.

Developing the earlier critical example into a gentle start up would look something like 'I'm feeling a little left out of our talk tonight and I need to offload. I appreciate you needed to process what has gone on for you today, and hoping we can now talk about my day?'

Be being more gentle in your start up than a harsh approach, you will help keep the other parties rational and logical brain activated. This will enable them to respond rather than react, increasing your needs being both heard and understood, and hopefully met.

Questions to ask yourself:

- When you face a conflict, do you lead or engage by criticising the other party?
- Can you evolve your critical lens and turn it into a gentle start up instead?

Remember - Don't get furious, get curious.

DEFENSIVENESS = TAKING RESPONSIBILITY

The antidote to defensiveness is taking responsibility. This is carried out in two parts. First each party takes the time to understand each other's position in the area of conflict. To do this, there are seven steps you can follow:

1. Ask the other person to clarify their position regarding the conflict.
2. Reflect only what you've heard and ask if what you've understood is correct.
3. If incorrect, ask them what you've misinterpreted so you can gain clarity.
4. When correct, validate their position 'I can understand how you came to that position.'
5. Ask if there is anything else you need to know about their position.
6. Once steps 1-5 have been completed, the roles swap until the process is completed.
7. When all parties have spoken, establish if a pathway forward can be reached.

If a pathway forward can be reached, as in there isn't a stalemate in the conflict, then each party takes responsibility for the part they played in the conflict. To do this, there are seven steps you can follow:

1. Take accountability for the part you have played in the conflict.
2. Acknowledge and apologise for the factors that have played into the conflict.
3. Share what you can do differently next time.
4. Check if the other party accepts your accountability and apology.
5. Ask if there is anything else they would appreciate you doing differently.
6. If this is possible for you to do, acknowledge you will incorporate this moving forward.
7. Once completed, move to the next party, until all members of the conflict have spoken.

An example could look like this. '(1) I can understand that when I was short with you when I returned home from work, it left you feeling hurt and unsupported. (2) I've been having a stressful time at work recently and have been taking it out on you. (3) Moving forward, I'll make an active effort to leave my stress at the door before entering our house, by going boxing in my lunch breaks when feeling stressed. (4) Would that make things better? (5) and is there anything else I can do?' The other party may respond, 'That would help.' Before they go on to acknowledge their responsibility for the conflict. '(1) I can understand that after a long and stressful day at work, you may feel overwhelmed when you arrive home, and being on you as soon as you walk in the door to support me with the kids isn't helpful. (2) I've been struggling with managing the housework and children recently, and when you come home, I want to pass the heavy lifting onto you. (3) In the future, I can ensure I give you time to unwind when you get in before asking for help, and also look into getting additional support. (4) Would that work? (5) and is there anything else I can do?'

By co-creating a space, to look at the conflict, contributing factors and misunderstandings that may have occurred, it can allow for new approaches to be explored, that can work for both parties.

Questions to ask yourself:

- Are you able to take the time to understand the other persons position in a conflict?
- Are you able take responsibility for how your actions may have impacted others?
- Are you able to come up with a different approach moving forward in an attempt to prevent the conflict from repeating?

Remember - Sometimes it's better to lose the battle, so you can win the war.

CONTEMPT = BUILD A CULTURE OF APPRECIATION AND RESPECT

The antidote to contempt is to build a culture of appreciation and respect. When you have contempt for someone, you are likely to view them as beneath you, worthless or not worthy of your time and energy. This perspective creates an imbalance in the relationship and will lead to resentment on both sides. Instead, if you look to focus on areas of appreciation and respect for the other party when addressing the issue that's causing the conflict, the other party is probably going to be a lot more receptive to addressing the issue.

For example, when expressing contempt in a conflict, you may say, 'You forgot to send the report to me again. Ugh, you're so incredibly lazy and useless.' An alternative way of addressing the conflict and building a culture of appreciation and respect could be. 'I see how busy you've been lately and appreciate how hard you must be working. I know you've got a lot on but if you could please remember to send me the weekly report before my meeting, so that I can be prepared, I'd appreciate it.' This approach will ensure the other person feels seen and understood and is more likely to engage with you than if they feel attacked through contempt.

Questions to ask yourself:

- Do you show contempt for the other party in a conflict?
- Is there a way you can express appreciation and respect whilst addressing the issue?

Remember - A spoon full of sugar makes the medicine go down.

STONE WALLING = SELF-SOOTHING

The antidote to stonewalling is self-soothing. When you are engaged in a conflict, it is understandable from time to time you will become overwhelmed and flooded with emotions. As mentioned earlier, if your heart rate exceeds a certain beat per minute (BPM) you have a complete breakdown in cognitive functioning, impairing your ability to think rationally and logically. It is likely that once you start going above 100 BPM, you will start to shut down, stop talking, and disengage. This may lead to the other person saying things including 'You're not listening to me!' and 'Say something!', but in a state of overwhelm you may be unable to (or in some cases unwilling to do so, through fear of further escalation of the issue).

At this point, or before, if possible, it is important to follow these three steps:

1. Acknowledge you are overwhelmed and need a break.
2. Provide a time when the conversation can be revisited.
3. Convey how important resolving the conflict is for you.

An example may look like this. 'I'm feeling overwhelmed with emotion, and it is affecting my ability to listen to and understand what you are saying. What you have to say about this issue is important to me, and I want to understand where you are coming from. To do this properly, I need to take 30 minutes just to regulate myself, so that together we can work on this issue and reach a resolution.' This will give you the opportunity to step away from the environment, to go and self-soothe for 30-minutes. It will help regulate your heart rate and bring you back down to a calmer disposition, so that when you return, you can hopefully discuss the issue that is causing conflict and be able to reach a resolution. To help self-sooth, you can engage in a number of activities including, breathing exercises, guided meditation, going for a walk, having a bath and stroking an animal.

Questions to ask yourself:

- Do you ever feel flooded when in conflict?
- Does this lead you to shut down, stop talking, and disengage from the other party?
- What helps you to self soothe to bring down your heart rate?

Remember - Arousal leaves us mind blind.

These examples show different ways to handle conflict, particularly when the four horsemen of the apocalypse are present. Two additional ways within which you can navigate conflict to lead to a healthy resolution are:

1. Notice the language you use.
2. Start from a point of agreement.

Have you ever noticed that when anyone begins a sentence and then the word but appears, what comes next undoes what is said before it? 'I like the idea, but I'm not sure it's right.' But has negative connotations to it. It can mean except, it can deny, renounce, reject something, leaving the person feeling unheard, hurt, rejected. Evolving your language to use building blocks to find solutions, rather than using language that takes away, could help engage rather than enrage or disengage the other party. Using the same example, an alternative could be 'I like the idea, and I'm wondering if there are other ideas we can look at alongside this to compare with.'

Here are a couple of initial questions to ask yourself:

- What word/s do you use that could be replaced in your sentences with more positive language to lead to more productive conversations? Particular words to pay attention to include but, should, have to, must.
- When entering conflict, we often start by focusing on the differences and the chasm that lies between the two (or more) positions that are held.
- What would happen instead if you switched your focus when entering a conflict and highlighted all the areas which you agree upon, before moving to the area/s of contention?

If two founders are in conflict about business growth and investment, they can start by acknowledging their shared desire for the company's success. A building point could look like, 'We both agree that the business needs to pivot in the wake of AI, and we both agree we need to invest a portion of our annual earnings into research and development.' Whilst the two founders may disagree on where to invest their money and how much, by continually bringing it back to points of agreement and building from there, it can help the founders to focus on us vs the problem, rather than me vs them.

Further questions to ask yourself:

- What areas of agreement do you have with the other party when entering a conflict?
- Do you explicitly share these with the other party?
- Can you keep circling back to these when you deviate to keep you on track?

Whilst many conflicts can be resolved or an agreement can be reached if it's a perpetual problem, not all conflicts can be resolved. Some conflicts may require a mediator or a couple's therapist to sit in and support the parties as they navigate their way through the conflict to reach a resolution. In these situations, it is important to seek the help of a trained professional and to not be afraid to ask for additional help and support in navigating your way through the conflict.

There are also some conflicts where maybe they, not you, are the problem. Roy Cohn, an influential lawyer in the twentieth and early twenty-first centuries, and Trump's mentor, was known for saying 'Never apologise. Never admit defeat.' This in part goes a long way to explaining Donald Trump's ongoing behaviour in light of him losing the 2020 presidential election and the subsequent legal issues that have come because of this outlook on life. Not everyone you enter a conflict with has the ability (be that a willingness or ableness) to reach a healthy conflict resolution. Most of the time, these individuals have sociopathic or narcissistic traits. They can't think about anyone but themselves because of their own psychological wounds. This is not to judge them, but to understand them. For if we understand that we cannot engage in healthy conflict with them, we reclaim our power and can decide whether we choose to engage with them, get enraged by them or disengage with them, or as a therapist friend once shared you either make-up, break-up or buckle up. The choice is yours.

Our ability to show up in relationships can be influenced by what we're going through in our personal life, leading to conflicts. Things such as a loss of a job, a bereavement, financial difficulties, loss of a relationship will affect your mood. Being in a helping profession such as a psychotherapist, carer, nurse that demands you to be compassionate to others may leave you feeling compassion fatigued and unable to show much, if any compassion at the end of your day. In those instances, communication is key from both parties to be able to support one another and help to avoid things from escalating.

Presenter and author Mel Robbins (2017) shone a spotlight on a technique that helps partners to show up for one another. When you and your partner connect, be that at the beginning of the day, at work, after work, start by asking a simple question; What percentage are you able to show up at today? Each partner takes turns to reflect on where they are at that day. If one person is at 20% and the other is 80%, the person with the higher percentage, asks 'In what way/s can I help you today to lighten your load and support you?' This may result in helping take on some responsibilities the other person usually carries out to help them, through to offering them a space to just offload what they're currently going through without judgment. If both parties are below a combined 100%, say at 20% each, both parties acknowledge this and ask each other, 'How can we be mindful that we are both running on empty, and where else can we turn to, to support ourselves, so that we don't resent each other for not being able to show up?'

By creating an open dialogue each day, this enables each partner to understand rather than assume what is going on with the other party. For when we assume we make an ASS out of U and ME. One last thing to pick up on that can complement this is making the time to meet regularly at an agreed time with your partner, to look at the state of your union. This gives each party the opportunity to share and reflect upon the strengths of the relationship, as well as look at the areas of development that need to be focused on to strengthen the relationship further. When entering the state of the union discussions, it is important to keep the focus on it being a discussion, not a debate. That the language used is conversational rather than confrontational by focusing on the antidotes as opposed to the four horsemen. Regularly doing both tasks allows you to handle problems promptly and view conflicts as opportunities for resolution.

Reminder - Be humble in your victories and gracious in your defeats.

TURNING YOUR ATTENTION INWARD

So far, we have focused on external conflicts, but many of our conflicts occur within us rather than outside of us. For some, it may manifest because of beliefs or rules we grew up with that cause the internal conflict. Looking at the story at the beginning of this chapter with Zac and Ralph, if you have been told not to express your thoughts, opinions and beliefs to keep the peace, to not upset others, you end up introjecting (swallowing down) those thoughts feelings and beliefs. If the feeling you swallow down is anger, it will turn into depression. By swallowing down your feelings, the wounded part of you doesn't have time to express itself, for the protector part of you is trying to keep you safe. The negative implications of that is then a war rages within between these two different parts. Your wounded part feels silenced by the protector part. Your protector part feels misunderstood by the wounded part because they are trying to protect the other from being hurt by what's going on outside. As a result, neither part feels heard and understood, resulting in each part of you feeling neglected.

This approach can lead to the defence mechanism of displacement occurring, where the feelings of the wounded part/s are misdirected onto a different person or object than the one in which they are intended for. We see this happen a lot in school where the bullies are often subjected to bullying or abusive behaviour at home by their parents or older siblings. Without the ability to retaliate, they instead take it out on someone they perceive as a weaker or an easier target. It can also show up in passive-aggressive behaviour, where aggravations are aired either to the person directly or to parties who know the cause of the conflict, because it is an easier or safer way to show displeasure at a situation. This often occurs because outright anger/frustration wasn't allowed or tolerated growing up, and this became a way for those feelings to be processed.

When you aren't provided with a healthy way to deal with conflict and come to a resolution, you will create adaptive behaviours such as displacement or passive-aggressiveness, that enable you to survive your formative years. However, as you move into adulthood, those adaptive behaviours that served you may now hinder you. Another way this conflict avoidant behaviour may show up is with a lie.

TELL ME LIES, TELL ME SWEET LITTLE LIES.

Sarah and Tom got caught up in a whirlwind romance. Falling fast for each other, they both couldn't wait to spend time with each other. Tom liked Sarah's go get it attitude to life and Sarah liked Tom's easy and agreeable approach to everything. The honeymoon period seemed to last longer than the previous relationships that Sarah had been in, where conflicts would arise due to her bull like attitude to everything, but Tom was different. Tom was happy to go along with everything that Sarah wanted to do. But the reality was far from the truth. Tom didn't want to go along with everything that Sarah wanted to do, but he wanted to keep the peace as he hated conflict and actively wanted to avoid it, so he lied. As the relationship went on, Tom would continue to agree to things he didn't want to do, ending up sacrificing his needs for the needs of Sarah, and slowly but surely, he felt the weight of the relationship pile on top of him.

Tom's need to do what he wanted to do were not getting met in the relationship and, feeling neglected, he started looking elsewhere.

It wasn't long before he found comfort in the arms of Sinead and began having an affair. Whilst Tom's agreeableness was still present in the affair because he and Sinead had a more similar outlook to life, he didn't have to lie as much. Things came to a head a couple of months later when Sarah found out that Tom was having an affair with Sinead. Sarah was heartbroken because she didn't realise there was a problem in their relationship, as Tom had been so good at keeping up appearances. Tom, wanting to avoid conflict, agreed with Sarah's proposal that they break up, when Sarah really wanted Tom to fight for their relationship, with Tom's agreeableness once again, getting in the way of a healthy conflict resolution.

In this story, we see that Tom's avoidant behaviour contributed to the breakdown of his relationship with Sarah. Tom's aversion to conflict resulted in him lying to keep the peace in his relationship, but also led to him feeling discontentment in his relationship. The leading cause of breakdowns in relationships is because of neglect, not conflict. Because of Tom's needs feeling neglected, he searched elsewhere to get his needs met, with better (although not complete) success. Relationship guru Esther Perel (2023) observes that when it comes to avoidant behaviour in relationships and the subsequent need to lie to keep the peace, 'The secret turns into a lie. The lie turns into a deception. The deception turns into a betrayal and now it has become a fiasco.' Through avoidance of dealing with an issue/problem/conflict when it shows up, you become the main facilitator in a problem blowing up further down the road.

SELF-REFLECTION TIME

Do you identify as someone that is conflict avoidant in your relationships? Consider these questions to gain insight into how conflict avoidance affects your life and relationships.

- How is my avoidance of conflict contributing to a breakdown of my relationship/s?

- Is there a healthier way I could deal with the conflict?
- What steps can I take today to become better at dealing with conflict?

Internal conflict not only arises towards people, but situations. Author Sarah Sifers (2006) identified that internally there are three main types of conflict:

1. Approach-avoidant conflict
2. Double approach conflict   and
3. Double avoidant conflict

APPROACH AVOIDANT CONFLICT

Approach avoidant conflict occurs when an individual has reason to both approach a goal and avoid it. It could be a desirable goal, such as having children at an early age, that has an undesirable goal of postponing going to university to gain a qualification.

Questions to ask yourself:

- Do you have any approach-avoidant conflicts?
- How do you decide on which option to take?

DOUBLE APPROACH CONFLICT

A double approach conflict occurs when two desirable offers appear simultaneously, and you are left to decide which one to choose. For example, it could be the choice between two attractive job offers. Although a positive position to be in, the stress it invokes in deciding can negatively affect you.

Questions to ask yourself:

- Do you have any double approach conflicts?
- Does making a decision cause you stress?

- How do you come to an informed decision?

DOUBLE AVOIDANT CONFLICT

A double avoidant conflict occurs when you have to choose between two undesirable options. An example can be of an elderly individual who must choose between a painful and risky operation and continue to live with a painful and debilitating medical condition.

Questions to ask yourself:

- Do you have any double avoidant conflicts?
- Do you avoid making a decision in this instance?
- How do you come to your decision?

If you have problems making decisions, Chapter 12, All I Do Is Win will help make the process a lot easier for you.

SELF DEVELOPMENT TIME

Before we head to Chapter 5, It's A Mad World, let's take a moment to reflect on how you will evolve your relationship with conflict moving forward, to create less problems in your life:

- How will you enter new situations when conflict arises differently moving forward?
- If you're conflict avoidant, will the techniques in this chapter help you to address your issues more easily?
- Do you know where your boundaries are and what your non-negotiables are in a conflict?
- Can you articulate them healthily so that you have a starting point to build from?

- Does it help to view conflict instead as a conversation, a discussion, a debate, or an argument? Are one of these alternative words more palatable?
- If you've unconsciously repressed your thoughts, feelings and emotions in your formative years and now consciously suppress or have unhealthy ways of dealing with them through passive aggressive behaviour or displacement, are you willing to look at processing them in a healthier way?

Take the time to sit with these questions. Give yourself time to address any problems you have or create because of your relationship with conflict.

SUMMARY

Conflict can show up in different ways and different forms. The way with which each of us navigates conflict is often based upon how we were exposed to conflict growing up. If you were shown a healthy version of conflict, where there is a rupture in the relationship and an active repair, you will attempt to model that yourself. If you witness unhealthy conflict growing up, including the avoidance of a repair, or avoiding conflict in the first place in an attempt to keep the peace, then a war is going to rage within you, leading to rupture and despair.

Not all conflict is bad. Some conflict helps us to grow as individuals and evolve our views and positions on things we previously wouldn't have addressed. A healthy ratio to conflict is 5:1 five positive interactions to one negative one, an unhealthy ratio is 0.8:1. When conflict occurs, the four horsemen of the apocalypse can appear. Criticism, defensiveness, contempt, and stonewalling will exacerbate a conflict, leading to a stalemate or breakdown in the relationship. The four antidotes that counter these horsemen to lead to a healthier conflict resolution are using a gentle start up, taking responsibility, building a culture of appreciation and respect and self-soothing.

Not all problems can be solved, with 69% of problems being perpetual and 31% being situational. Alongside this, not all parties are willing or able to partake in healthy conflict and when we realise this, we have the choice to either put up or break up with the other party. Conflict can also occur within us, as well as with others. Our avoidance to conflict can create a war within, when our true thoughts, feelings and opinions aren't honoured. If your avoidance leads to agreeableness in a relationship at the sake of your truth, it will lead to lies, which will lead to deceit and ultimately a betrayal to both yourself and your partner, when you inevitably end up having to deal with the conflict as it blows up, rather than when it shows up.

The internal conflicts also show up as either an approach-avoidant conflict, a double approach conflict, or a double avoidant conflict. This can cause unnecessary stress and pressure, or analysis paralysis, stopping you from making a decision (which in itself is a decision), the fear of missing out, and projected regret if you make the wrong decision.

5

MAD WORLD

Environments

At the turn of the century, Aryia was born in the West Bengal region of India, to her two parents, completing their family, as the younger sibling to her sister Nirvana, who was two years older than her. Aryia's family were practicing Hindus. Both her mother and father came from Vaishya backgrounds, known in Hindu culture as the third rung of the caste system, where they are believed to be cut from the Brahma's (God's) thighs and are comprised of traders. Shortly after turning two, Aryia contracted meningitis. The illness ravaged her body, and at hospital it was touch and go for a moment, with the doctors having to operate and amputate both of Aryia's legs to save her life. Following a lengthy period in the hospital, Aryia returned home, wheelchair bound, as a result of the amputation of her legs. Her parents believed Aryia's illness was the workings of karma. It was fated, or in the Hindu tongue, it was kismet. Many a creative adjustment had to be made to accommodate Aryia's change in physicality, none more so than for Aryia herself. Having only learned to walk a year before, she had to become accustomed to a new way of navigating her way through life, which would often be tricky on the roads of her town with uneven roads and pathways.

Though her physicality had become impaired, Aryia's intellect had not, and she excelled as she worked her way through school. Initially going to a local school that catered primarily to other Vaishya families in her neighbourhood, one teacher noticed Aryia's potential and convinced her parents to move her to a school slightly further afield that could nourish Aryia's potential, allowing her to excel. Despite their trepidation, Aryia went to the school, that mostly comprised of children from Kshatriya backgrounds, the second rung of the caste system. Aryia was used to being at a disadvantage in life, because of her physical impairment, but it wasn't until she attended this new school that the disadvantages played a much more significant role in her life. Throughout the school, from the teachers to her fellow students, Aryia would find that she would be overlooked, left out, or discouraged from other students' parents from hanging out with her. Only one of a handful of students from a Vaishya background, she found herself segregated from those with a Kshatriya background. The problem for Aryia was that she found little commonality with the Viashya students.

Still, Aryia persevered. She worked hard in all of her classes and took a real shining to computer programming. For two years, she had been begging her family to buy a computer for the home, so that she could keep up with the workload and not be at a disadvantage to those from a more privileged background. On her thirteenth birthday, her parents, who had scrimped and saved, finally gave Aryia what she wanted more than anything in the world, even prosthetic legs, a laptop. With any free moment, she would spend her time at the computer learning and developing her programming skills. Coming on leaps and bounds in computer programming, Aryia became frustrated that despite being more competent than anyone else in her class, or even those a couple of years older than her, her work was continually overlooked or dismissed by her teacher, in favour of Kshatriya students. This slowly but surely wore away at Aryia, who felt unfairly treated. Confiding in her mum about what was happening to her, and that she was feeling depressed, Aryia did not receive the support she was hoping and looking for. Instead, her mum grew worried. Psychological disorders are viewed in Hindu culture as bad blood that has been inherited from ancestors. It could tarnish the family name and would impact Aryia's marriage prospects in years to come.

Aryia became aware more than ever of the impact the Hindu caste system had on the ability of people to grow and thrive, feeling stifled more by this than her physical impairments to progress through life, but still, she persevered. Despite her school responsibilities and helping her family with their shop, Aryia dedicated every free second to improving her programming skills. Aryia's face lit up one evening, when one of the many programming websites she used detailed a competition being held in Delhi, where the prize was a scholarship to Stanford University to study computer programming. Seeing this as her escape from the trappings of her life, Aryia, like she had with her laptop, pleaded with her parents to help pay for the trip to Delhi. Her parents, who had been putting money away to buy their daughter prosthetic legs for her 17th birthday, deliberated back and forth. The prosthetic legs would increase her prospects in terms of marriage, the competition would increase her career prospects. The odds were extremely slim that Aryia would win, and this weighed on Aryia's parents' minds, but ultimately seeing how hard she worked, and how so many people in the community had told them how talented she was at programming, they agreed to send her to Delhi, with her mum attending also, whilst her dad and sister stayed back to run the family shop.

The trip was a whirlwind for Aryia. Having never left the state of West Bengal before, everything was exciting and new for her. She arrived at the competition full of hope and as she worked her way through the rounds, Aryia saw off her competitors one by one, until she reached the final two. It was Aryia versus a male student one year older than her, from a Brahmin background, the top rung of the Hindu caste system. The scholarship was within her reach, and it looked like the prize was hers as the final round played out, but

Aryia was pipped to the post by her competitor, who was declared the winner of the competition, to much fanfare and awarded the scholarship in front of a captive audience. Aryia, left heartbroken and hopeless, was consoled by her mother. She was reassured that she gave it her best shot, but told 'that us Vaishya people haven't been afforded the same opportunities in life.' Aryia was then taken aback by the next line. 'Maybe it's time to give up the dream of becoming a computer programmer and turn your attention instead to finding a partner and settling down?' Aryia couldn't hide her outrage, but before she could express her feelings, a woman, also from a Vaishya background, approached.

'Sorry to interrupt you both. I wanted to offer my condolences on losing the competition but also share my absolute admiration for how well you did in the competition.' Aryia looked perplexed. Who was this woman and what did she want? 'I have overcome a lot of challenges in my life to get where I am today,' she shared as she lifted her right trouser leg to reveal a prosthetic leg 'and I'm now the Senior Vice President of a successful tech company here in Delhi.' Aryia's face lit up. In front of her stood a woman that not only looked like her but had also navigated the loss of a limb and the challenges of being a Vaishya to forge a career, much like the one Aryia had dreamed of. The woman continued, 'I had hoped this year, we would finally see a Vaishya win the competition, but once again we see not only a Brahmin win but a male too. It breaks my heart to see someone like you with such potential, miss out on the opportunity to further your goals, and so if you were open to it, I would love to offer a full scholarship to study at Stanford University and a job at the company I work for when you finish to allow you to continue to harness the extraordinary talent I witnessed today.' Aryia's mum looked at her daughter in disbelief as tears ran down Aryia's eyes. That evening, the women headed out to dinner together, bonding over their backgrounds, dreams and more, at which point Aryia, who already decided the instant it was offered, formally accepted the invitation from this kind woman, Kara.

Joy followed in those next few months, as Aryia returned to celebrate with her father and sister. There was a sense of justice that prevailed when she let her school know that she was off to Stanford that September on a full scholarship to study computer programming. Envy was rife amongst her fellow students that she would continue to flourish, leaving them all behind in West Bengal. Aryia had also reclaimed her power from the teacher who had stifled her growth at every turn, and though the teacher tried their best to continue to cut Aryia down to size, she had outgrown the environment. Kara had facilitated the opportunity to flourish in a new environment, the teacher's power no longer holding any weight.

Before leaving India, Kara had also arranged for Aryia to be fitted with a pair of prosthetic legs, which had taken some getting used to, but had allowed for Aryia to move more freely, no longer requiring the wheelchair to get around. Eternally grateful to Kara, Aryia jetted off to Stanford, where she finally felt like she was in an environment that would allow her to flourish and thrive. With the campus and course more multi-cultural than anything she had experienced before, and with her physical impairment greatly improved by the aide of the prosthetic legs, Aryia felt treated more like an equal than ever before. She was not treated differently because of her physical ability, nor overlooked for her Vaishya background. And though she continued to experience some form of racism or sexism from time to time, given what she had to navigate through childhood, Aryia grew from strength to strength. Aryia's work in her sophomore year garnered international attention, with tech companies from around the world wanting to meet with her. Aryia, flattered by all the attention and the offers to come and work for a variety of companies, remained loyal to Kara. For Kara had offered her the golden ticket, affording Aryia's dreams to come true. Upon completing her degree, Aryia returned home for the summer, before relocating to Delhi, where Kara had recently taken over as CEO of the company. As Aryia began the next chapter of her life and career, in a job that she had dreamed of, ever since she first laid hands on a computer, she thought to herself, I'm finally where I was destined to be.

Aryia's story is unique in terms of the challenges and obstacles that she faced during her life, but the underlying issues that came up for her are something that anyone can face. The environment you find yourself in will have a significant impact on how you approach life. One of the biggest challenges that Aryia faced was that of the second school she visited. Her classmates ostracised her, and her teacher held her back to keep her in the position, the teacher felt she should be in. Though in Aryia's case, this was because of cultural issues and the teacher wanting to uphold the Hindu caste structure, this plays out day in and day out around the world with individuals in environments where their growth is stifled by others. In Australia and New Zealand, they refer to it as tall poppy syndrome. This is where somebody who is believed by their peers to be too successful or bragging about their success faces criticism and scrutiny and is cut down to size. Over in Japan, there is a similar common expression where 'the nail that sticks up gets hammered down'. In the Netherlands, the expression is 'don't put your head above ground level.' And in Scandinavia, they have an expression that derives from a novel by Aksel Sandemose (1933) 'You're not to think you are anything special' known more commonly as the Law of Jante.

On one hand, these various perspectives introduce a level of humility in the approach to life and work, but on the other hand, it can stifle growth. In Aryia's case, her parents had resided to the trappings of the Hindu caste system they were born into, but Aryia wanted more and not be beholden to the trappings of the environment that she found herself in. This can also play out when the emotions of jealousy (threatened, protective or fearful of losing one's position or situation to someone else) and envy (the painful feeling of wanting what someone else has) are thrown into the mix. People that are happy for your successes in life won't stifle you through jealousy or envy. They will encourage and support you. As venture capitalist Marc Andreessen (2016) notes, 'Every billionaire suffers from the same problem. Nobody around them ever says, "Hey, that stupid idea you just had is really stupid.'" Whilst billionaires may incur adversities in certain environments, they are likely to gravitate towards environments that encourage and support their ideas and avoid environments that proactively try to stifle or tear their ideas or growth down.

As you grow through life, different people come into your life whilst others leave. They may be in your life for a reason, a season or a lifetime, and often you don't know at the time which one they will be. Friends that you have grown up with, you may grow apart from. They may use lines such as 'you've changed' or throw comments around, including 'you're getting way too big for your boots.' This is less a reflection of your growth and more a reflection of their own stagnancy. They are projecting their feelings onto you, hoping to regain what once was. The problem arises if you choose to pay heed to what the individual/s are saying, and adapt accordingly to fit in. Regressing to old ways, at the sacrifice of your own growth, as opposed to finding a new environment that facilitates and encourages you to grow further. These individuals are what I refer to as The External Shitty Committee, that drain you of your energy, your motivation, your dreams and more, leaving you feel worse about yourself than before you interacted with them. They don't facilitate or enable you to become the best version of yourself.

SELF REFLECTION TIME

Think about the current environment you find yourself in. Look at the people, the culture, the religion, the politics in the environment and ask yourself if any of those factors cause problems in your life.

- Is there a manager that stifles your ability to grow in your company?

- Is there someone who's a bad influence on you and has an adverse impact on your career?
- Do you have a friend that never celebrates your successes or complains about them?
- Are there family members that cannot see challenges as opportunities to grow?
- Does your culture discriminate against part or all of your identity, preventing you from growing?

Unpack these issues and look at the impact they have had on your life, your relationships, your career.

- What limiting beliefs have they formed?
- Where would you be if you found yourself in a more supportive environment?
- What would you gain by evolving your environment into a more supportive environment?
- What would you have to give up or relinquish to be in a more supportive environment?
- What is keeping you in these environments that are stifling your growth in life?
- What is the secondary gain you derive from staying in those environments?

The physical environment you find yourself in may not be the only issue causing problems in your life. Different cultures within the same environment can cause just as many problems for you as the next story will highlight.

LOST IN TRANSLATION

An English man, German man and American man walk into a bar in the hustle and bustle of Shibuya, Tokyo, just around the corner from the hotel they are staying at. At just after 8pm, they arrived in the bar, where a Japanese man, with whom they all work alongside as part of a rapidly growing finance company, greets them. The German guy, seeing 8:01pm on the clock, apologises profusely to the Japanese man, much to the bewilderment of the American and English men. As the gentlemen are seated at a table, they wonder where their Brazilian counterpart is, and chalk it down to him being held up with some last-minute work bits before the big meeting the next day. Various senior leadership team members from around the world had been called to the company's headquarters in Tokyo, to help address some teething issues the company is experiencing with its rapid expansion from a domestic to global force in the financial world.

There had been several issues with communication between international offices. Delays and confusion on timelines and project deliverables. Complaints about certain markets holding up others. The list went on. The hope was by bringing the various teams together, they could work through the issues, identify the problems and implement solutions. Exchanging pleasantries and making small talk about families at home, as the second round of drinks arrived at the table, the Brazilian man finally joined them, at 8:32pm. With a beaming smile on his face, he greeted each of his colleagues with a hug, ignoring the hands that both the English man and Japanese man offered. Confused by his timekeeping, the American asked if something had held him up en route, but the Brazilian shrugged it off, saying 'No, No', and redirected the conversation to discuss the evening's plans. The German man reeled off a clear agenda of talking points they needed to cover that evening, impressing the American, but leaving the English and Brazilian men caught slightly off guard. For they thought this was an informal get together before the big meeting tomorrow.

The Japanese man quietly observed everything playing out, being agreeable for the most part, and being selective with what he said when not. As the third round of drinks was brought over, accompanied by some bar snacks, the conversation had turned to one point on the German man's agenda; communication issues. As the group shared some of the issues they were experiencing, the

German man, who was first to share, was frank, blunt, and honest in his feedback. Not sugar-coating it at all, he laid into all the issues he and his team were experiencing, which had the rest of the team taken aback. The American man was thinking to himself, he didn't even lead in with a positive statement before going to the areas that were causing issues in communicating between international offices. Next up was the Japanese man who spoke in metaphors. His team felt like a rock, caught in the throes of a river, not knowing which way was up and which way was down. The English man, who by this point, was five drinks in and feeling the effects of the Sake and Asahi beer he was drinking, looked at the Japanese man perplexed. 'I'm not sure if it's the alcohol, but I don't understand a word of what you're saying. You're talking in rhymes, and I don't get what the problem is?' The table all shared a laugh, and the Japanese man, realising his metaphor didn't work, attempted his best to explain the problems he and his team were facing. Though clearer, there was a lot of reading between the lines that left the other men still confused as to what the problem was.

As the dynamics continued to play out that evening, the Japanese man continued to be taken aback by his international colleagues. Though there was a level of respect between the men, the Japanese man had been taught to respect your elders and give the table to the most senior person in the room. As the eldest and most senior member of the company, the behaviour of the other men was not something he was accustomed to. In Japanese culture, you always ceded to the elder or most senior person in the room, but he remembered what he had been taught in the Japanese constitution (1947). 'Harmony should be valued, and quarrels should be avoided. Everyone has biases, and few men are far-sighted.' And with that, he let the issue pass. With all the points on the agenda covered, the German man went to sum up the meeting, looking to go around each of the men to reach an agreement and discuss the next steps. This was at odds with the Japanese man. Used to a hierarchal approach to decision-making, he instead stepped in and took over, wrapping up the meeting points, before sharing that they should all head around the corner to one of his favourite karaoke bars. The Brazilian man was excited to go out and get to know his colleagues more, and the English man, though a little worse for wear, was agreeable to this unforeseen plan. This curve ball caught the American and German men off guard. They hadn't accounted for this late-night social obligation, and both said they had to leave and head back to the hotel. With the group splitting off into the night, the American and German guy felt more anxious about the next morning than they had when they started the evening and set about planning what they needed to do to be prepared, glad that they didn't follow the other guys out. The English, Brazilian and Japanese men continued to the karaoke bar, where they spent the next couple of hours drinking the night away, sharing stories from their respective countries and understanding the differences and similarities between them all.

The next morning, a little worse for wear, the English man and Brazilian man grabbed themselves a large cup of coffee each as they prepared for the meeting. They went to sit with their American and German colleagues from the night before, who looked apprehensive about the challenges that lie ahead. Standing at the front was the Japanese man, who looked as fresh as a daisy, without a trace of a hangover from the night before. As he began his speech, he shared with the room that last night over drinks with some of the team and at karaoke; he realized what the main issue was, that was causing the global organisation to run into so many problems. Coming from a variety of different cultures, with different approaches, things are continually getting lost in translation. The Japanese man had arranged for a culture specialist to come in at short notice, and over the next two days, work with the team to iron out the issues that they were experiencing. A year on at the same bar, the gentleman all got together again, this time with much more understanding of all the nuances that shaped their individual perspectives to life. The many issues that plagued the company the previous year no longer caused any of them major issues, and with a celebratory sake bomb, that the English man quickly regretted, they toasted to each other and the progress they made.

As the Japanese man in this story came to discover, the issues that the company was facing were down to the cultural differences that each regional office had comparative to one another. Though in some areas, certain cultures may closely align, in others, they would be miles apart. For each regional manager was doing what was normal for them in their culture, but the trouble often occurs cross-culturally with the word normal. Normal for whom? Author and culture expert Erin Meyer discusses the invisible boundaries that occur in cross-culture communication in her book The Culture Map (2016), identifying eight key areas that cause challenges when it comes to communicating between different cultures. The eight areas are:

1. **Communicating** - Low Context vs High Context
2. **Evaluating** - Direct Negative Feedback vs Indirect Negative Feedback
3. **Persuading** - Principles First vs Applications First
4. **Leading** - Egalitarian vs Hierarchical
5. **Deciding** - Consensual vs Top Down
6. **Trusting** - Task Based vs Relationship Based
7. **Disagreeing** - Confrontational vs Avoid Confrontation
8. **Scheduling** - Linear Time vs Flexible Time

In the story we saw how scheduling was linear for the Japanese man and the German, less so for the American and English man and very flexible with the Brazilian. For evaluating, the German man was very direct with his negative feedback comparative to the American who was used to a more positive first approach rather than straight to the negative. The Japanese man was high context in his communication using a lot of metaphors to convey his points, which was at odds with his American colleague who was low context, being clear and concise with his communication. The German man embraced disagreement, which was at odds with the

Japanese man who avoided confrontation wherever possible. When it came to leading and decision making the group were all happy with an egalitarian approach, though not averse to a hierarchical approach, but the decision making was less consensual through the eyes of the Japanese man, who pulled rank to confirm the outcomes, before moving the events of the evening onto the karaoke bar. Here is where Meyer (2016) notes that the Japanese and Brazilian men are aligned, as they build trust through relationships, whereas trust for the German and American man, they build trust in others upon results.

A fish doesn't realise it is in water until you take it out of its environment, where it quickly becomes apparent that air is different to water. The same is true for us. If we never leave the same environment we are in, we aren't exposed to different ways of communicating, working and learning that there are different ways to do things. It still blows my mind that according to the US State Department (2023), nearly two-thirds of Americans don't own a passport, with 11% of Americans never leaving the state they were born in.

Before I became I psychotherapist, I spent 18 years of my life working in the music industry for Sony and Universal, travelling the world with artists and working on projects including Enrique Iglesias, Kanye West, Spice Girls, Mariah Carey, George Michael, Sean Paul, Chainsmokers, Davido, Kygo, Labrinth, and countless more. Each of the artists came from a different cultural background, and each of the artists I travelled with were exposed to cultures different to the ones they knew. Some assimilated quickly, whilst others grew frustrated with the culture clashes around things such as scheduling or communicating. Having now visited over 155 countries in the world, I understand the importance of cultural competency and how easily problems can arise when a clash of cultures occurs due to a misunderstanding. But the question is do you?

SELF REFLECTION TIME

Think for a moment about yourself.

- What is your cultural background and how has that shaped the person you are today?
- What is the lineage of your parents?
- Do you live in the same country you were born in?
- How well travelled are you?
- How much exposure do you regularly experience to different cultures where you live?

SELF DEVELOPMENT TIME

All of these factors influence the person you are today. Let's go a step further. Take a moment to go back and look at the eight areas Erin Meyer identified, and see where you sit on each of them, acknowledging you may be between the two positions in one or more of them.

- Does your position on any of the aforementioned eight points cause any issues in your relationships, professionally, personally, romantically with others?
- If you have issues in communicating with others because you are low context and they are high context, using metaphors and expecting you to read between the lines, would it help to ask the other person to be clearer? Or the opposite, if it's the other way around.
- If you are experiencing issues with the delivery of the feedback of the other person, could you explain your feedback style, or understand theirs better, so that adjustments can be made to help smooth out any problems?
- When looking at persuading others to see or agree with your point, are you using the wrong approach and could moving to the opposite approach work for you? If you

are the one having a hard time being persuaded, could you share you need to understand more from a principle perspective (facts and opinions first) or applications perspective (theories and concepts) to help you reach a decision?
- As leadership clashes emerge, have you taken the time to understand the other person's approach and shared yours, so that a pathway forward can be agreed upon?
- During decision-making processes, are clashes occurring because you are using a top-down approach versus a consensual one? Is the opposite problem occurring? Do you understand what decision-making process is required in different relationships?
- When building trust, do you prefer to let hard work earn your trust, or do you like to build the relationship to earn trust? Is this affecting your ability to build trust with others who have an opposite approach to trust? Can you adjust your approach to accommodate these differences?
- If disagreements arise, how do you approach them? Is your confrontational approach or avoidance of confrontation compounding the problem? Could a different approach make the disagreements easier to work through?
- Are you always late, or extremely punctual? Does this impact your relationship with others? Would being more punctual, or more relaxed with your timekeeping, improve your relationships with others?

In each of these eight areas, it is likely, with different relationships, that you will have to adjust your approach slightly, tailoring it to the nuances of each individual. As humans, we can either be like ice cubes, fixed and rigid, or transform into water and be free flowing, adjusting to the surrounding environment. With a willingness and ability to look at how your cultural touchpoints may contribute to problems in your interpersonal relationships, and a proactive approach to evolving elements of yourself, to accommodate these differences, it is likely to significantly improve many of your relationships and reduce the number of problems in your life.

What happens if you find yourself entering into environments that you feel are healthy for you, but actually end up being unhealthy and problematic for you? The next two stories will help to highlight how a perceived healthy environment can quickly turn unhealthy for individuals.

WHERE DID IT ALL GO WRONG?

Emily arrived at her aunt's council estate the day after her parents' funeral. Their unexpected deaths as a result of a deadly car crash meant that Emily's aunt had become her legal guardian. At twelve-years-old, Emily had moved from rural-England to the hustle and bustle of Brixton. Her world completely turned upside down in the space of a matter of weeks. Gone were her parents, her home, her school friends. In place was a completely new environment. A small bedroom, in a high-rise tower block, on a large estate in what felt like the epicentre of the world. Emily did the best she could to adjust to her new life, and her aunt Michelle did the same, attempting to become a guardian to her niece, whilst juggling a full-time profession, all on her own. As the new kid in school, joining halfway through the school year, Emily was thrown into the deep end. Still processing her grief, she largely kept to herself and did the best she could to make it through the day.

Over the following year, Emily came out of her shell. Michelle, though rarely home because of the demands of her job, always attempted to make sure there was food in the fridge and to spend time with Emily when she could. This left a lot of time outside of school for Emily to be alone. She missed the sense of family and community that she had back where she was from and longed for that connection once more. She knew she couldn't get her parent's back, but she hoped she could find something similar to replicate it.

Her wish came true, when one day, just before her fourteenth birthday, when getting the lift to her floor, a stylish woman got into the lift and started talking to Emily. 'I've seen you here once or twice before haven't I' Kerry said. 'Yes, I moved here eighteen months ago.' As the two got talking on the short ride up to the same floor, Emily felt drawn to the magnetic energy of Kerry, and was pleased when she invited her to join her and her friends just along the hallway to a little gathering, they were having.

Emily began to spend more and more time with Kerry and her friends. The youngest of the group, by at least six-years, she was treated like an adult and finally felt like she was part of a family once more that her aunt could not create. Across the estate, people respected Kerry and by proxy, this meant that Emily was respected too. Emily enjoyed hanging out with Kerry, and as the relationship deepened, Kerry would ask Emily to do little errands for her, dropping off some packages here and there, and picking up the money for them. At first, Emily was naïve, not realising what was in the packages that were cleverly concealed, but it soon dawned on her she was selling drugs to people from all walks of life. Morally, Emily felt conflicted. Her parents had warned her just before they died that drugs were bad, but they weren't here anymore and Kerry had quickly become the closest thing to family. She didn't want to lose that, and so she pushed her morals to one side.

Things were slowly becoming more difficult with her aunt Michelle. Michelle had got a new boyfriend, who was coming over more and more. The two didn't get along, and Emily, wanting to spend more and more time with Kerry and her friends, would stay out later and later. Her schoolwork was being affected, and she'd started to drink, which all came to a head one day, when Michelle received a call from the school, saying that they were concerned about Emily's attendance and behaviour. Confronting Emily, Michelle, who was unaware of her dwindling attendance at school, offered her an ultimatum. Either Emily pull herself together, stop hanging out with these people she'd been skipping school for and get her grades up, or she'd have to leave the apartment. It surprised Michelle when she thought Emily had gone to her room sulking, conceding to what she'd said, but returned a few minutes later with all her belongings in various bags and marched out of the house.

Calling Kerry up and explaining her situation, Kerry invited Emily to move in to one of the groups apartment's across the estate, reassuring Emily she'd made the right decision and that these were in fact her family, albeit chosen family, as opposed to Michelle who was just family by blood. Not long after, Emily found herself deeper integrated into the group, and on her fifteenth birthday, dropped out of school so that she could spend more time with the group. Doing daily deliveries for Kerry at all hours of the day and night, Emily made enough money to cover the rent she now paid, and also live a comfortable life.

Emily's confidence grew, as did her cockiness and complacency, which came back to bite her in the ass, when one night, just short of her sixteenth birthday, whilst out delivering packages, one customer was an undercover police officer, busting her and Claudette, arresting them both and throwing them into the back of the car. Petrified, Emily had never been in trouble with the police before. The seriousness of the situation Emily was in quickly dawned on her, and turning to Claudette for reassurance that everything would be okay, Claudette turned, looked at Emily and said 'snitches get stitches' and turned back to look out of the window.

At the station, Emily was interrogated by the police. Establishing that she was a minor, she would go to juvenile detention as opposed to an adult prison, but was still facing time locked away. The officers wanted Emily to tell them who she was working for, that she would face less time locked away, but all she could hear was the words Claudette said, 'snitches get stitches' circle round and round in her head. Sat despondently in the chair, Emily said nothing, and was returned to a cell, where she sat alone. How did it end up like this? Emily thought, staring at the prison wall. Three years ago, everything seemed perfect, and now not only had her parents had been taken from her, but her home, her education and now her freedom too. A day passed before she had any visitors, and it surprised Emily when it was her aunt Michelle that turned up with her partner and not Kerry or any of her group of friends. She felt like a penguin, who abandon the weakest or struggling member/s of the group, as opposed to an elephant which rally round and nurtures the weak back to health. When the going gets tough, the tough get going, she thought, and Michelle, with no judgment in her eyes, only love and support, reassured Emily they would get through this, and sort it all out.

Emily's story is one that plays out all around the world. An individual looking for connection and belonging, who overlooks their morals, making questionable choices, that result in negative consequences. It can be on the more extreme end, like in Emily's case, falling into a life of criminal behaviour, all the way through to falling in with the wrong crowd at school, work, friendship groups, who have questionable behaviour. The need to feel connected and to belong clouds the ability to make rational and logical judgments that, over time, can lead to problems occurring in an individual's life.

SELF REFLECTION TIME

Think for a moment about any negative relationships you have or have had in your life.

- What drove you to connect with those individuals?
- Did you question or overlook your morals to stay connected with these individuals?
- Did you do something you knew was wrong but threw caution to the wind and did it, anyway?
- How have those decisions impacted your life?

- What problems have they bring up for you?
- Was your performance at work or in school impacted?
- Did you get suspended/expelled from school or fired from your job?
- Did other relationships become adversely impacted?

Sit with these questions and explore what comes up for you, whilst we take another look at how another perceived healthy environment can become problematic over time.

MY LONELINESS IS KILLING ME

Laurence sat across from me in my therapy office with tears rolling down his face and shared, 'I've never felt so alone.' We'd only just began our first session together, but I got a sense of where this would be going. This is a theme that continues to become more common over time in my private practice. A study by Cigna (2022) revealed that 58% of American's feel lonely. The City Index Survey's (2023) list of the loneliest cities revealed that 56% of Londoners felt lonely, 52% in New York, 50% in Dubai, 46% for Hong Kong and Sao Paolo. This figure is surprising to many, though in the dawn of the digital era, and taking a quick look at commutes around the world, everyone's faces are buried in their phones as opposed to engaging with the real world. It's no surprise that, whilst the world is more connected than ever, it is also lonelier than ever. Laurence had grown up with the internet and social media. It is where all his 'friends' spend the majority of their time.

A self-proclaimed nerd at school, Laurence didn't have many friends. He sought out chat rooms to make connections with others. On his various social media platforms, he followed accounts and content displaying interests that he had, including war games and history, and would have content fed into his algorithm that correlated to these interests. There were some out there individuals in the chat rooms, sharing conspiracy theories and controversial statements that, for the most part, Laurence laughed at, but nonetheless engaged with, through a like, a comment or a share. Laurence, like so many individuals these days, spent the majority of his time online. A quick look at his iPhone showed he spent around 13 hours a day on his device. A statistic that becomes even more startling when he acknowledged he would sleep roughly 8 hours a night. Laurence acknowledged it was now a problem for him, but at the time it provided him with a community, a sense of belonging in the chat rooms and across his social media platforms. He felt seen and heard online, whereas in the real world, he felt invisible. His views were also views others agreed with in the spaces he spent his time online, forming somewhat of an echo-chamber, where opposing views were shut down and pushed out.

Over time, Laurence's positions evolved, as the algorithms fed him more sensationalised content related to his interests. Influencers like Andrew Tate would show up, and though he didn't agree with some of what he shared, Andrew spoke to the part of Laurence that felt marginalised by society and women. He rarely had any luck on dating apps, either. The women he liked never seemed to like him, and the only women he seemed to receive an interest from were the women he didn't like. When he did finally match with someone, and agree to a date in real life, the date was awkward. His real-life social skills were limited, as he was so used to communicating in written form. His views had become more like convictions on certain subjects and he was unable and unwilling to see his date's side, convinced that his view was right and hers wrong. Unsurprisingly, this meant there was no second date on the cards, and he was back to feeling alone once more.

Laurence had a slim demeanour, and to keep in shape, he used his virtual headset and downloaded fitness apps, rather than attending a gym. He would compete with others online in these fitness games, but once the headset came off, he was back on his own again. His life was filled with AI. Not artificial intelligence, but artificial intimacy. The likes, comments and shares on his posts. The competition with others on digital games. The matches on dating apps. They all provided a sense of connection, but they all existed in the digital world. Though he knew these individuals, apart from the odd unsuccessful date, he never actually met any of them in the real world. The rise of AI, artificial intelligence, further compounded the artificial intimacy he was experiencing, where he would converse with an AI platform like ChatGPT, or hardware such as his Alexa, more than any real-world communication.

Laurence's job was fully remote based, meaning he could work from home. Apart from his job interview and a monthly zoom meeting with his team, he was left to his own devices to do his job. This further compounded his sense of loneliness in his one-bedroom apartment in Central London. Laurence would sit at home all day, every day, living his life online. The only interactions with real life humans would be the food delivery person, or the Amazon driver with his packages. But online he was desperate to form connections with others. Continuing to swipe on dating apps in the hope of a match that would work out this time, or posting content in the chat rooms and on his socials looking for engagement and interaction. As author Noreena Hertz (2020) notes, 'It is the constant process of having to sell oneself – and the constant fear that no one will want to buy – that's the problem.'

Laurence had noticed, the more divisive the content he posted online, the more engagement he would receive, and so he started ramping up this content, which saw his popularity soar, until one day, he posted something across his socials and on the chatroom's he visited that was so out there, that it saw his accounts suspended. He already felt cut off from the real world, but now he had been cut off from the world that had given him a lifeline. Laurence didn't know what to do, and that had resulted in him seeking therapy to work through the problems he was facing. Over our time working together, Laurence slowly but surely stepped out more into the real world. Joining a gym that ran classes so he could meet other people. Looking up groups that had similar interests that met in person.

Finding a new job that had a hybrid working structure, so that he could meet and interact with his colleagues in real life. It didn't always go smoothly for Laurence, and there were often more downs than ups, but over time, the connection and belonging he spent all his time looking for online, he began to find in the real world.

The internet, and more recently, social media, is an environment the majority of the world is now immersed in, with over two-thirds of the global population having access to the internet. Whilst it has a lot of positive aspects to it, there is also a darker side to it. One of the major problems it is causing is artificial intimacy. Real world connection and intimacy are being replaced by likes, shares and comments, leading to people feeling more alone. Social media has turned from a platform of connection to a platform of self-promotion where vanity validation is sought. Users are all fed different content, based on an algorithm that shares content it thinks you will like, from previous content you have engaged with. According to digital expert Wylie (2019), 'using Facebook likes, a computer model reigned supreme in predicting human behaviour. With ten likes, the model predicted a person's behaviour more accurately than one of their co-workers. With 150 likes, better than a family member. And with 300 likes, the model knew the person better than their own spouse.' Pre-internet era, if you appeared on Terry Wogan's TV chat-show on BBC 1 and on his Radio 2 show, you could reach 70% of the UK population. These days, with individualised algorithms, it becomes harder to reach a mass audience, yet the personalised feeds that every social media user scrolls through can leave users feeling that everyone is seeing the same content as they are.

Cambridge Analytica was able to weaponise this during several elections around the world, most famously in the 2016 US presidential election. By targeting people based on a psychological model known as OCEAN, that helps to construct people's personalities based on their Openness (O), Conscientiousness (C), Extrovertedness (E) Agreeableness (A) and Neuroticism (N), Cambridge Analytica could influence people's thoughts, beliefs and behaviours. Through feeding them bespoke content that would compound their position or alter their position on certain subject matters, it would have the result of moving them or cementing them in voting for the candidate that Cambridge Analytica was working for. Following several successful campaigns, Cambridge Analytica was exposed by whistle blowers and shut down, but it shone a spotlight on the dark side of social media and the internet, how easily it can be to manipulate human behaviour, stoke division amongst cultures and society and cause mass problems. The dawn of AI, that can replicate voices and create realistic deep fake videos, looks set to be the next wave of problems humanity will face with this online environment the world finds itself living in.

SELF REFLECTION TIME

Think about your own relationship with the internet, social media and digital devices.

- In what ways and how do they improve your life, and in what ways and how do they cause problems?
- Do they make you feel lonelier?
- Do they cause you to have a negative perception of yourself?
- Does the content that fills your feeds evoke certain negative reactions within you?
- How much time do you spend engaging with digital devices daily?
- Does your interaction with the digital world have an adverse impact on your interaction with the real world?
- How many of your followers in the digital world are real world friends that you could call up if going through a difficult time and would answer the phone and come to support you?

- Are there ways that you can evolve your engagement with the digital world to spend more time in the physical world?

For Laurence it was joining fitness classes, real world group meet-ups on hobbies and interests he has, and moving jobs to interact with colleagues in real life.

- What would that look like for you?
- Could a digital detox for a period of time improve your mental health and well-being?

These are just some questions to help you begin to look at the digital environment you find yourself in, identify any areas that may be problematic and explore what you could do to change that. The digital world we all find ourselves in has a lot of positive aspects too and we appreciate that, but for the purpose of this book, Maybe You're The Problem, it's about looking at the problematic areas of your life; and in this chapter the environments you find yourself in, and working on these problems to create a better life for you.

SUMMARY

The environments we find ourselves in can allow us to flourish and thrive or stifle our growth. Different plants have different needs, even in the same environment, in order to survive. A cactus can go for days without water, whereas tomatoes need watering every day or two. Like plants, we can be similar to others, but have different needs in the same environment that allows us to grow and thrive. Certain environments, because of cultural, religious or societal rules and beliefs, can stifle and individuals' growth, causing cognitive dissonance. Switching to different environments can remove some or all of these problems. In certain cultures, poppy syndrome (or its equivalent) can occur where a person is cut down to size, for daring to stand out amongst a crowd, be successful or celebrate their successes. If this is causing problems, look to find environments that allow you to grow without restrictions that impede your growth. Living in a multi-cultural society or working for an international corporation can lead to problems, where a lack of understanding of the different cultural references is likely to lead to communication getting lost in translation. Taking the time to understand, learn and immerse oneself in different cultures can remove the invisible barriers that different cultures can bring.

Loneliness can be a key driver in falling into environments that cause problems. The need to feel connected and to belong can cause individuals to overlook or bypass their morals, all to be a part of something. Falling into the wrong crowd can down the road cause issues in inter-personal relationships, in work and with the criminal justice system. The same is true for the digital world. The rise of AI, artificial intimacy, is causing problems for people around the world, where over 50% of the global population now feels lonely on a regular basis. Though the internet and social media has brought many positive changes to the world, it also has a dark side. With social media being weaponised by the likes of Cambridge Analytica to influence human behaviour, the rise of divisive characters like Andrew Tate who hold extreme views on subjects, or terrorist organisations who radicalize impressionable people online, the digital world we all live in is continuing to create more problems for individuals and society than solutions. It is important we monitor our usage and our intentions when engaging online, to see where problems may arise, and to form real world connections to nourish the part of ourselves that yearns to feel connected and to belong, rather than become dependent on artificial connections in the digital world.

6

TALKING ABOUT MY GENERATION

Generations

Brian sat alongside his brother nervously on the couch, watching TV with the rest of his family, as numbers began to be called out on the screen. The year was 1972 and Brian had only recently turned eighteen. The Vietnam war had carried on for over sixteen years at this point, and since 1969, young men in the United States, between the ages of eighteen to twenty-six, were being drafted based on their date of birth. With 366 blue plastic capsules placed in a large plastic container, one by one balls were being pulled and read out, notifying viewers which individuals based on their birth date had been drafted. Brian's brother Daniel, who was fifteen at the time, idolised his older brother and did not want Brian's birth date to be called out. There was a moment of relief when the family thought all the numbers for that year had been called, but one last ball was to be drawn, and as the number was read out on TV, the family's heart sank. Brian's birth date had been drawn, and he would be called to serve in the US army on a conscription for two years in Vietnam.

Leaving for the war, the family wished Brian an emotional farewell, with him promising to write letters home to keep them updated as he embarked on serving his country. Brian was against the war in Vietnam and had even joined in some protests that had unfolded on his high school campus. But duty bound to the country, he went off to serve his time. The war was tough on Brian. During his assignment, he lost several of his friends through various attacks that broke out, and he often wondered to himself, what are we even fighting for? Without the ability to go home for the holidays or special occasions, Brian had to make do with corresponding via letters and the occasional call, when he would find himself in Saigon as it was then known. Reaching the final stint of his conscription out in Vietnam, Brian was counting down the days until he would return home, noting that he would make it back just in time to see his brother Daniel turn eighteen. A week before Brian's return, he notified his parents about his return, but told them to keep the surprise from Daniel, for he wanted to knock on the door and surprise him on his birthday. The ultimate present for Daniel was getting his brother back.

The day in question came, and Daniel's eighteenth birthday party held at the family home was in full swing. When the doorbell rang, Daniel's parents shared a knowing look at each other in anticipation of the surprise that was behind the door. Daniel, distracted by his friends, was encouraged by his mother to answer the door, for his last present was being delivered later than planned. As Daniel opened the door, excited to see what the present was on the other side of the door, he looked confused when he was greeted by an army officer holding a folded American flag. Initially confused, his heart sank as the reality set in and the officer asked if Mr. and Mrs. Winterfeldt were home. The surprise was not the surprise the family were expecting or the one they had discussed just a few days earlier with Brian. On the last day before being discharged, Brian's unit had been caught in an offensive attack by the Viet Cong. Looking to protect his unit from the onslaught of bullets raining down on them, Brian attempted to launch a counter-offensive, but was taken out by a grenade, his body blown to bits.

With his remains returned to the US, as the family prepared to say goodbye to Brian, Daniel was inconsolable. He was now the same age that Brian was, but US citizens were no longer being drafted for the war. The war was beginning to wind down, ending less than a year later in 1975. Daniel was full of what ifs in his mind. What if Brian had been born two years later, like he was? He wouldn't have had to fight a war he didn't believe in. What if Brian had been born one day later? His birthday wouldn't have been called and he wouldn't have been called up to serve. What if Daniel was born a few years earlier? Would he have been called up to serve? If the war carried on even longer, would the same fate have befallen unto him?

Brian was born during a generational period that meant he would be old enough to serve in the Vietnam war, and young enough to not be ruled out of serving on determination that his age was disadvantageous to the US army. His brother born, but two years later, escaped this fate, being too young to serve. His father Samuel born in 1934, who had lost his own father Eric (Brian and Daniels Grandfather) in the second world war, was deemed too old to serve by the time the drafting for the Vietnam war occurred. The generation that Samuel and Daniel had both respectively been born into, had aligned with the time in history that they didn't end up serving in a war, whereas both Brian and his grandfather Eric, found themselves in generations that made them eligible for duty.

Fast forward, fifty years from the day the Winterfeldt family sat around the TV watching the drafting being called out on live TV, a chill filled the winter air, on a frosty night late in February 2022. I was meeting two of my dearest friends, Frank and Ivanna Borin, for dinner. The couple are two amazing video directors and executive producers, who had just flown in from Los Angeles, ahead of another major video shoot they would do, this time for Harry Styles 'As It Was.' The talented Tanu Muino had also flown in to direct the video, and the amazing Nikita Kuzmenko would be director of photography for the shoot. As we all sat down to dinner, on the eve of what would become a game changing song and video for Harry Styles, sending his profile stratospheric, the mood was not that of excitement, but a whole mixture of emotions. It was 24th February 2022, the day that Russia invaded Ukraine. Ivanna, who now lived in Los Angeles, was born and grew up in Ukraine, and both Tanu and Nikita were living in Ukraine at the time. Their ability to navigate shooting the music video, whilst simultaneously having to process the war that was unfolding in their homeland, is a testament to the incredible mental agility each of them has. A million different questions were flying around each of their heads, many similar, but some unique, to each individual. For Ivanna, would her family be safe where they lived, and could safe passage be arranged for them to leave? For Nikita, upon his return to Ukraine, would he be called up to serve in the army? For Tanu, would she be able to return home after the video shoot, or would she become a nomad?

The war would impact them, their family members, people all over Ukraine and beyond, from different generations in different ways. Children would be forced to leave their education behind, with schools being bombed and families fleeing. Young adults would be called up to serve in the army, having to put any careers on hold, and become separated from their loved ones. Parents and elder generations would witness all that they had worked hard for; their businesses, their homes, destroyed in the conflict of war. Torn between the decision to stay if perceived safe to do so and being forced to become refugees, displaced because of the war. No one from Ukraine, or with ties or relations to Ukraine, would be unaffected by the war brought on by Russia. Yet the impact of the war, still ongoing as this book is being written, is still to be realised. How will losing out on an education impact those children who were forced to flee in their later life? How will being drafted for the army impact those who had to put their lives and careers on hold? How will those who worked hard to build their businesses and own their own homes navigate losing it all and have to build a life for themselves again? How will the effects of the war shape the way future generations of Ukrainians are raised? Many of these questions remain unknown and unanswered, but history provides us with clues. For whilst history never repeats itself, it often rhymes. History offers us the ability to look at what happened in previous generations, allowing us to learn of patterns that have played out over centuries, to make predictions and forecasts of how the future may play out.

As we grow through life, we begin to identify that certain key events we have experienced and gone through (Brexit, 9/11, Great Recession) have shaped who we are. How these key events shaped us has a lot to do with how old we were when they happened. This is how generations form. Historical events shape generations differently depending on the stage of life they are in. In other words, generations are shaped by the intersection of the stage of their life and time. A generation is the aggregate of all people born over a span of between roughly fifteen to twenty years, or about the length of one phase of life: childhood, young adulthood, midlife, and old age. Combining the insights of writers, including John Stuart Mill (2004), August Compte (1997) through to Karl Manheim (2013) and Ortega and Gassett (1931), three primary criteria that help to define a generation, were identified.

1. Members of a generation share an age location in history. They encounter key historical events and social trends while occupying the same phase of life. For example, Generation Z (1997-2012) came of age during the advent of social media. Millennials (1981-1996) entered adulthood, the workforce, and the property ladder in the aftermath of 9/11 and during and post the 2008 global recession.
2. Members of a generation will be shaped by the eras they encounter during their formative years. They also tend to share some common beliefs and behaviours, including basic attitudes about risk taking, culture and values, civic engagement, and family life.

3. Members of each generation who share similar experiences and traits will form a sense of community with their generation. They view other generations as different to their own with a unique perspective towards life, that others don't share.

Focusing in on the second point, generations are shaped by the events that will have occurred during their formative years. If growing up during the depression in 1929 or the great recession in 2008, that resulted in a period of austerity, you are likely to experience a different environment than growing up in a boom or growth period, resulting in the likelihood of a different relationship to finances. If growing up during a period of war, as opposed to growing up during a period of peace, you are likely to have a different relationship to safety and freedom. Your primary caregivers may be more frugal with their finances to make them go further. They may be more protective because of the lack of safety experienced in the world. These behaviours shape the beliefs of a generation that have long-lasting impacts on the way each generation approaches the world.

Authors William Strauss and Neil Howe (1992) identified correlations between generations when reflecting on human history from 1584 into the future up to 2069, noting that patterns emerged and repeated every eighty to ninety years. Split into four cycles, they discovered that through time, based on what a generation was exposed to in their formative years, it would dictate the majority of that generation's outlook and behaviours to life during different periods of their lives, as different key events; wars, recessions, pandemics, booms unfolded. They identified four turnings over an eighty to ninety-year period, and below I've highlighted the most recent cycle in human history:

1. **High (First turning)** – Post Second World War Boom (1946 – 1960)

2. **Awakening (Second Turning)** – Consciousness Revolution (1961 – 1981)
3. **Unravelling (Third Turning)** – Thatcherism, Reaganomics and Culture Wars (1982 – 2006)
4. **Crisis (Fourth Turning)** – Great Recession, Brexit, Global Pandemic (2007 – 2027)

Dependent on when you are reading or listening to this book, you are likely to be, at this moment in time, in the fourth turning; crisis, or heading into the next turning from 2028 onwards, when history tells us we will return to the first turning again; high. Looking at the current generations inhabiting the planet, each can be found in the following turnings;

- **The Silent Generation (1925 – 1945)** were born into the fourth turning; Crisis.
- **The Boomer Generation (1946 – 1960)** were born into the first turning; High.
- **Generation X (1961 – 1980)** were born into the second turning; Awakening.
- **Millennials (1981 – 1996)** [though some variations to this time frame occur dependent on who you ask] were born in the third turning; Unravelling.
- **Gen Z (1997 – 2012)** [again some variations occur here] were born into the tail end of the third turning: Unravelling, and into the fourth turning; Crisis.
- **The Alpha Generation (2013 – 2027)** [with this generation still occurring, exact dates are still to be determined] born into the fourth turning, crisis.

Looking at the current climate we find ourselves in over the past fifteen to twenty years, it is not surprising to see we are in the fourth turning; crisis. From the great recession of 2008 that led to a period of austerity around the world, through to the rising of cult like leaders from Donald Trump in the US and Jair Bolsonaro of Brazil, sowing division rather than unification between their population.

The global COVID-19 pandemic of 2020 to the wars between Ukraine and Russia, Israel and Hamas, a prolonged period of crisis during this turning, will have different impacts on different generations. We can see this in the Figure 6.1, which highlights how different generations will feel at different periods of their lives, based on which turning they are in.

BIRTH YEAR (ACROSS) AGE (BELOW)	1920 - 1940 CRISIS	1941 - 1961 HIGH	1962 - 1982 AWAKENING	1983 - 2003 UNRAVELLING	2004 - 2027 CRISIS
ELDER AGE 66-87	Sensitive	Visionary	Reclusive	Busy	Sensitive
MIDLIFE AGE 44-65	Moralistic	Pragmatic	Powerful	Indecisive	Moralistic
YOUNG ADULT AGE 22-43	Alienated	Heroic	Conformist	Narcissistic	Alienated
CHILDREN AGE 0-21	Protected	Suffocated	Indulged	Criticised	Protected

Figure 6.1 - The Generational Diagonal of the Past 100 Years.

To identify your own pathway through the different turnings follow the below steps:

- Start by going across the top column and find the row, which aligns with your birth year.
- Next, head to the bottom cell of that row to identify what your childhood was likely to have been.
- Then move right to the next turning, and move up one cell, to the next period of your life (young adult). This will highlight a key perspective your childhood will have given you.
- Next continue across one turning, and up one cell to identify your outlook in midlife.
- Finally, move across one last turning and up one cell to identify how you feel as an elder.

If you reach the last column on Figure 6.1 before reaching the elder age range, i.e you are only at midlife, for your elder column, move to the second column 1940-1961 High, to discover your next word, and continue the steps, until you reach the elder column. An example of this would be, if you were born in the silent generation (1925-45) you will probably have grown up protected, turning into heroic young fighters of the forties and fifties, into powerful midlife leaders in the sixties and seventies, before becoming busy in your elder years.

Strauss and Howe (1992) also gave each generation one of four archetypes over the eighty-to-ninety-year cycle:

1. **Artists (Silent Generation and Gen Z)** – The artist generation is often unfulfilled coming of age. Their focus as they enter adulthood is improving, transitioning in midlife from conformist to experimental. Their leadership style can often be pluralistic and indecisive, and as they grow older, they become more sensitive. The artist generation is generally seen as caring, open-minded and an expert in their area of expertise. However, they can also be seen as extremely sentimental, yearning for what was, with a very complicated outlook and approach to things, and very indecisive.
2. **Prophets (Boomer Generation and Alpha Generation)** – The prophet generation is usually seen as spirited. As they enter adulthood, they become very reflective. Their leadership style can often be quite righteous and austere, leading them to be seen or want to be seen as wise and respected. The prophet generation is generally seen as principled, resolute, and creative. However, they can also be seen as narcissistic, presumptuous, and ruthless.
3. **Nomads (Generation X)** – The nomad generation often feel alienated as they come of age and have, as a result, become self-sufficient. They are seen as solitary and pragmatic, with a tough outlook on life. Their leadership style is seen as frenetic to exhausted. The nomad generation is generally viewed as savvy, practical,

and perceptive. However, they can also be viewed as lacking feelings towards others, uncultured and amoral.
4. **Heroes (Millennials)** – The hero generation are often empowered as they come of age. There is an energetic and hubristic outlook to life, and a yearning to build. Companies, a better life, and so forth. Their leadership style is seen to be collegial and expansive. The hero generation is generally viewed to be selfless, rational, and competent. However, they are also viewed to be unreflective, mechanistic, and overbold.

Reflecting on both the chart above and the archetypes, do you resonate with the descriptions of the generation you were born into? It's important to note that correlation doesn't necessarily imply causation. For there are always exceptions to every rule. These are patterns that Strauss and Howe identified over a period of five-hundred years. Their viewing being that a broad demographic within each generation, exposed to the same events, will react similarly and acquire certain personality traits.

Let's look at how one of these archetypes move through the generation periods.

A MUSICAL HERO

Daniel Ek was born on 21st February 1983, in a small suburb called Rågsved (population 9,000) just outside of Stockholm, Sweden. Born into the millennial generation, Ek's father was out of his life early on, and he and his younger brother Felix were raised by his mum Elisabet and his stepfather Hasse Ek. The family was an average Swedish household with not much money. His grandmother was an opera singer, whilst her husband played the nylon string guitar that Ek played during childhood, his music teacher even noting he was a gifted singer and guitarist. The rise of the digital era exploded in the 1990s, as Ek headed into adolescence. With personal computers becoming a staple in many family homes, schools incorporating IT into the curriculum and the world wide web going from strength to strength, Ek had ample opportunity to explore his interests in computing.

Ek enjoyed the internet and started coding at thirteen. He built websites that showcased his skills, working hard in school and college. He even ran websites and offered web hosting services from his bedroom. In 2002, he left college after a short period of studying IT/engineering because the course emphasized theoretical mathematics rather than the subject matters that he was interested in. Instead, Ek focused on working for a number of digital companies, including Tradera and Stardoll, before starting a digital advertising company called Advertigo, utilising and honing his IT and coding skill set along the way. In 2006, Ek sold Advertigo and became a millionaire, with enough money in the bank at 23 to retire. Yet, after a brief spell enjoying the trappings of his success, Ek grew bored and depressed, and felt like he needed a new challenge. He briefly worked at µTorrent before they sold it, and he was looking for a new challenge.

Daniel had two main loves in his life: the love of music and the love of computing. He had, back in 2002, had an idea for a digital music service, off the back of Napster (the illegal file-sharing platform), which had come in and disrupted the recorded music industry. In 1999, when Napster launched, the global music industry was worth $25,2 billion USD. By 2002, over 10% of the global market share had been wiped from the music industry, falling to $22.6 billion USD. Even as Napster was shut down through legal proceedings, similar services including LimeWire and Kazaa would pop up in its place. By 2006, when Ek was ready to explore a new venture, the global music industry had fallen 23% from 1999s peak to $19.4 billion USD. By this point Apple had launched the iTunes store, but the music platform wasn't generating enough income to offset the rapid decline in revenues from digital piracy, with the music industry continuing to head into freefall.

With the financial backing of Martin Lorentzon, who had previously bought Ek's company Advertigo, Ek revisited his idea from 2002, a music service that did not involve charging for song downloads, but instead a streaming service. Where access to every song you could ever want would be at your fingertips, similar to what Napster and others had offered, but with a monthly fee instead of being free, allowing you to stream, rather than download high quality songs whenever and wherever you wanted. Pulling together a team of talented IT programmers, Ek set to work, bringing his vision of Spotify to life. Yet it wasn't plain sailing from there. The recorded music industry is renowned for its ruthlessness. Over the years, many artists from the likes of Prince to Michael Jackson have spoken out at their perception of the corrupt nature in which the music business operates. The recorded music industry was reluctant to change, which had landed them in the situation they found themselves in. Blindsided by the explosion the internet era brought, and decimation caused by illegal downloading websites, the recorded music industry, were reluctant initially to Spotify, clinging on to the old model of the CD format, and only wanting to embrace the digital download. Too much change, too soon, seemed overwhelming for them. But still, Ek pushed forward. Money was tight and continuing to keep the vision of Spotify alive proved challenging, but with the music industry continuing to decline; by 2008, the global music industry was down by a third of its peak value in 1999 to $16.9 billion USD, and with trends continuing to point to further declines, Ek's perseverance would pay off.

By 2008, Ek had finally convinced the major labels to come on board, with a reported agreement in place that they would receive 18% of the shares in the online streaming service. Spotify initially launched in Sweden in 2008. By 2010, Spotify launched in the UK, where registrations surged following the launch of the platform as an app on mobile devices and the launch in the US market in 2011. In Europe, Spotify gained one million paying subscribers by March 2011 and reached two million paying subscribers six months later. By 2014, when the global recorded music industry had reported its lowest annual figures in decades at $14.2 billion, some 44% down on the peak of its annual earnings, Spotify had by contract amassed 75 million subscribers (20 million on the paid subscription model and the rest on the free ad-supported tier). At this turning point, Spotify continued to grow, becoming a force in the industry. Artists who had famously held out from the platform, including Taylor Swift and Adele, finally joining the platform. Spotify is currently the number one music outlet worldwide, where, as of the second quarter of 2023, Spotify has amassed over 551 million users, including more than 220 million paid subscribers in over 180 markets. In 2022, Spotify generated €11.72 billion in annual revenue, tripling its revenue over the previous five years.

Daniel Ek was born into the millennial generation, placing him under the Hero archetype. From Sweden, which, as mentioned in the previous chapter, is known for its Law of Jante 'You're not to think you're anything special', the culture creates an environment of humility. An individual can be subjected to criticism if they raise their head above the parapet (protective wall), which ties into the criticism outlook shared in Figure 6.1 that millennials experience in their childhood years. Able to harness this critical judgment when looking at opportunities in the marketplace, as Ek moved into the next chapter of his life, young adult, which for millennials is known as the alienated period, this played into Daniel's strengths. He self-identifies as an introvert, and his brief enjoyment of the trappings of his success, following the sale of his company, reaffirmed this. Leaning into the alienated period allowed Ek to work tirelessly to build Spotify, and he was not put off when he was continually alienated by the major labels, and pushed through to find a way to make Spotify the success it is today. As Ek begins to enter the next phase of his life in 2027, the midlife period, that is known for millennials to be the pragmatic period, it stands to reason, that it will be Ek's pragmatic perspective to his business and life, that will help him navigate problems as they arise.

Ek was born on 21st February 1983. A small but not insignificant detail. When the internet exploded in the mid-1990s, Ek was a teenager, and with the resource of a home computer and access to the internet, he was able to devote countless hours of his time to honing his skill set and developing his craft, the way that someone ten-years younger than Ek in the mid-1990s wouldn't be able to, because of their developmental age. And someone ten-years older than Ek unlikely to, because of the time commitments they are likely to have to their career and to a family. Ek dropped out of college at 19 years old to pursue his dream of working in computing. Again, this is something that would be a lot harder for someone from the Boomer generation to do, owing to the financial commitments they are tied to, to keep a roof over their heads and food on the table. This flexibility that is often only afforded to the youth, with fewer responsibilities, allows for more risks to be taken.

Ek's access to resources growing up, in terms of a home computer and technology at school, along with the financial resources the sale of his company and his investor and co-founder offered, provided the first building block for Ek's success. The second building block was his hard work, built through tens of thousands of hours since his teenage years coding, meant that by the time Ek turned 23 in 2006 when he started Spotify, a decade or so after he began coding, he was equipped with the skill set to take advantage of the third building block, the opportunity of timing. Ek's success launching Spotify was at a pivotal point in the music industry. With the music industry revenue in freefall, an opportunity opened up that wasn't there five or ten years before, for someone from a previous generation (most likely Generation X) to take advantage of.

Think this is a coincidence? Look at some of the other founders of the largest tech companies in the world, and you begin to see a pattern emerging. Mark Zuckerberg founder of Facebook; now Meta, the leading social media organisation in the world, was born 14th May 1984, a millennial. Airbnb founders Brian Chesky (29th August 1981) and Joe Gebba (21st August 1981) are both millennials. Many of the founders of the leading tech companies of today are all born at the beginning of the millennial generation. Other clusters of successful tech founders also appear close together, when you look at the tail end of Generation X. Jack Dorsey founder of Twitter (born 1978), Garret Camp (born 1978) and Travis Kalanick (born 1976) founders of Uber, and Jawed Karim (born 1979) and Chad Hurley (born 1977) founders of YouTube. All of the Generation X examples are born within three years of each other, and when combining Gen X with Millennials, the majority of today's biggest tech company founders are all born within a 7-year period of one another.

In fact, as Malcolm Gladwell highlights in his book Outliers (2009), if you look through human history and review a list of the seventy-five richest people, fourteen of the American entrants that stem from the 19th Century are born within nine years of each other. This aligned with the industrial revolution in the US in the 1860s and 1870s, when railroads were being built and Wall Street emerged. If you were born in the 1840s you were too young to take advantage of the opportunities that the revolution brought, and if you were born in the 1820s, you were too old, with Gladwell acknowledging that those from the older generation were shaped by the mindset of the pre-Civil War paradigm that prevented them from taking advantage of the opportunity before them. The perfect period to take advantage of the revolution was the period in between. Those that were born in the 1830s.

If you look at the richest people in the world at the end of 2023, three of the top 5 richest people in the world: Elon Musk (1971) founder of Tesla, Space X and Nueralink (amongst other companies), Larry Page (1973) founder of Google and Jeff Bezos (1964) founder of Amazon, are all born within nine years of each other. The other two entrants that made up the top five richest people in the world: Bernard Arnault (1949) founder of luxury goods company LVMH, and Larry Ellison (1944), founder of tech company Oracle, are born within five years of one another.

Canadian psychologist Roger Barnsley (1983) discovered this phenomenon on a micro level during his research on sports teams. Looking at ice hockey teams, he noticed a correlation between the players emerge when reviewing the month within which they were born. Looking at the Ontario state junior hockey league, he noticed that more players were born in January than any other month of the year. The second month? February. The third? March. His analysis highlighted that when looking at the best ice-hockey players in Canada, 40% were born between January to March, 30% between April and June, 20% between July and September, and the remaining 10% between October and December. Trying to understand why the top players' birth dates were so heavily skewed, he turned to the academic model.

In Canada, the academic school year starts in January. In the US, it is August, the UK September, with further variations displayed in different countries. If a child has not got any developmental impairments in their earliest years, then a child going to school born in January in Canada is going to be eleven months more developed than a child born in December of that same year. At those early developmental ages between four to ten, that can account for a significant difference between skills and capabilities. From talking and processing thoughts all the way through to the ability to pick up and learn things. An invisible advantage that permeates through traditional academia favours students born at the start of the academic year, offering more opportunity for their advantage in developmental age. This can be seen by teachers as the older children being more gifted, talented, academic in the class, and these students being placed in special programmes, where higher grades become more attainable through more time and opportunity for the talent to be nurtured and grown. It will probably widen the developmental chasm between those at the start of the academic year who received preferential treatment, and those who didn't. Who don't get to benefit from additional support and hours spent honing a skill or talent. This preferential treatment can lead to the developmental chasm widening further down the road, where, for example. scouts for sporting teams and institutions pick those students who have been given more time to work on their skill, or scholarships for those students who were identified as gifted and academic, and placed into the higher graded classes, where their talents were nurtured.

It's important to remember that correlation doesn't imply causation, for there are exceptions to every rule. Yet patterns do emerge on a micro level, where the month you were born in relation to the start of the academic year can have a positive or adverse effect on opportunities afforded to you. The same is true on a macro level, where within every generation there is a window of opportunity. Those born in the 1830s were born during the right period within their generation to take advantage of the industrial revolution. Those born in the late 1970s and early 1980s were born in the right generations to take advantage of the digital revolution. Timing can favour those born in one generation, whilst be disadvantageous in another generation.

We can see a painful example of this across three different generations in relation to the AIDs epidemic. Those from both the Boomer Generation and Generation X, were of, or coming of age during the eighties when the AID's epidemic broke out. Infected individuals were rarely taken seriously, where stigma was abound that HIV and AID's was a gay disease, with the illness disproportionately affecting gay males. By 1987, HIV had infected 32,000 people in the US alone, with more than half of them dying. A culture of shame and blame permeated through the mainstream media, and little was being done to find treatment or solutions. Focusing specifically on America, by the height of the pandemic in the early 1990s, it was the leading cause of death for all Americans aged 25 to 44. Countless lives were lost, including Queen frontman Freddie Mercury, to the disease. Treatments were slow to be developed and approved. Drugs, such as AZt, were seen as breakthroughs, but provided no cure. They had serious side effects, such as causing liver problems and low blood cell counts that could be deadly. Combined with a hefty price tag of $16,500 in today's US dollars for a one-year treatment, it made the treatment an unviable option for many. With those who contracted HIV before 1995, provided with little to no effective treatment for AID's, the disease was seen pretty much as a death sentence. In 1995, the Food and Drug Administration (FDA) approved Saquinavir, the first in a different antiretroviral drug class called protease inhibitors. A year later another class of antiretrovirals were approved NNTRI's.

The combination of these two therapies, expanded the lifeline of people who contracted HIV, that was sadly too late for so many from the Boomer Generation and Generation X, but a welcomed introduction at the time that many Millennials were coming of age and beginning to explore their sexuality. Combivir furthered this process in 1997 by combining the two anti-HIV drugs, making it easier to take. This advancement in the treatment of HIV in the AID's epidemic, meant that contracting HIV no-longer was a death sentence, with many individuals managing to live a normal life, and further advances in the treatment of HIV, meant that many individuals would become undetectable, meaning that they could not pass HIV on to another person.

A further step forward in the treatment of HIV, came in the form of PrEP. A medication that not only helped those who were HIV positive but could also protect healthy people from becoming infected. In 2012, the FDA in the US, approved the PrEP drug Truvada, and over the course of that decade, the United States Preventive Services Task Force recommended anyone who's at risk for HIV infection take PrEP. This time, it would be Generation Z, who would benefit the most from the introduction of PrEP, coming to age when their sexuality is beginning to be explored following the roll-out of the drug. Today, PrEP is commonly taken by people from the LGBTQIA+ community. Having been labelled as the 'gay disease', with an increased awareness and a proactive approach to the disease, and through taking PrEP and practicing sex safely by the LGBTQIA+ community, statistics now show that each year, more heterosexual people become infected by the disease than homosexual people, highlighting a changing of the tides.

Sadly, those who were born in the Boomer Generation and Generation X and had an active sex life in the eighties and early nineties didn't have access to the antiretroviral drugs, that could prevent them from dying from the disease. Equally, individuals from those two generations and Millennials who were having an active sex life didn't have access to PrEP to bring the chance of contracting HIV down to almost zero. The timing of each generation engaging in sex, determining the chances of contracting HIV and living with the disease.

Timing plays a part in both the problems and opportunities that arise in each generation's lives. If Daniel Ek had been born a decade later, would he have still gone on to invent Spotify, or would another talented programmer born at the start of the millennial generation gone on to create what Ek did? With Brian, who we met at the start of the chapter, had he been born a year later, he would not have been drafted owing to the drafting of new recruits for the Vietnam war finishing the year he was selected. In a crueller turn of events, if he had been born just 37 minutes later, after the stroke of midnight, the day he would have been born, was one of the dates that weren't called.

SELF REFLECTION TIME

Let's now take some time to reflect on how the generation you were born into has played a role in your life, creating both opportunities and problems for you.

- How has the generation you were born into, impacted your life?

- What global events occurred during your childhood that shaped your outlook on life?
- What opportunities are afforded to your generation, in terms of global developments, that weren't available to previous generations at your age?

For example, if you are coming of age now, as we embark into a new chapter in the digital revolution and the advancement of AI, is there an opportunity to develop your skill set, to turn it into an opportunity for a career and life progression, similar to that of Daniel Ek?

- Have there been setbacks for your generation, such as the COVID-19 pandemic, that have adversely affected you and your peers?
- What have you done to address this problem?

The founders of Airbnb and Uber launched their companies during the Great Recession (2008), seeing an opportunity for people to make a secondary, or in some cases primary income, from resources they already had, whilst going through financial hardship. Remember what happens to you that is out of your control, is not your fault, but what you do as a result is your responsibility.

- Do you let the key events in your generation define you, or do you define it as a moment in time that brought about change?

Now that you are aware of the eighty-to-ninety-year cycle that occurs between generations, and the behaviours and outlooks that define each generation, as you move through the key milestones within your generation as highlighted in Figure 6.1; children, young adult, midlife and elder, are you able to harness the characteristics that define each chapter to support your growth through life, or do you let those characteristics define you? Each generation faces different hardships during the key developmental stages in their lives. Yet we are all individuals within each generation with different variables alongside the generation we were born into shaping who we are and who we become.

SELF DEVELOPMENT TIME

As we come to the end of this chapter, take some time to look at generational problems you may encounter and what you can do to address them.

- Are you able to distinguish between what is a generational issue (an issue that affects those of you born in the same generation) and what is a personal issue (an issue that is specific to you)?
- If you could do one thing today within your control, to address a problem that impacts you because of the generation you were born into, what would you do?

If the problem persists, continue to ask yourself these two questions daily. Put yourself in the best position not to let the generation define you, but for you instead to define the generation.

SUMMARY

The generation you are born into can play a significant role, in what shapes you as an individual. William Stauss and Neil Howe (1992) identified the cycle of generations occur over a period of eighty-to-ninety years breaking them into four turnings. The high, the awakening, the unravelling, and the crisis. Patterns emerged, showing how dependent on the generation you were born into, you would become one of four archetypes, the artist, prophet, nomad, or hero. Though correlation doesn't automatically mean causation, these archetypes could identify how different generations would approach different phases of their lives.

When in the 1980s Roger Barnsley discovered the phenomenon of relative age, it helped to identify how certain periods of time within both a macro and micro scale of generations can benefit some members of a generation more than others. Many of today's leading tech titans are born within a seven-year period of each other and separate to these individuals three of the five richest people on the planet being born within a nine-year period. The different windows of opportunity that are open to each generation, relative to the time of coming of age to take advantage of that window, can occur during recessions, depressions, war, pandemics, technological revolutions and more.

Alongside windows of opportunity for generations, there is also unfortunate timing for certain generations too, as seen both at the beginning of the chapter with Brian and his drafting for the Vietnam war, and people like Freddy Mercury who died of AIDs before the advancement in medicine could help him, like it does so many today, to both treat HIV and prevent contraction.

Each generation will have significant milestones that shape the generation, leading to both problems and opportunities. Some problems are out of an individual's control, whilst others are within the realm of control. As we begin to leave the turning of crisis, and enter the next turning of awakening, what will you do, at this point in your life and within your generation, to make any changes needed, to both address problems you face as a result of the generation you grew up in, and to live a more fulfilling life?

7

PLEASE HAVE MERCY ON ME

Shame

Carl grew up in a broken home on the outskirts of Houston, Texas. He was raised by his mother, following his father's incarceration mere months after he was born for attempted murder. On alternating weekends and some evenings, he was looked after by his aunts from his father's side, who lived nearby. Born to a white-Christian mother and black-Christian father, Carl's dual-heritage was apparent in his home and family, though to the outside world, if someone were to look at him, he would be seen to pass as white.

Carl's upbringing was strict. As a devout-Christian woman, Carl's mum Judy would insist on Carl going to church twice a week, where he would be reprimanded by Judy if he got distracted or bored during the lengthy sermons he was subjected to. Anger also held no place in the household. Any time Carl would experience anger or frustration, as children do from time to time, Judy and also his aunts, would tell him, 'Boys like you, aren't allowed to be angry. You need to swallow that anger down, for it doesn't have a place in this world.' Unaware why his mother and aunts would tell him this, he listened to them and slowly learnt to disown the anger from himself and feel shame any time it would come up.

Carl's interactions with his father were limited. The jail he was serving his sentence in was over an hour away, and so he would only see him once a month. Any time anyone at school asked about his father, he was told to use the line that his father was away serving the country. This left it vague enough, so that people assumed he was in the army, but also left Carl feeling ashamed to have a father in prison. Carl was academically gifted and would find himself at the top of the class when it came to any tests in elementary school all the way through to middle school. On the rare occasion that he would receive a B, rather than an A, his mother would scold him, telling him he must work harder and that he needed to work harder than anyone else in his class to get ahead in life.

Because of the district Carl went to school in, there was a lack of diversity within the students, who were predominantly either white or Latino. Owing to the absenteeism of his father, and his mother picking him up, along with his complexion, no one knew about the black side of his identity, and he was encouraged not only by his mum, but his aunts to play up his whiteness and down his blackness, for it would make life easier for him. Carl wasn't sure what that meant at such a young age, but as he got older, he started to notice it. His cousins, who were all black compared to his dual heritage, would point out he wasn't black, that he didn't look black, and he felt left out from the family, not quite fitting in. He never felt like he fitted in around his white or Latino friends either, because even though he could pass as white, he was still different.

As time went on, he grew further apart from his cousins and aunts, not through choice but because his cousins, who were all older than him, didn't want to hang around with a 'whitey like him' anymore. Not only had he had to disown the truth about his father, but he was now being disowned by his cousins and the black side of his family, which lead to him further disowning the black side of his identity, along with the anger he had learned to disown. Carl was accustomed to his mum or the barber's giving him a buzz cut, but in his early teens he wanted to grow out his hair, like his friends, and copy the hairstyle of the day. As his hair grew, the curls and texture reflected that of his father, rather than the straight blonde hair of his mother, making it harder to near on impossible to replicate the hairstyle of his friends. Judy, who had become busier as her career took off, eventually noticed one evening that Carl's hair had grown far beyond the usual buzz cut, and went to get the clippers. An argument ensued, when Carl wanted to keep his hair and attempt to grow it out, but gave in to his mother, whose strict upbringing always prevailed over Carl's will.

Another change was occurring in Carl. He had never had a girlfriend during childhood, which his mother had chalked up to his focus on his schoolwork and being the best he could be. Yet he noticed his interest in men was more than just friendship, and that concerned him. For being raised in a strict-Christian household, and going to church twice a week, even now he was in his teens, he had heard many a sermon and also read in the bible that being gay was a sin. Yet these feelings grew stronger as puberty kicked in, and Carl would experience cognitive dissonance (where two opposed beliefs are held at the same time). How could something that he was repeatedly told was wrong in his faith, also be something he was feeling inside of himself?

Not feeling safe to explore those feelings with anyone in the community, Carl decided to do with his sexuality what he had been taught or made to do with both his anger and his ethnicity and split himself from it. With all the repression and splitting off from parts of himself that formed his identity, Carl, who over the years continued to lose parts of himself, felt completely lost and also shamed by the various parts that he had disowned. Making his way through high-school, Carl graduated with a scholarship to go to an Ivy-League college, leaving rural Houston for Princeton in New Jersey. Free from the strictness of his upbringing, Carl felt freer to be himself, though still kept certain parts of his identity hidden from others, until he met Jevan. Jevan could see Carl in a way no one else did, and straight away they got on like a house on fire. On the first time of meeting, Jevan, who was black, could distil that Carl was of dual heritage. Though there was an initial denial, Carl conceded and felt freer to embrace a side of him that he'd hidden for so long.

Carl also grew out his hair. Jevan took him to get cornrows for the first time and brought him to the bars and clubs filled predominantly with black people. Though he was often made fun of by Jevan's black friends for being the whitey of the group, which brought up issues he'd had with his cousins in the past, unlike his cousins, Carl felt included within the group. Several of them like Carl, had incarcerated fathers, such was the justice system. Carl often noticed he would get preferential treatment at places over others, or be the only one not singled out by security when at shops, or going into clubs. Was this what his mother and aunts were protecting him from he thought? Carl was angry at the mistreatment of his friends, but they had been used to it all their lives and had told Carl that getting angry would make matters worse and not saying anything would be easier for everyone. It was all making sense now. Carl's mum and aunts were trying to protect him from what his father, uncles, and cousins were subjected to. Because he could pass as white, it made it possible for him to avoid the racial profiling. Which in some ways only made Carl feel more guilt and shame for disowning part of who he really was.

Carl had always known that Jevan was gay, but was never open about his own sexuality, often overcompensating for it, by leaning into sport more than he ever really cared for, and casually dating girls that never lasted more than a couple of weeks. One night, drunk at a club, Carl was taken aback when Jevan leaned in and kissed him. Initially protesting, Carl could feel feelings he'd repressed for so long stirring up inside of him. Jevan shared that he always knew Carl was gay, or at least bi-sexual, but wanted to give him the space to figure it out for himself. Jevan, however, grew bored with waiting and was willing to hedge his bets. That night their relationship took itself to a new level, and they quickly became boyfriends.

A few weeks later, Carl was caught off guard when his mother arrived with his recently released father to surprise him, but the surprise was on his parents, who were shocked to see Carl in a public display of affection with Jevan. Carl, happy to see his father finally out of prison and a free man for the first time in Carl's life, went to greet his father, who quickly turned away from his son and straight to Judy. 'You never told me we had a faggot for a son.' Noah said. Judy was quick to respond, 'It's the first I'm learning of it, too.' They both turned to Carl, who sensed a conflict about to occur alongside the anger rising inside of him, but he would swallow it down again, as he always had. Instead, trying to diffuse the situation, Carl went to introduce Jevan. 'You're mistaken if you think I'm gonna stand here and approve of this.' Noah stated. 'Tell me we've got it wrong Carl, that we didn't see what we just saw.' Judy added. Carl, taking a long breath and deciding which answer to give, knowing that whatever he said would ultimately determine his future relationships with the three most important people surrounding him, said, 'It's true what you saw mum, Jevan is my boyfriend.' And with that, Noah punched Jevan, sending him flying, and grabbed Carl, dragging him out of the store. 'We'll find a doctor that can cure you of this disease.'

But as they attempted to leave, with Judy following behind him, Carl unsuccessfully trying to escape his father's vice like grip, and Jevan lying motionless on the floor, a police car turned up and arrested Noah. Noah looked at his son, saying 'It's all a big misunderstanding', attempting to get Carl to confirm this to the police. Instead, Carl looked away, feeling ashamed of his father. His mother, watching this unfold, pleaded with her son not to send his father back to prison once more, and reaffirm what his father was saying. Turning to Judy, he asked one simple question, 'Will you accept I am gay?' Judy responded, 'I can't. It's a sin to be gay in the eyes of our Lord.' And with that, Carl had his answer. He never saw his father again, and his mother disowned him for being gay. Though he went on to live a happy life with Jevan and have his own family, the pain he'd felt through being disowned by his cousins for being too light-skinned, his parents for being gay, and having to split from parts of himself including his anger because of the shame he felt, Carl never truly recovered from all his shame until his dying day.

As seen through Carl's story, shame can manifest in many different ways. It showed up initially when he was shamed for his anger and told to swallow it down. Shame was also present in his interactions with his cousins, who disowned him for his light-skin that enabled him to pass as white. In many environments, he was encouraged to disown the black part of himself by his mum, forcing him to code-switch (adapt to a different environment) to fit in. From his hair, to the story he would tell about his father, he leant more into his whiteness than his blackness, but ended up never feeling like he belonged anywhere. His religious upbringing came at odds with his sexuality in adolescence, causing cognitive dissonance, and feeling internalised shame that who he was, according to his religion, was wrong, once again leading him to disown that part of himself for several years.

Shame is one of the strongest emotions an individual can experience, and is likely to have severe implications on an individual's mental health, causing a number of problems in their life. Psychotherapist Joseph Burgo (2018) identified the four leading causes of shame.

1. **Unrequited Love**

The first area of shame is unrequited love. Unrequited love is the love that is rejected, not realised or reciprocated, which can lead to humiliation and shame. From the unrequited love of a mother to their child, who cannot provide the love that child needs through to a rejection from someone you are attracted to, this kind of shame experienced can feed into one of the two negative core beliefs we hold as humans 'I am not loveable'.

2. Unwanted Exposure

The second area of shame is unwanted exposure. This can happen at all stages of one's life. From a parent berating you in public, or a teacher telling you off in class, through to bullies picking on you in front of your classmates, or a boss or colleague calling you out in front of the office. At some point or other, we will have all felt what it is like to be publicly humiliated in front of others unwantedly, leading to feelings of shame.

3. Disappointed Expectation

The third area of shame identified by Burgo is disappointed expectation. Disappointed expectation is when you set out to do something and you fail. This could be both your own expectation of yourself, or the expectation of others put on you. This can often show up in sporting professionals, who feel a sense of shame when they don't win a race, game, hit a target or standard they have set. It can also show up when there is an expectation by others that you internalise, such as grades needed to get into university, and if you fall short, the disappointment can lead to shame. It can also be a disappointment at the end of a friendship, relationship, that can also lead to shame that you couldn't make it work.

4. Being left out

The last area of shame is exclusion or being left out. Within all of us, there is a need to feel connected, like we belong. From work colleagues to friendships, family members to romantic relationships, we all want to be a part of something and place a lot of value on being liked and not feeling like an outsider. When something threatens that, a break-up, disownment, bullying, firing, we can take that pretty hard, leading to feelings of shame and fuelling the other negative core belief we all have as humans 'I am not enough.'

Not all shame is bad, as John Bradshaw notes in his book Healing The Shame That Binds You (2006), 'Without healthy shame, moral behaviour and ethical responsibility are impossible.' Healthy shame often occurs in early childhood when a primary caregiver reprimands a child to protect them from a danger. The child may initially feel a sense of shame for doing wrong, but comes to learn that the caregiver was protecting the child from a dangerous situation or environment that could cause harm. It's also important to point out that guilt and shame, although cousins, are very different in how they are internalised by an individual. Guilt is how you feel about something you have done that goes against your own values or beliefs. Shame, on the other hand, is a negative perspective of how you see yourself, impacting your sense of self, self-esteem, and your overall identity.

The problem with shame arises when it is internalised and compounded. It can lead to an individual believing that they are inherently flawed. That they are inferior to others and defective as a human. So strong can the feelings be, that defensive strategies are developed by the individual to mask the shame felt inside. With Carl, it led to a splitting of himself, disowning the parts of him that brought a sense of shame. In extreme cases, it can lead to toxic adaptive behaviours that not only impact the individual but others, too. It can lead to addiction as a coping strategy to avoid the shame. Bradshaw (2006) also notes it can have roots in violence, criminality and even war. And as Mary L Trump (2020) notes, it can lead to narcissistic personality disorder, as with her uncle Donald Trump, where an individual seeks to avoid shame at all costs because of the shame experienced in their formative years. Instead they constantly seek out validation and approval. Through splitting off from the part of oneself that brings about shame, and embracing the other part/s of oneself that are more favourable, it can lead to a grandiose view that they are better than others, and lead to questionable ethics and morals.

NAVIGATING A NARCASSIST

Samantha is one of the most charismatic characters I've ever met working as a psychotherapist. My supervisor, Jennifer had warned me ahead of beginning with this client at the rehab centre I was at, that she would use all kinds of tactics and techniques to avoid dealing with her issues, try to make me collude with her way of thinking and seeing things, and to stay at the surface level at all times to avoid any deep diving. During her psychiatric assessment, Samantha had been diagnosed with narcissistic personality disorder, and as Jennifer pointed out, narcissists seldom find their way into a therapeutic space, because they have disowned any part of themselves they feel is wrong about them, and only allow the good in themselves to be seen, for fear of the repressed or disowned feelings of shame returning.

Pace and grace were the name of the game with Jennifer. Through each of the initial sessions, I would get to know her story and what had led her into rehab. Jennifer didn't come willingly. It was an intervention by her family owing to her drug usage and lady of the night activities. Like an onion, slowly peeling back layer after layer, over time I began to earn Samantha's trust. She would open up more and more about her past, but anytime we got too close to something uncomfortable, she would become quickly flooded with emotion and shut down, with the drug cravings returning to ease the discomfort she felt. Samantha would also lean into her charm offensive, trying to flatter me with how well the sessions were going, or use her sexuality and sensuality to deflect from any painful areas were approaching.

As trauma specialist and creator of The Voyage (2023), Lou Lebentz discusses when working with traumatised clients, before you can take a client on a journey of healing through their trauma (and shame) you must first land them in the sand, through grounding techniques to make sure they are safe and stable within themselves, before they can swim in the discomfort of the sea and the feelings they feel. With Samantha, there was a lot of landing in the sand, and dipping toes in the water. The shame of her childhood was so strong that Samantha had built up a whole host of defence mechanisms to protect her from the past that had so traumatised her. The problem Samantha faced was that her partner Daniel, with whom she'd been in a relationship with for nearly two decades and built a business with, was looking to file for divorce. Gain sole custody of their children. And work with the board of their company to have her removed from the business. He also feared that one child was displaying many of the same qualities in Samantha that Daniel had worked hard to protect their children from.

This reality was painful for Samantha, as she didn't want to lose her business. She was confident she could find another Daniel, she stated, and was still young enough to have more children if they were taken from her, but her business she was unable or willing to lose, as it was a marker of her success and compounded the feelings of grandiosity. A painful few months followed, as together we delicately danced around Samantha's past, slowly uncovering many of the shameful events that had occurred during her childhood, that had led to Samantha becoming the woman that sat in front of me. As the feelings increased, so did the urges to use, and relapse was a high possibility. Samantha, though, determined not to lose her business, decided to extend her stay in rehab. To fight through the urges and find a better way of coping with the toxic shame, any time it would rear its ugly head. Also, conscious of switching one vice for another, though Samantha's exercise routine increased somewhat during her stay, we monitored it to ensure it didn't become the new unhealthy coping strategy in place of drugs.

The narcissistic wounds were deeply embedded in Samantha. During our time working together, Samantha was able to work through much of the toxic shame she felt because of the relationship with her mother, but some scars were too deep to heal. Her father was that scar. She idolised her father, and was unwilling to see the role his abuse, invalidation, criticism and more played in shaping the woman she'd become. In therapy, you can only take the client as far as they are willing to go. As the saying goes, you can take the horse to water, but you can't make it drink. Sometimes you can't even get the horse to move to begin with. I realized here that this would be a stalemate for Samantha, and feeling I had done all I could do, it was time to bring the therapeutic relationship to an end.

Though changes were definitely visible in Samantha, as the therapeutic relationship went on, I could still very much see many of the narcissistic traits continue to play out in our sessions, and wondered if she would ever be willing or able to truly deep dive into the past and change her ways. For the defence mechanisms were serving a purpose. They were protecting her from her shame and allowing her to use whatever she needed to get what she wanted. I am unsure what unfolded with her marriage, children, and business beyond the therapeutic relationship, as my files weren't requested in any court proceedings for the prosecution or defence, but I do hope that the work, somehow helped to heal some of the shame Samantha had carried with her throughout her life.

Samantha's story is a rare example of a therapist working with a narcissist on their narcissistic wounds. According to a study carried out by Psychology Today (2022), only 2%-16% of all therapeutic clients have narcissistic personality disorder or narcissistic traits. Even then, in most cases, it is to deal with an external problem that they feel has nothing to do with them. For unconscious survival mechanisms and adaptive behaviours, such as denial, idealisation, repression, and dissociation have allowed them to lose touch with the shame, hurt and pain they felt. As I often say to my clients; To heal is to feel. But we can only do that when we reveal that which we conceal. Without recovery from the shame that we have felt, it can get carried on for generations. For trauma and shame that isn't treated, is transmitted. So the choices are simple, either process and hand back (symbolically) the shame you felt or you continue to pass it on.

SELF REFLECTION TIME

Take a moment to reflect on any moments of shame that you have experienced in your life that you can access.

- Alongside the shame you felt, were there other emotions that came up for you?
- What were the contributing factors that enabled the shaming incident to take place or to compound the shame?
- Did the weight that these individuals hold and/or the environment hold compound the shame, and if so, how?
- Was an outlet provided to process the shame you felt, or did you swallow it down?
- What adaptive behaviours did you seek out to navigate dealing with the shame you felt?
- Did you split off from/disown the part of you that was shamed?
- Did you create an idealised version of yourself?
- Were different defence mechanisms utilised, such as denial, displacement, repression, to avoid the feelings of shame?
- Did you reach for something; alcohol, drugs to escape the feeling of shame?
- Did that escapism lead to a dependency on the vice of choice over time?

It is important here to remember with the shame you experienced, that what happened to you in most instances wasn't your fault. You were at the receiving end of an experience that left you with feelings of shame, and more than likely, not an outlet to process it. In those scenarios, you did the best you could, with the resources you had at the time, to navigate the feelings of shame that consumed you, leading to adaptive behaviours to survive those feelings. However, at some point those adaptive behaviours, that will have served you well to deal with the shame, are likely in some way, shape or form to have become maladaptive, and cause you problems, be that in the relationship with yourself, your life, your work and/or your relationships.

Again, this is not to judge or blame yourself for that, but to acknowledge that this is happened, to be aware of it and to take accountability and responsibility for the path you chose as a result. It is only when we accept ourselves as we truly are that change can come about. Through this process, you can start to move from a victim of your circumstance to a survivor. As you continue to work through and process the shame, you can once again move states, this time from a survivor into a thriver. Processing the shame that compounds you is not something I would recommend that you do by yourself, owing to what can occur when you open pandora's box. I would actively encourage you to do this with a psychotherapist like myself in private practice, or through support groups that navigate themes and topics relating to the area of shame that speaks to you. It could also be through rehab, if the shame is underlying a substance misuse issue. Whatever pathway you choose, it is important that you find a space that is free from judgment, that is supportive and nurturing, as you navigate the uncomfortable thoughts and feelings as they arise.

One of the most common defence mechanisms that appears when processing shame is intellectualisation. As Abraham Low acknowledges, 'Intellectualizing about our problems is complex but easy, whilst doing something about them is simple but difficult.' Intellectualisation keeps you in your head and away from your feelings. The very thing you are likely to be avoiding. For the feelings of shame and other feelings can be somewhat overwhelming. It is also likely that at the beginning of the process of exploring shame, one will guard themselves from exposing the inner thoughts and feelings to others. This is through fear of further shame being placed by others on top of the shame that is already there. Additionally, the defence mechanisms in play will guard the individual against exposing themselves to the shame, and these will need to be honoured and worked with, rather than against.

During the process, it is likely that two other prime emotions appear: anger and sadness. Anger is the emotion that gives us strength. Sadness is the emotion that gives us the ability to heal. Both are necessary emotions to process shame and should be welcomed equally in the process. Again, if there is an avoidance of these emotions, because of beliefs around them, these too must be honoured, worked through, and then welcomed into the space for the healing process to take place.

The problems that shame may cause in an individual's life can vary widely. For some, it may have resulted in limiting beliefs. They may have grown up with a parent who made them feel that their needs were selfish, and so they feel a sense of shame anytime they express their needs. The shame is reaffirmed anytime someone cannot meet those needs, causing them to be unable or unwilling to express their needs. For others, it may have led to a dependence on a vice to avoid feelings of shame that are now having an adverse impact on their life, their career, their health or their relationships. As one client of mine expressed in the rehab, 'I was caught in a vicious cycle. I drank to avoid the shame I felt, but when I woke up the next morning, I would feel shame for what unfolded because of my drinking. And so, I would repeat the cycle again, to avoid feeling.'

My client was stuck in what is known as a shame cycle. There are varying models of the shame cycle that differ slightly dependent on the catalyst and the coping strategy. Figure 7.1 provides an example of how the shame cycle works.

SHAME CYCLE

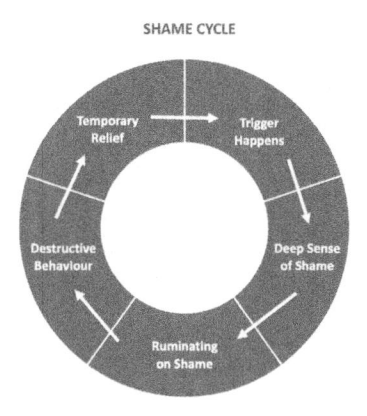

Figure 7.1 - Shame Cycle

- **STEP 1** - First off, a trigger happens usually from an external stimulus. Examples include a mistake made which has been reprimanded. An intrusive memory of a past shameful experience.
- **STEP 2** - This leads to a deep sense of guilt, which can turn into shame.
- **STEP 3** - As time prevails, the shame ruminates, bringing up uncomfortable and often unbearable emotions, alongside the shame that the individual is unable or unwilling to process or deal with.
- **STEP 4** - This results in the individual leaning into the vice or behaviour that has historically helped them to escape from their thoughts and feelings. A dependence is likely to form over time, that it is likely to cause destructive behaviour to the individual and to their relationships.
- **STEP 5** - As a result of the vice or behaviour being engaged with, at that moment, temporary relief from the situation, thought, feeling, is provided.

The cycle is likely to repeat once the effects of the vice has worn off, and the reality, returned to, which can lead to the individual quickly re-entering the shame cycle, especially if the destructive behaviour has significant consequences, such as loss of job, relationships, family, or home. In other instances, the individual may step away from the shame cycle for a while, as the coping strategy has provided a longer temporary-respite from the shame, until another trigger activates the individual again.

For other people, shame may manifest in stagnation as they navigate their way through life. If someone has toxically shamed an individual, they are likely to become more guarded than others, secretive and often quite defensive. Their inability to form long-term relationships or be close on an intimate or emotional level can stifle their development romantically and/or professionally. Perfectionism and controlling behaviour can be two qualities that arise in the individual, which are demanded of themselves, but can also be projected onto others, further hampering the ability to sustain relationships. Through avoiding the chance to be shamed by being guarded, it also avoids the chance to form deeper and more intimate connections with others, leading to isolation, loneliness, feelings of hopelessness and despair. Sometimes, this can develop into suicidal ideation, intent, or an attempt.

SELF DEVELOPMENT TIME

Having looked at the four areas of shame and the shame cycle, here are some questions to ask yourself:

- Which of the four areas of shame have you experienced the most?
- Have you ever noticed yourself caught in a shame cycle?
- What destructive behaviours do you lean into?
- What does the destructive behaviour result in?
- Does dwelling on the mistake lead to more feelings of shame and the shame cycle repeating?
- Are you willing and able to explore any shame you have that lies underneath the surfacee? To work through the

impact the shame has had on your life. The adaptive behaviours it resulted in, and the impact those behaviours have caused?
- Are you open to evolving the way you process shame, to gain a healthier relationship with yourself, to work through and no longer be partially defined by the shame that binds you?

If you are, then why not begin today, by seeking out a psychotherapist such as myself to help you process and work through any shame you have experienced in your life. Alternatively, identify a support group that aligns with an area that brings up shame with you, that you can join to explore and discuss your feelings of shame. If an addiction covers your shame up, and you wish to seek help for both, reach out to a professional for help, support and guidance, such as a doctor, a rehab or a fellowship group such as alcoholics anonymous. Help processing shame comes in many forms. If one option doesn't work for you, don't be deterred. Try another. The process won't be easy and sitting with the discomfort will probably be hard. But in the long run, it will be worthwhile, when problems caused by the shame that binds you are no longer problems you have to navigate in your life.

SUMMARY

Shame is an emotion that we all feel as humans from time to time. There is healthy shame that helps to protect us and provide us with a moral compass and an ethical responsibility and negative shame that adversely affects us and our relationships with others. The four principal ways in which shame shows up are through unrequited love, unwanted exposure, disappointed expectation, and exclusion. Guilt, shames cousin, is how you feel about something you have done that goes against your own values or beliefs. Shame is a negative perspective of how you see yourself, impacting your sense of self, self-esteem, and your overall identity.

Shame is one of the most powerful emotions and can lead to an individual utilising whatever resources available to them at the time to avoid the feelings of shame. From splitting off from the part of the self that has been shamed and creating an idealised grandiose version of oneself that can be found in people with narcissism, through to individuals who lean into a vice to avoid feeling, which can lead to a dependency. Over time, these adaptive behaviours can become maladaptive, causing problems in an individual's life, their health, their relationships, and their career. Individuals can often get caught in a shame cycle, that sees them repeating the same patterns again and again to avoid dealing with the shame, but then compounding it further.

To process and work through the shame, it is important to find and/or create a safe and supportive environment, free from judgment. Pace and grace are the name of the game, going slow and steady to ground an individual, to be able to increase the window of tolerance for the emotions that come up. Honouring whatever defence mechanisms or emotions show up as the process develops and allowing them to be understood allows the individual to move from victim to survivor, and as the journey continues from survivor to thriver.

8

MAN IN THE MIRROR

Self-Awareness

Every morning started the same for Karen. Three alarms had to be set to get her out of bed before she stumbled into the kitchen to pour herself a cup of coffee. An hour later, after showering, deciphering which outfit to wear and applying her make-up, Karen would hop into her car and drive to work. Arriving at the office, her assistant Celine would meet her at the entrance with what resembled an iced coffee, where she had been patiently waiting for 15 minutes. 'Always late' Michelle would say, 'But worth the wait' Karen would reply, as the women would laugh together, making their way through the office, to discuss the agenda of the day. Though Celine ran a tight ship for Karen as her executive assistant, she, as well as everybody else in the office, knew that Karen's ability to be on time for anything was not a skill she was born with or had learned over time. So much so, that Celine would intentionally hold spaces in Karen's diary to account for her tardiness, so that her perpetual lateness didn't have a further domino effect on each day's agenda, which may result in meetings having to be cancelled or rescheduled after they were scheduled to begin.

On the fourth Wednesday of every month, Karen and her small, trusted circle of friends would come together over dinner and drinks, at whatever the latest new hotspot in London was. Having known each other for twenty-one years, as a result of all going to university together, the three other women, like Celine, were well aware of Karen's time-keeping skills. They would joke about the old days and her always being late to class, turning in assignments at the eleventh hour, and holding up group presentation preparation because she couldn't keep up her side of the workload. But hey, that was Karen. With the restaurants that the ladies would frequent always requiring a booking and having limits on the occupation time at the table, the other three ladies would put the reservation back by thirty minutes, knowing Karen ran at least forty minutes late on a good day. The ladies would tell Karen 7:30pm for dinner, turn up at 8pm for their reservation, and Karen would totter in around 8:15pm.

This catch up was different, for they were planning Karen's fortieth birthday celebrations to be held that weekend. The ladies had it all planned out. They were all going to be celebrating in Manhattan, with the other three ladies flying out ahead early Friday morning, whilst Karen would join them following a later flight at lunchtime. Though Karen was always late, the one thing she was always on time for was flights. For a flight would not wait around for Karen if she was late, so she would have to adjust her time keeping skills to reflect this. Landing in NYC and making her way to the hotel, Karen dumped off her stuff in her room and got ready. Without work distractions or domestic tasks needing attending to, it surprised Karen when she looked at the time to see that she would, in fact, be running on time and maybe even early for once. Ordering an Uber to take her to Manhatta for dinner, a restaurant in the financial district, Karen pulled up and made her way into the restaurant.

Being seated at her table, Karen was slightly shocked to be the first of the group at the restaurant, but she was there at 7:50pm a full ten-minutes before the dinner reservation and actually sat smugly, looking forward to seeing the look on her friends faces, when they saw her already sat at the table waiting, for what possibly could have been the first time ever. With 8pm coming and going, Karen looked slightly confused when guest after guest arrived in the restaurant, but her friends were nowhere to be seen. Momentarily, she questioned whether she had got the wrong restaurant, but the maître-d had confirmed the booking and directed her to the table she found herself sat at. Her patience grew thin, when by 8:30pm there was still no sign of the women. Reaching to her mobile to call the women, for some reason the service on her phone was out preventing her from being able to contact them, adding to Karen's frustration. An hour had passed, when at 8:50pm, the three ladies came walking over to see Karen, already sat at the table, three glasses of wine in, looking infuriated.

'We weren't expecting you here for at least another ten-minutes', Claire shared. 'What do you mean? The reservation was at 8pm and I've been here since 7:50pm.' The women looked at each other, shocked, both that she had been here all this time and for once was not only on time but in fact early. 'Oh, you didn't actually think the reservation was at 8pm, did you?' Emma laughed. Karen, clearly not seeing the funny side of things, retorted, 'Well, that's what time you told me.' The women all looked at each other and laughed. 'There's Karen time, and then there's actual time. We always give you a different time to the actual time we meet, and even then, you are invariably later than the actual time.' Karen, now less furious and more intrigued, asked the women how long they'd been doing this, and they said since university, when they grew tired of always being kept waiting. Karen was mortified. She knew she was always late, but she hadn't realised the impact her lateness had on others and the creative adjustments people in her life made to accommodate it. It wasn't until that night, when she got a taste of her own medicine and was left waiting for others, that she finally got a sense of how others felt because of her time-keeping skills.

As the women laughed and reminisced over their friendships,

Karen reaching level four, aka forty, and what she plans to do entering her forties; the last of the group to do so, she shocked the group when she said she planned to be on time from here-on-out. Fast forward a year, and true to her word, Karen changed her ways. Celine could now schedule meetings and have them run on time. Her friends would tell Karen the real reservation or meeting times and she would show up promptly on time, or sometimes ahead of schedule, with a round of drinks waiting for them. Karen even adjusted her morning routine, realising she'd not given herself enough time in the morning to get herself ready and get into work on time. All of these tweaks had a positive impact on Karen, and though or a rare occasion Karen would run late, it would now be the exception and no longer the rule.

Karen's story is a great example of one of the four different ways in which a problem can occur, because of our values, beliefs, or behaviours. Psychologists Harrington Ingham and Joseph Luft (1969) created a framework called The Johari Window, to help understand the conscious and unconscious bias's that we all have as humans, that if explored and unpacked can lead to an increase in self-awareness and our understanding of others. Split into four quadrants, as highlighted in Figure 8.1, the first quadrant are things that are known to ourselves and others, referred to as the open self. The second quadrant, the blind-self are the things that are known by others, but unknown to us. The third quadrant, the hidden self, is information you know, but not shared by others. And the final quadrant, the unknown self, is information about yourself that neither others nor you currently know.

	KNOWN TO SELF	UNKNOWN TO SELF
KNOWN TO OTHERS	**OPEN SELF** INFORMATION ABOUT YOU THAT BOTH YOU AND OTHERS KNOW.	**BLIND SELF** INFORMATION ABOUT YOU THAT YOU DON'T KNOW BUT OTHERS DO KNOW.
UNKNOWN TO OTHERS	**HIDDEN SELF** INFORMATION ABOUT YOU THAT YOU KNOW BUT OTHERS DON'T KNOW.	**UNKNOWN SELF** INFORMATION ABOUT YOU THAT NEITHER YOU NOR OTHERS KNOW.

Figure 8.1 - Johari Window.

In Karen's story, we see the first quadrant in Figure 8.1 the open self playing out, whereby everyone, including Karen, is aware of her lateness. It has become a behaviour that Karen has gained over the years because of her inability to manage her time, that formed part of her identity. As a result of her time-keeping, her friends and her assistant, amongst others in her life, made creative adjustments in their lives, colluding with her behaviour, that enabled Karen to continually run late. But Karen never missed a flight in her life. She could always show up before the flight left, showing that this wasn't a fault in her operating system per-say, but a maladaptive behaviour that, in certain environments and with certain people, had been enabled. It was only when Karen showed up on time, but unbeknownst to her, in fact early, that she realised the impact her behaviour had on others. Feeling the way she felt at the perceived lateness of her friends gave Karen insight into the feelings other people may have had as a result of Karen's perpetual lateness. Karen felt the group didn't value or appreciate her time. She felt she was less important in that moment, and realised if she was feeling this, then other people may have felt this way towards her. This insight allowed her to reflect upon her own patterns and led to a change in her ways.

SELF REFLECTION TIME

Turning the attention from Karen to you, if we begin by looking at the first quadrant, the open self:

- Are there any problematic behaviours, values or beliefs you have that everyone knows about, that have an adverse impact on your life?
- Are you perpetually late, like Karen?
- Are you overly giving with your time, finances?

Take a moment to reflect on this. It must be something that all the key people in your life know about you, including yourself.

- Are there people in your life that enable this behaviour to happen and collude with you?
- Do they make adjustments for your lateness like Karen?
- Do they take advantage of your kindness and time by letting you always pick up the bill or hog the conversation?
- How does your behaviour affect the relationship? The relationship with yourself? Your relationship with others? If comfortable asking other people, the relationship they have with you specifically because of this behaviour.
- What would happen if you changed or evolved this behaviour?
- Would your life become incrementally better?
- Would you have a better relationship with yourself and with others?
- Would you gain deeper relationships and remove those superficial relationships that don't serve you?

As you ponder over those questions, let's next turn our attention to the blind-self, the area that is known by others about us, but not by ourselves.

WHEN IGNORANCE ISN'T TRULY BLISS

Beaming with delight, the doctor carefully wrapped the baby in a blanket and passed the new-born daughter to Sarah, who, lying in the hospital bed, had just become a mum for the second time. Her partner Adam, who sat alongside her during the delivery, was over the moon, proud to become a father once more. As their families came to visit, Sarah's parents brought in their elder daughter Daisy, who got to meet her sister Poppy for the first time. Initially intrigued and confused by this recent addition to the family, Daisy showered her sister with kisses and Sarah and Adam were relieved to see the siblings get along with one another, alleviating their concerns that Daisy may reject Poppy. But the alleviation was to be short-lived.

With Poppy taking up so much of Sarah's time, like many new-born's do, Daisy started to feel resentful. Sarah was prepared for this to happen, for she had read extensively about the terrible-two's and with Daisy now a toddler, acting out and playing up; Sarah attributed Daisy's behaviour to this. Daisy would often become frustrated when her parents wouldn't play with her if they were busy tending to Poppy. She would go off and sulk and become stubborn with both of her parents. At dinner time Daisy would refuse to eat her food, not because she wasn't hungry, but to prove a point to her parents. Though Sarah and Adam both parented equally, the weight of navigating two children under the age of three was weighing heavily on Sarah. The constant need to appease Daisy, whilst having to take care of Poppy who was completely dependent at 3-months old on her parents, was exhausting.

Owing to both Sarah and Adam's parents living far away, getting help or support from the extended family wasn't easily accessible, but Sarah relished the times her parents would come down to see their grandchildren, whilst also granting Adam and Sarah a reprieve. With Sarah's parents coming down for the weekend to visit the family, Sarah and Adam took advantage to have a night off from the children and spend it in a hotel not too far away. Daisy was in full-blown temper-tantrum mode when Sarah's parents arrived, and despite Sarah's best efforts to appease Daisy, she just couldn't settle her down. Her mum, who Sarah had not had the easiest relationship with over the years, stepped in and was able to calm and soothe Daisy and take her up to bed, where Poppy was already asleep next door.

Sarah was making a final list and checking all the various things her parents might need, when Sarah's mum, having come back down from putting Daisy to bed said 'Your Daisy's a right chip off the block isn't she.' Silence creeped over the room, as Adam and Sarah's father stared at each other and then at Sarah, not sure how she was going to respond. 'What do you mean?' Sarah asked quizzically, with a hint of passive-aggressiveness thrown in for good measure. 'Well, she's stubborn, just like you. When your dad and I arrived earlier, she was sulking because she didn't get her own way. You always used to do that as a child, and you still do to this day, isn't that right, Adam?' Adam, like a deer in the headlights, froze, as all attention turned to him. Sarah's glare, like the eye of Sauron, left Adam flustered, not knowing how to approach this. He did not want to get caught up in the grenade Sarah's mum had just thrown into the conversation that was about to detonate at any second. Sarah's father, stepped in to take the pressure off Adam, trying to pivot the conversation, sharing 'What I think your mum is trying to say, is that Daisy is like a mini-you in some respects. She has inherited a whole host of your qualities. The great parts of you, and also some of the area's that we've come to accept about you.' 'Accept?!' Sarah's frustration at this point turned to rage and fury, but rather than blow up in the house, Sarah instead turned and walked out to the car, waiting for Adam to join.

As they drove to the hotel, Adam knew it was best to leave Sarah to calm down before engaging in conversation. After a while, Sarah began to vent at Adam. The audacity of her parents to say that Daisy's stubbornness and sulkiness was a byproduct of Sarah. Adam was having to tip-toe on eggshells, nodding and sharing mmmhmms to appease his wife, for he was driving and didn't want her to erupt in the car, which could lead to a crash. Once they'd checked in to the hotel room, and settled down, Adam bravely broached the subject, asking Sarah, 'Now you've had time to settle down a bit, do you think your parents may have a point?' 'What are you trying to say?' Sarah's stern tone made it clear that this was going to be less a conversation and more a confrontation. 'It's just that I think maybe your mum has a point. One of the many things I love about you is that you hold strong to your convictions, but sometimes that leads to stubbornness, when you aren't willing to look at things from a different perspective.' Sarah, slightly disarmed at Adam's softer approach but still slowly bubbling up with frustration, sat staring without saying a word, leaving Adam to continue. 'When we argue, have you noticed that you rarely are the first to re-engage? It seems that your stubbornness impedes your ability to reconnect after an argument, and it ends up being me that has to apologise.' 'That's not true!' Sarah was quick to respond. 'Why don't I let you finish up getting ready, whilst I go down and grab a drink at the bar and meet you down there? That way, it may give you some space away from me and your parents, so you can think about everything.'

As Adam made his way downstairs, Sarah was left reflecting on what her parents and Adam had shared. Was she stubborn? Did she sulk? Did it only happen with her family, or did it also play out with her friends and at work? Quickly texting one of her friends and colleagues Ryan, she asked, 'Do you think I'm sulky and stubborn? Be honest!' Ryan, her gay-best friend, was quick to respond, 'Of course you are, but that's why we love you.' Ryan was always a straight shooter, and so she knew if he said it, then it must be true. Not that she didn't trust her parents or Adam. And with that, Sarah could finally see, what everyone else saw in her, and in that moment she decided, she needed to do something about it, so that her daughter Daisy didn't continue to act like her mum, or that Poppy didn't pick up the same traits.

It's often the case that when someone becomes a parent, the

blind spots in a person's character are pointed out. The way their child does things, says things or interacts with others, can offer insight into what you do naturally on auto-pilot without realising. Having a child can often be the easiest way to see a blind spot, as they are a reflection of at least half of you, if they are your biological child. Friends, family members, colleagues can also point out blind spots in your patterns of relating that may be unknown to you. I recall when I worked in the music industry, one colleague Ryan got me 'The Book of Aggravation' as a secret Santa present, and when everyone laughed saying that was the perfect present, I had to self-reflect and see that actually I get aggravated quickly in a lot of situations, which allowed me to work on my patience and communication skills to become less aggravated in everyday life.

SELF DEVELOPMENT TIME

We all have blind spots, and me asking you to identify them right here and now is almost an impossible challenge without the help of others. If you are willing and able to do so, why not take the time to reach out to a colleague, friend, family member or loved one, and ask them to help you identify some of your blind spots, that may be affecting your life unbeknownst to you and causing issues in your ability to relate to others.

It is important that you set the parameters here with the individual sharing these insights with you, meeting their disclosures with curiosity, not furiosity. Listen to understand, not to respond. It's natural to want to defend your reputation if it feels like your character is under attack, but remain calm and collected. If you are triggered by what someone says, then it is often a sign there is an unhealed part of yourself that has been activated, and whatever has been shared, likely to have an element of truth to it. Start slow, it's all about pace and grace. You don't want to become flooded with emotion and be unable to hear or process what is being shared. If you want to gain more self-awareness and work on any areas of your life, that may be problematic, then making steps in this direction towards learning about your blind spots is a great area to begin.

Next up is the hidden self. The parts of us we don't want others to see or know about us. Often this can be a survival strategy, required to be implemented to protect us from the world around us, but it can show up in many different ways, as Alexis' story shows.

HIDING IN PLAIN SIGHT

Alexis seemed to be the woman who had it all. In her late-thirties, Alexis had dropped out of Berkeley in the first semester to launch her own tech start-up Perspective. Ahead of the curve, the AI company paved the way for many of today's other leading AI companies including Open AI and Chat GPT, and on the eve of it being publicly listed on the New York Stock Exchange, the company was valued at over $40 billion USD. With the majority stake in the company, overnight, Alexis was due to overtake two women she admired most, Oprah and Rihanna, to become the richest black female in the USA.

Alexis had a steady partner in Rodrigo whom she had dated since Berkeley University, and though they didn't yet have children, it was something in the pipeline that they had explored committing to once Perspective had become listed and Alexis could take a step back. Perspective had been Alexis' child for the past 16 years. It had, in many ways, consumed every waking moment. This meant that there was little time for her to catch up with friends or family. With Rodrigo, they did their best to make Alexis' schedule work for them both, though weeks could sometimes pass without them seeing each other, such were the demands of her job.

A year before Perspective's listing, Rodrigo and Alexis' mum had noticed a change in Alexis' behaviour. Though she had always been quite guarded, Alexis had become more so. She was short on the phone, avoiding meeting up when she was in town, often only conceding when her partner or her mum insisted on seeing her. Alexis blamed it on work, and both Rodrigo and her mum bought the lie, though they noticed Alexis was looking a bit more gaunt than her usual slim frame portrayed, and a little more ashy. Concerned for her well-being, her mother made a fuss, sending nutritional tips and making sure her daughter looked after herself, but Alexis assured her she would be okay. One evening, it surprised Rodrigo when he returned home to their apartment in Silicon Valley to find Alexis set-up with a drip going into her arm and a nurse nearby. Confused and alarmed, Alexis quickly reassured him it was just an IV drip full of vitamins to re-energize her after a long week, like the ones that were all the rage, down in Los Angeles.

Alexis once again, managed to hide the truth from those closest to her, but the veil came all crashing down, when during a celebratory dinner with her friends and family in NYC two nights before the public listing, Alexis collapsed whilst giving a toast. Unresponsive, Rodrigo called an ambulance, and she was quickly rushed to the hospital, where her friends and family eagerly awaited news in the waiting room. When Alexis had been stabilised, the doctor came out to let all who were gathered know the good news. Many wanted to go in and see her, but the doctor noted that Alexis had specifically asked only to see Rodrigo and her mum. As Alexis shared the news she had been keeping a secret for a year, her mother broke down and cried. Rodrigo, in a state of shock at the news Alexis had just shared, could do nothing but just look straight into Alexis' eyes. Terminal Cancer. Stage 4. Disbelief filled the air, the silence deafening. Alexis had known for a little over a year and had been given twelve to eighteen-months to live.

The secrets and the lies, the adaptive behaviours that Alexis had to make to keep up the pretence, had all taken its toll on her body. Finally, being forced to reveal the truth and no longer hide what she was going through, a lightness came over Alexis. No longer was she weighed down by the additional burden of having to hide a part of herself from the two people closest to her. Reassuring both Rodrigo and her mum that she was going to tell them the day after the public listing, so that it didn't affect Perspective's floating on the stock exchange, Alexis made both of them promise to hold the secret amongst themselves for a couple more days, so that she could get her affairs in order. Rodrigo told the friends and family members that she had collapsed from exhaustion and that they just want to keep her in overnight to monitor her, and give her some more fluids before discharging her in the morning. As Alexis lay in bed in her private suite that night, she sat there, tears falling down her cheek, wondering why she had kept this a secret for so long from the two people she cared about more than anyone else in the world. For it felt as if it was the weight of the secret that nearly killed her, not the cancer itself.

Alexis' story, though uncommon, is one many can relate to. How hiding a part of ourselves from others results in us having to lie, change the way we do things, alter our schedules, all so that we keep up appearances and not let others in to see the truth. Sometimes this is through imposter syndrome and fear of being exposed, as covered in Chapter 9, Who Do You Think You Are. Other times, as mentioned earlier, it is a survival instinct to protect us from bullying, from being subjected to racism (if you can pass as another race to the one you identify with), homophobia, transphobia, classism and so forth. In other instances, it may be to hide a past that you are ashamed of, your family, your culture, a prison record, all in the hope that if you hide that part of you, it will prevent others from labelling you or defining you wholly based on the part you have chosen to hide. We all hide parts of ourselves, especially when we first met people. For trust needs to be formed in a relationship, and until we can trust someone, we need to be wary about how we interact with them. Many of you will have grown up with 'Don't talk to strangers' etched into your head by your parents when you were a child. In our formative years, most of us won't have been exposed to the harsh realities of the world, and grown up somewhat in a bubble, under the protection of our parents. So through their guidance, we don't talk to strangers, because they aren't to be trusted, and this plays out into adulthood, that only when we know and trust someone are we more likely to let them in.

SELF REFLECTION TIME

There is nothing wrong with hiding parts of yourself in certain situations, but in this book, we are looking at how the hidden self may cause you problems in your life, in your patterns of relating to others, and how it can actually result in impacting your physical health as well as your mental health. Let's take some time now to explore the hidden parts of yourself.

- What parts of yourself are hidden from others?
- What is the reasoning for doing this?
- Is it hidden from everyone, or only in certain settings?
- What would happen if you disclosed that hidden part of yourself with someone?
- What would happen if someone found out about the hidden part of yourself without you sharing?
- How does hiding a part of yourself affect your everyday life?
- Would life be easier for you in the long run if you could share that hidden part of yourself?

These are some initial questions to ask yourself, to see how your hidden self is impacting you and if it may be causing problems in your life. You may, through exploration, come to the decision that you no longer wish to hide that part of yourself, and that is great. You may also decide that it is important to keep that part of yourself hidden, and that is okay too. For your safety and survival is most important and in some parts of the world and some cultures, you may have to hide a part of yourself; your sexuality, for example, as if exposed it could lead to imprisonment or even death, as is the case in roughly a third of countries around the world who view homosexuality as punishable by imprisonment or death.

The last of the four quadrants in the Johari Window is the unknown self, that which is unknown to both you and everyone else.

ERUPTING LIKE A VOLCANO

Killian was a mild-mannered child. He was always attentive and caring, never complained, and always supported his family members at home. At school, he was quiet to the point that he would almost go unnoticeable. Killian was bright and got all of his work done on time, but was happy to be an observer rather than a participant in life. This approach worked well for him, and throughout primary school, Killian went through his days without many problems.

The same was true for Killian for the first couple of years of secondary school until a new kid moved to his school and started to cause trouble. Sam had been excluded from his previous school and he found himself in Killian's school, where they shared a couple of classes. At first, Killian went unnoticed. Killian had always strategically placed himself in the classroom, where he would not be noticed, but also not in a space where problems would occur; usually the unruly children were at the back of the class. By this point, Killian had shot up in size. Almost overnight, Killian was 6ft tall. At fourteen, this made it harder for Killian to hide, and when Sam had fallen out of flavour with some of the group at the back of their class, he took up a seat next to Killian instead. Killian was still polite and courteous to Sam, but had no intention of befriending him. Sam, however, was desperate to form a new alliance and would continually distract Killian, impeding him from his ability to concentrate and learn in class.

It all came to a head a couple of weeks later when Sam continued to mess around in class, distracting Killian. Killian, politely asking Sam to keep quiet, but this did not go down well with Sam. Sam launched into an argument with Killian, which set off a rage inside of Killian. He had been like a dormant volcano sitting alongside him. But now, suddenly, he could feel the lava bubbling up inside, and then, before he knew it, Killian exploded into a fit of rage, unleashing a tirade of words on Sam. As the altercation ramped up, it finally caught the teacher's attention, who tried to break up the unfolding fight, but before the teacher could get to them both, Sam had taken a swing at Killian and missed. Killian, who until this point had never laid a finger on anyone, went on the counterattack, and with one sharp blow sent Sam stumbling backwards, falling flat on the floor. By this point, the teacher had reached them and sent them to the principal's office, where the boys' respective parents were called in.

Killian's parents, Courtney and Reggie, were shocked and surprised when they heard what had happened in the class and when asking Killian what had happened, Killian shared, 'I don't know what came over me.' Killian got off with a warning, whilst Sam, who had caused two other fights to break out that week, was suspended from the school. When they got home, Killian's mum Courtney shared that she was proud of her son for standing up for himself, but concerned that he'd resorted to violence to address the issue. Killian understood and went on to re-clarify that he was only defending himself. Sam was making sexist and racist comments in class, and that clashed with Killian's values, and he could not let that slide.

There will have been a moment in most of our lives when we are caught off-guard by our emotions, our feelings or our behaviours. Those things that we've never thought of, that blindside us at 4pm on a Tuesday afternoon. When confronted with something that we may not have previously given much thought to, we may have to take some time to evaluate and work out our position on something. In other cases, like Killian's story, we may go into auto-pilot and our reactions and actions seem to come out of nowhere. Often these reactions can occur when we are asked of our opinion on a divisive figure like Donald Trump or our views on two countries at war, like Ukraine and Russia. The unknown self is, in essence, the unexposed self. When we expose ourselves to certain environments or situations, the unknown self is able to come to the fore. This quadrant, the unknown self, unlike the other three quadrants, the known self, the hidden self, and the blind self, can be harder to uncover because we don't know what we don't know. And if no one else knows either, then where are we to begin?

SELF DEVELOPMENT TIME

As Socrates famously once said, 'The unexplored life is not worth living.' And so, to uncover that which is hidden, we must be open and willing to explore the parts of ourselves we have yet to uncover. Here are some initial questions to get you started:

- How much time do you set aside to look inwards to explore the parts of you that have yet to be revealed?
- Have you established what your values and beliefs are in relation to the key topics and themes that play out in not only your daily life, but in current affairs, both domestically and around the world?
- Are you living in an echo-chamber that reaffirms your values and beliefs on a position, or do you seek out and explore alternate perspectives that may challenge and evolve the way you see and do things?
- Are there problems that occur in your life for which you don't know what the root cause of them is?

As you answer these questions, it can help to externalise your thoughts and feelings. Journalling them, discussing them with friends, family members, in support groups, and in therapy can all help in increasing your levels of self-awareness.

SUMMARY

Self-awareness comes when you stop looking outside at the

world and begin the journey inwards. Using the Johari Window, there are four different ways in which you can increase your self-awareness. First, by examining your open-self and exploring whether values, beliefs, or behaviours you have, that are known both to yourself and to others, like Karen's time-keeping, you can identify the areas that are having an adverse effect on your life. By examining, your blind-self, through speaking with those closest to you, or working with a therapist, you can uncover patterns of relating that are causing you problems. As the saying goes, you can't recover from a problem unless you know what you are recovering from. By addressing your blind spots, you then have the opportunity to address and work through the issues. For what we can name, we can tame. When looking at the hidden self-aspects of your life, through evaluating how hiding these parts of yourself are affecting your day-to-day living, you can work through whether or not to disclose these parts, and where if anywhere it is safe to do so. If you are willing and able to go on a journey inward to discover that which is hidden, you can gain further enlightenment about that which was previously unknown or unavailable to you. As the Vietnamese Buddhist monk Thich Nhat Hanh shared, 'Enlightenment, for a wave in the ocean, is the moment the wave realises that it is water.'

Through gaining self-awareness and addressing problems as and when they arise, you can change the pathway forward for you. If there is problematic thinking that you have inherited, through gaining self-awareness and changing your approach, you pass the problematic thinking/behaviour backwards instead of passing it on to the next generation of your lineage.

9

WHO DO YOU THINK YOU ARE

Imposter Syndrome

Claire was what her parents described as a 'gifted child'. The elder of two siblings, during childhood, it seemed whatever Claire turned her hand to she was good at. From playing the piano and singing through to drawing and playing sports, Claire took to each like a duck to water. Growing up in a small village on the border of England and Scotland, the pride Claire's parents had in her ability to capture people's attention every time she sang led them to enter her in local singing and talent competitions. Still only six-years-old, Claire remarkably showed few nerves when she performed and quickly found herself winning each competition that she would enter.

As the years passed by, Claire would spend many of her weekends driven by her parents from competition to competition in neighbouring villages and towns, and on the odd occasion a bigger city a couple of hours away from home. The medals and trophies were quickly accumulating, and by her teenage years, there was barely any space in her room or around the house to place them. A high achiever academically at school, Claire found the subjects she studied a breeze, with the exception of history that didn't come easy to her. It was no surprise when it came to choosing which elective subjects she was to take exams in, history was quickly dropped. As the exams approached, Claire's parents secretly shared concerns her singing or her exam results may take a hit with the amount she was doing. They recalled how hard it was for them to pass their exams at her age and the amount of time and effort they put in to pass had meant they had to sacrifice in other areas, but Claire breezed through her exams and continued to win the competitions she entered, finding both easy to manage and without having to apply much effort or energy into them.

The day of her exam results, Claire's school had been selected by one of the national morning breakfast TV shows to reveal students opening their results live on air. Encouraged by her parents to do so, Claire opened her results to reveal she had received top grades in all of her subjects. As the host asked her parents how they felt, her father shared, 'We're so proud of our Claire. She's so gifted and there is nothing she can't achieve when she sets her mind to it.' One of the local crew filming the news segment overheard Claire singing and, taken aback by her abilities, approached her father and asked if they'd ever considered entering her into a popular new TV singing competition. He was working as part of the production on the show and could put in a word for Claire and have her fast-tracked through the audition process.

Claire jumped at the chance, when her parents shared with her the opportunity, and true to the producer's word, Claire could jump the audition line where many of the auditionees were waiting in the auditorium busily doing their vocal warmups and continuously rehearsing their audition pieces. Claire sailed through the audition and the subsequent elimination rounds with relative ease to become one of the final group of contestants to make it to the live shows. The first live show was exhilarating for Claire. Her performance went well and when it came to the results show, her name was the first called out to go through to the following week's show.

Filled with confidence, Claire entered the second week walking on air. The song selected for her to perform was one she was familiar with from her days doing the competition circuit. Whilst the rest of the contestants, who all shared a house together, busily rehearsed their songs and accompanying routines, Claire took it easy, knowing she had this performance in the bag. For she'd performed Celine Dion's 'It's All Coming Back To Me Now' hundreds of times. It was her show-stopping piece. As the live show rolled around, Claire's performance was to close the show. Working her way through the song with relative ease, as she reached the climax of the song, Claire choked on the high note. Her pitch was off, and as she held the note, trying desperately to correct the note she'd sung, she lost her way and the rest of the performance fell apart.

Inconsolable after the show, despite reassurances from others that it happens to us all from time to time, Claire was bereft. For this had never happened before. Everything had always come so effortlessly to her. When the voting results came in, Claire anxiously awaited, hoping for her name to be called out. The week before she had gone through first, but as name after name was called out, she found herself in the bottom two and up for elimination. A familiar face was also in the bottom two, Paul, whom she'd competed against numerous times growing up and always came out on top. Paul went first, and managed to put in a stellar performance, much better than the night before. The pressure was now on Claire. As she worked her way through the song, she pushed herself and once again when it came to the big note at the end, her voice cracked, and right there, right then, she knew it was over.

As each of the judges confirmed it was Paul they would be sending through to the next round, Claire's heart had sunk. She'd never lost anything before. After the show, as her parents came to console her, she could see the disappointment in their eyes. For Claire, their gifted child, maybe wasn't so gifted after all. Had she fooled everyone all this time, and finally she'd been found out not to be so gifted? These thoughts and many more began circling through Claire's head. Claire had never 'failed' at something before and was mortified at doing so; twice, on such a public platform, and so she hid herself away. Reluctant to appear on the grand finale of the TV competition, Claire finally agreed, but opted to take a smaller singing role in the group performance, through fear of choking again.

The performance went smoothly, and at the wrap party Claire was approached by the bosses of the TV show to join the tour of the finalists next year. Usually, they only take the Top 8 out on tour (Claire had finished eleventh) but they were willing to make an exception for her, as they felt she had a great voice but had just been unfortunate on the live show. However, Claire had declined. There had also been interest expressed in her by several record labels too, but she'd passed on all of those too. For Claire had started to question her talent and abilities. 'Maybe I'm not as good as everyone thinks I am.' 'Everyone told me I was gifted growing up, and I believed them, but the show exposed me to not be so gifted after all.'

Following the TV show, Claire withdrew from singing in public. Riddled with fear that she'd lost the gift that she'd been given as a child, she didn't want to put herself into situations where she might deliver a less than perfect performance and have that thought reaffirmed and be exposed as an imposter. And so Claire's dream of becoming a pop-star went to the graveyard to die, as she hung up her microphone and opted to pursue a regular nine-to-five job instead.

Stories like these fill my private practice all the time. Young, talented individuals who seek out my support for imposter syndrome, feeling they have the curse of the gifted child. From singers like Sarah above, to young sports players who find themselves dropped from the academy all the way through to premier league footballers, who struggle with finding themselves on the substitute bench match after match. These individuals share a commonality. Their natural talent gave them a head start in life, but as time prevailed, their talents may have plateaued. Others who didn't have that natural talent began to overtake them. What came so easily to them had now become more difficult.

THE ORIGINS OF IMPOSTER SYNDROME

Before we delve deeper into this, it may help to take a step back and look at imposter syndrome more broadly. Imposter syndrome was a term first coined by Pauline Clance and Dr. Suzanne Imes in 1978, when they published their research on 'The Imposter in High-Achieving Women'. Their study found that there appeared to be an internal experience of intellectual phoniness that was particularly prevalent amongst a select sample of high-achieving women. This came as a result of early family dynamics and later an introjection of societal sex-role stereotyping that appeared to contribute significantly to the development of the imposter phenomenon. This would come despite any outstanding academic and personal accomplishments, with the women studied believing that they were not really bright, and they will have fooled anyone who thinks otherwise.

Since 1978, numerous studies have been carried out with the mean average of these studies, revealing that roughly 70% of people experience imposter syndrome at some point in their lives. Imposter syndrome isn't limited to just females. It impacts all genders, as well as all age ranges and demographics. As we move further into the 21st century, imposter syndrome seems to be on the rise where a 516% increase in google searches for imposter syndrome has occurred on Google over the past few years. With the rise of social media, it seems imposter syndrome rates will continue to rise amongst the general population, as imposter syndrome moves beyond the intellectual phoniness first identified in 1978 and to a broader chasm between what is believed to be the true self and the idealised self that is presented to the world.

Dr Valerie Young (2011), an expert in imposter syndrome, identified five main sub-groups for imposter syndrome, which are:

1. The gifted child
2. The perfectionist
3. The superhuman
4. The expert   and
5. The soloist

Let's take a moment to briefly understand what each of the imposter syndrome sub-groups looks like and how it can show up.

THE GIFTED CHILD

The gifted child is someone whose talent in one or many areas has come naturally to them. They judge their competence based on the ease and speed with which they can do things, rather than the effort they put in. If something takes a long time to complete or master, they feel shame, like an imposter. There is an expectation to get things right on the first attempt, and if that doesn't happen, an internal alarm bell sounds, that they aren't good at that thing, and if found out, they will be deemed an imposter.

THE PERFECTIONIST

Perfectionists are individuals who set extremely high goals for themselves, and if they fail to reach them, they experience self-doubt and concern about measuring up. The perfectionist may focus on being perfect in one (work) or all areas of their lives, and can live in a constant state of fear, that the perfect standards they have set for themselves, may not be reached, that the image they are conveying, be that in real-life or on social media, may be exposed, and they may be seen as flawed, as an imposter. Anxiety is often rife in the perfectionist, with the need to feel like they are always in control, to try to manage their perfectionist image.

THE SUPERHUMAN

Superhumans are high-achievers who convince themselves that they are imposters. They push themselves to work harder and harder in an attempt to prove otherwise, but this is to cover up for their insecurities. If they succeed in achieving what they set out to do, it will often be chalked down to luck, or to others who contributed to the success. When a failure is perceived to occur, this will re-enforce their feelings of being an imposter, leading to intense feelings of shame, and a desire to work harder once more to prove they are not an imposter. The risk of burn-out, because of their relentless work ethic, is high amongst this sub-group of people who suffer from the superhuman imposter syndrome.

THE EXPERT

The expert bases their competence on what they know, and how much they know, or can do. Believing they can never know enough, they fear that no matter how much knowledge or understanding they have in their area/s of expertise, they will be exposed as inexperienced and unknowledgeable by someone when they are questioned. There is often an insatiable appetite for trainings and certifications, to validate their expertise, an aversion to apply for any position unless they meet every criteria, and an avoidance of being labelled expert by others.

THE SOLOIST

Soloists are individuals who feel as though asking for help from other people reveals their phoniness. They choose to be independent in most, if not all, areas of their lives. If they keep people at bay, then they won't be able to find out that they are an imposter in one or many areas of their lives. For the soloist, they take being independent to the extreme. Being independent in itself is okay, but only being able to rely on oneself and refusing assistance so that you can prove your worth will lead to problems arising.

Before we delve deeper into your own imposter syndrome, let's get more acquainted with the second sub-group, the perfectionist.

KEEPING UP APPEARANCES

David was the guy who seemed to have it all. Deemed to have what is called pretty privilege (economic, social and political advantages or benefits solely based on one's physical appearance) David's natural good looks, saw him amass a significant following across his social media platforms, to a point where his 'influencer' status attracted the attention of companies and brands, who wanted to align themselves with the young and carefree attitude he portrayed. Paid-partnerships, endorsement deals and other opportunities followed, as his profile continued to soar.

At one of the many events David was regularly invited to, he met another 'influencer' Hannah. The pair immediately hit it off and soon after became a couple. This pairing seemed to be a match made in heaven and saw their respective followers and reach soar, as they portrayed this perfect life that many of their followers aspired to. The opportunities continued to flow in for David and continued to expose him to things he could never have dreamed of. Having come from a broken home, where he shared a small one-bedroom apartment with his mum and older sister, David was now finding himself going from one five-star hotel to another all around the world and generating enough money to buy a luxury apartment in a much sought after postcode.

As the requests continued to come in, the demands on David's time and energy increased significantly, leading to him feeling exhausted as a result of always having to be 'on', portraying the perfect lifestyle that would fill up his social media feed. With less and less time to do the things that brought David joy, instead being replaced place of things that would bring in David (and his partner) money, he slipped into a deep depression. Everything seemed perfect on the surface and across his social media feeds, but beneath, David was struggling to get out of bed. The loss of motivation led to his lack of routine in going to the gym, leading to the loss of the chiselled physique he'd become synonymous with. Alongside this, some of the former paid-partnerships and brand deals David had previously been top of the list for companies and brands, were starting to go to other 'influencers' whose reach and aspirational lifestyle matched, or in sometimes exceeded, what was being portrayed on David's socials.

With pressure from his girlfriend and manager to keep up appearances and promote a perfect lifestyle that was at odds with the reality David was facing, the gap between David's true self and the ideal self that was being portrayed across social media grew wider and wider. To the outside world, it looked like David had the perfect life, but he began to feel like an imposter, selling a lie to others and an image that was impossible to maintain. Yet at the same time, he feared losing everything that he worked hard to attain. A few months later, the pressure became too much, and I found David sitting across from me in my private practice. Hannah had, in his words, 'traded him in for another influencer to grow her brand'. Requests were still coming into his manager regularly to promote various products and a lifestyle he had built his own brand on, but the pressure to be this happy, go lucky, pretty boy with a perfect physique and not a care in the world, left him empty and disconnected from himself. It took several sessions to unpack and explore the root cause of David's conditions of worth, his need to seek approval and validation from others to feel good about himself. Coming from a father that had abandoned him, and a mother who only gave tough love, David yearned for acceptance and approval, but seldom received it from those who he wanted it from the most. As his attractiveness became apparent, he leant into that, gaining a form of love and adoration that he so desperately desired from his family. Yet, no matter how much he fed that part of himself through social media, it never filled the hole left by the emptiness of his parents' lack of love and attention. David took the time to mourn the loss of the parents he needed, to accept the parents he had. He evolved his relationship with his social media, separating himself as a person from the product his image was, and no longer chasing likes to validate his worth. Today David is in a much better place with his relationship to social media, and has learned to find love within himself, rather that solely seeking it outside.

Though David may be at one end of a continuum, in the digital world that most of us now occupy, it is becoming more and more common to see individuals experience imposter syndrome as our lives are played out online. According to a study by Statistica (2023), the average person spends roughly 2 hours and 31 minutes each day on social media alone. The bi-product of this is that we are continually fed and exposed through our own individual algorithms to how the people we follow are living their lives. Yet, as with my client David, the content on all our profiles, with the rare exception, is carefully curated to highlight the best of ourselves, whilst hiding the rest of ourselves. We become validated by the likes, comments, shares that acknowledge the content we share, which reinforces the underlying need to post more and more content that showcases a blessed and highly favoured lifestyle.

The wider the gap between your everyday life and the life that you present on social media, the higher the chance of imposter syndrome occurring. The pressure to keep up with others online can leave individuals feeling like imposters when the image portrayed doesn't match the everyday reality. Always having new outfits #OOTD to share online, may hide the reality you can't afford many of the looks and have had to beg, borrow or steal them to keep up the image, and the fear that someone is going to find out or even worse expose the truth. The cost isn't just financial, it's coming at the sake of your mental health as well.

With another client in my private practice, we spent an entire session exploring and unpacking whether they should delete a post on Instagram because it had got less than their typical one million likes. What was so important to them about reaching that threshold? What did it mean if they didn't hit that magic number? As the session progressed, the client's imposter syndrome became clear. If one of their posts didn't reach at least one million likes, it reinforced a belief that they weren't good enough, that people had lost interest in them and that who they truly were had been exposed. Therefore, it was better to delete the post and keep up the image that everything had at least one million likes, than risk a post receiving less.

Dr Sandi Mann (2016) identified three areas that are likely to underpin an individual's imposter syndrome:

1. Low self-confidence
2. Low self-belief   and
3. Low self-esteem

Self-confidence is the confidence in our abilities in any given area. Self-belief is what we believe about ourselves. And self-esteem is who we are as a whole, rather than specific elements about how much approval, acceptance, and worthiness we feel. Let's look at an example of two individuals, one who has a good level of all three and one with a low level of all three.

Two friends, Sam and Terra, both in their thirties, enter a 10km run being held in a local town for the second year in a row. Both completing the run at a respectable time, though slightly down on what they ran the previous year, the two friends had very different reactions to their race. Sam notes that though they were slower than the previous year, it didn't impact her confidence in her ability to run, her belief that she is a good runner, or that it reflected badly on her as a whole. Terra, who used to run cross country professionally as a teenager, had a different outlook. The finishing time, that was down on her target, impacted her confidence in her abilities as a runner, it knocked her self-belief leaving her feeling that she was now past her prime as a runner, and impacted her self-esteem where she questioned, 'If I'm no longer good at running (that had formed part of her identity) then am I good at anything?'

Martin Seligman (2018), founder of positive psychology, attributes these reflections to two different perspectives. Terra has a pessimistic outlook on life. Her negativity bias as she reflects on the result of her run has led her to believe that the situation is permanent, that it will go on forever more (I'm no longer any good at running). It's pervasive. That this one area will impact every area (I am no good at anything). And that it's personal. No one else is experiencing this issue (despite Sam also being down on her time). Sam, however, has a more realistic/optimistic outlook on life, acknowledging that this situation is temporary. This will pass (it was just one race). It's specific. This is only focused on one area of my life (not performing as well in my run, doesn't mean I'm not performing well overall). And it's impersonal. This isn't about me (everyone was down on their race time this year).

Individuals who struggle with imposter syndrome are likely to suffer from a pessimistic outlook and have a negativity bias. As a result, the likelihood is that their perspective on issues they have to confront will be seen through a permanent, pervasive, and personal lens, rather than a specific, temporary, and impersonal lens. But as we mentioned earlier, imposter syndrome affects roughly 70% of the population. So when does it show up? And who is more susceptible to imposter syndrome?

Imposter syndrome is more common amongst high achievers, as highlighted in the five main sub-groups of imposter syndrome. It can often show up in students who are striving to achieve top grades, but equally in those who feel they are performing beyond their means. It shows up in academics, who are held up as experts in their field of work. Many experts believe that they are put on a pedestal and they can't live up to the expert status, as whilst they may know a lot, there is still much to know and they fear being exposed for not knowing. Alongside these areas, it shows up in competitive arenas, sport especially. A good performance can be put down to luck or a fluke rather than hard work. If part of a group sport, an individual can feel they are not as good as the rest of the team. If an individual sport, they can feel they're not as good as the rest of the field. As in the story at the beginning of the chapter, it can show up in individuals that have early success in something and then a continued pressure to live up to that expectation. Imposter syndrome can show up when an individual starts their career after their education, where a lack of ongoing support can leave them feeling they don't know what they're doing. It can continue throughout the progression of an individual's career, as promotions, leading to new roles and more senior positions, demanding different skills and responsibilities, that an individual may feel they don't have and that were promoted before they were ready. That they are going to finally be exposed as a fraud and so on. It is likely to show up in an individual who wants to portray a perfect life but struggle to keep up with the many demands that it brings with it. One last example is that it can show up is in environments where an individual is a minority. They may be the only individual who is different to everyone else (gender, sexuality, ethnicity, physicality, religion, etc.). The weight of expectation that they carry to represent that part of themselves as a symbol of their community without guidance or support can lead them to question every decision they make and bring about feelings of imposter syndrome.

It shows up primarily in periods of transition, when moving from the comfort and familiarity of what one knows, into a space or arena that is unknown. It can lead to what Carl Rogers (1977) calls The Real Self vs The Ideal Self, the version of the self we are and the version of the self we present to the world. An individual may portray an ideal self through social media all the way through to attempting to live up to titles or view projected onto them. The wider the chasm between the real self and ideal self, the more likely that imposter syndrome is going to show up. The fear of being found out as not being the ideal self that is seen by others comes into play.

INTO THE UNKNOWN

Liana was taken aback when she was approached by the board of her company to become the interim CEO, whilst the company was navigating a changing of the guard at the top of the organisation. Impressed by her hard work and the results she had delivered, the company felt Liana would be the perfect person to steer the ship during this period of transition. Also unbeknownst to Liana, the board was also viewing this as a trial period, as they believed Liana would be the ideal person to take over the role. Initially grateful for the opportunity, Liana felt fear and doubt creep in. Thought's such as 'If I take this role, I'll finally be found out as a fraud' and 'I'm not good at my job' played over and over, but following discussions with her husband Anthony she decided to take on the role.

Another issue plagued Liana's thoughts as she took on the interim CEO role. Liana would become not only the first woman in the company's history to take on the role, but also the first person who was not white too. The board of the company was full of what is often referred to as the stale, pale, male club; older straight white men, and Liana was the complete opposite of this. Though Liana had got on well with the previous CEO, she hadn't had an opportunity to speak with them, to get any support or guidance on how to approach the role, and so Liana was left to make the role her own. This was exactly what the board was hoping and wanting from Liana, but didn't communicate this explicitly to Liana.

As the weeks went by, Liana became overwhelmed with imposter syndrome. Every decision she made, she second guessed. Was she doing the right thing? Is this the way the business should be run? And many other thoughts would continue to arise. Torn between trying to replicate what the previous CEO did and carve out her own pathway of how to be a CEO, Liana would often experience analysis paralysis, leaving her stuck. Not long into the role, I found Liana sitting across from me in my private practice. As we explored and unpacked her imposter syndrome, all the hard work and results that got Liana to where she was, Liana had written off as just luck. She questioned thoughts of whether she was a tokenistic hire because of her gender and ethnicity. The weight to represent those two parts of her identity meant that she was paralysed by fear, afraid to make any mistakes, because not only would this reflect badly on her, but whom she represented. Liana also had a very different approach to leadership than the former CEO. Liana was very nurturing and supportive, open and collaborative with others, providing a sense of agency and autonomy to individuals to perform their roles, which was at odds with the former CEO who operated from a position of fear and control, micromanaging all of his direct reports.

Through naming her fears and identifying her needs, Liana could carve out a plan where she could move forward in the interim role without being overwhelmed with feelings of imposter syndrome. Alongside the ongoing support she received through my private practice, she joined a community for black female executives, so that she could see reflected back to her what she was struggling to see in herself – for you can't be what you can't see. This allowed her to seek help, support, and guidance from other individuals not too dissimilar to her to navigate this new role. Liana also leant into her leadership style, relinquishing the desire to keep going the old CEO's approach, that was at odds with her own style. I'm pleased to report that owing to the changes and proactive steps she made, Liana became permanent CEO for the company six months later, and the company continues to grow to new heights under her leadership.

Many of the leading figures we see in the world today in different arenas have publicly spoken about their feelings of imposter syndrome. Former COO of Facebook (now Meta) Sheryl Sandberg (2015) acknowledged 'Every time I didn't embarrass myself – or even excelled – I believed that I had fooled everyone yet again.' Actor Tom Hanks (2018) shared, 'No matter what I've done, there comes a point where you think, how did I get here? When are they going to discover that I am, in fact, a fraud and take everything away from me?' And former chairman and CEO of Starbuck's Howard Schultz (2012) shared feelings not to dissimilar to what Liana experienced/ 'Very few people, whether you've been in that job before or not, get into the seat and believe that they are now qualified to be the CEO. They're not going to tell you that, but it's true.'

As human's we all hold two negative core beliefs:

1. *I am not enough.*
2. *I am not loveable.*

These beliefs often underpin and give fuel to the thoughts and feelings of imposter syndrome. When finding ourselves in environments or situations where these negative core beliefs are activated, then the imposter syndrome is likely to arise. This can often give rise to the If/Then rule. If I do X, then I will achieve Y. If I work really hard, then I will prove my worth in this role. If I win this award, then I will receive the acceptance, praise of my friends/family/peers/idol. The paradox that often appears here when imposter syndrome is at play, is that an individual is seeking praise but then will dismiss it when it comes, chalking it down to a fluke or luck.

Pressure and expectation often come into alignment with imposter syndrome. Pressure and expectation aren't always a bad thing. They can be a driving force within an individual to help them set out for what they want to achieve. The famous expression 'Too little challenge and we get bored. Too much challenge and we give up' comes into play here. Pressure and expectation provide individuals with a challenge. Yet, if the challenge feels overwhelming, like it's too much or insurmountable, then it is likely the individual will give up. It can also lead to a pattern of avoidance because of a fear of failure and being exposed if unable to meet the challenge.

SELF RELECTION TIME

Let's turn our attention away from the examples and onto you to explore if imposter syndrome is present in your life. Whether you identify with any of the imposter syndrome sub-groups and how imposter syndrome may be causing you problems in your life.

- Do you experience imposter syndrome?
- In what way/s does your imposter syndrome show up?
- Do you identify with one of the five sub-groups of imposter syndrome?

Perfectionism questions:

- Do you struggle with perfectionism?
- Do you have a need to control things?
- Are you a micro-manager?
- Do you have difficulty delegating, or get frustrated/disappointed in the results when you do?

Gifted child questions:

- Were you labelled a gifted child growing up?
- Are you used to excelling without much effort?
- When you face a setback, does your confidence take a blow, or do you give up?
- Do you avoid challenges at things you perceive yourself not to be great at?

Superhuman questions:

- Do you find yourself stressed when you're not working and find downtime wasteful?
- Have you let hobbies and passions fall by the wayside in pursuit of your career?

- Do you continuously push yourself beyond your limits to achieve your goals?
- Do you find that you spread yourself too thinly across all of your obligations?

Soloist questions:

- Do you feel you need to achieve things on your own?
- 'I don't need anyone's help.' Does this statement sound like you?
- Did you receive no help, or a lack of help from others, when asking for it growing up?

Expert questions:

- Do you feel like you haven't truly earned your title as an expert in your specific field?
- Do you struggle to put yourself forward for anything where you don't meet every requirement listed in a role, despite all of your achievements?
- Even if you've been in a position for a while, do you still feel as though you don't know enough?

Do you identify with any of the sub-groups of imposter syndrome? It may be that you identify with none, one, or several of these sub-groups. Below, we will begin to look at different ways in which you can start to overcome the feelings of imposter syndrome, both overall and within the different sub-groups.

SELF DEVELOPMENT TIME

There are several ways in which you can reduce or remove your imposter syndrome if you are willing to evolve your way of thinking and relating to things and situations. The first area we'll look at is perfectionism. Perfectionism, by its definition, is a refusal to accept any standard short of perfection. It equally is an aversion to failure or perceived failure. The problem is perfectionism is a myth. Whilst there may be moments in your life that are perfect, it isn't sustainable in the long run. Striving for perfectionism also will, at some point, lead to the thing that you are looking to avoid, failure, or perceived failure. This can be seen in Figure 9.1, the perfectionism cycle.

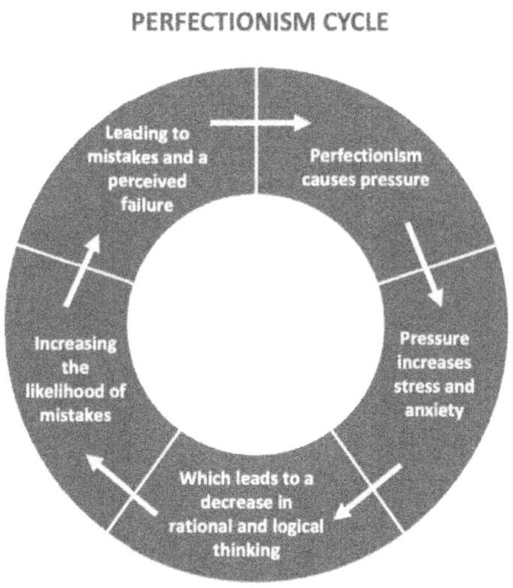

PERFECTIONISM CYCLE

- Leading to mistakes and a perceived failure
- Perfectionism causes pressure
- Pressure increases stress and anxiety
- Which leads to a decrease in rational and logical thinking
- Increasing the likelihood of mistakes

Figure 9.1 - The Perfectionism Cycle.

1. Perfectionism leads to pressure.
2. Press leads to an increase in stress and anxiety.
3. Significant increases in stress and anxiety leads to a decrease in rational and logical thinking.
4. A decrease in rational and logical thinking can lead to mistakes.
5. Mistakes lead to failure or a perceived failure.
6. Therefore, perfectionism equals failure.

The issue doesn't just lie with the relationship to perfectionism, but the aversion of failure. We currently find ourselves in a period of time where failure is something to avoid at all costs. We celebrate our successes in the light, nowhere more so than on social media, but our failures are to be hidden out of sight. However, it is important to continue to remind oneself that the people who are the most successful in life are not the ones that haven't failed, but the ones who have gone from failure to failure without a loss of determinism that what they are hoping or looking to achieve will eventually come.

Success happens in the darkness. Victory happens in the light. Usain Bolt was victorious in the 100m at the Olympics and became the world record holder at the World Championships, but that was as a result of the successes he made in the darkness when the eyes of the world weren't on him. When he was in practice in Jamaica. When he would falter getting out of the blocks and take the time to improve his start. When he'd train to review his strides and posture. Think back to your own beginnings. Your first attempt at walking didn't result in success. Your first attempt at talking didn't result in success. But still you persevered and now look at you, you walking, talking superstar. Your first workout/run will be hard and or bad. Your first attempt at public speaking will be hard and/or bad. But over time, it will get better. It will become easier as you build muscle memory. Every expert was once a beginner. Swap your expectation of what or where you should be and appreciate what or where you are and continue to build from there. Choose progress over perfection.

Let's turn now to social media and the issue with comparison. A study carried out by charity Scope (2024) shows that 62% of people feel social media platforms make them feel inadequate about their own lives. Comparison is the thief of joy. Social media itself isn't a bad thing, but the way it has evolved over time from a place of connection to a place of self-promotion has resulted in this need to keep up with others, and as mentioned earlier to only show the best sides of ourselves.

- Do you engage in periodical digital detoxes where you take a complete break from social media?

If not, why not try it for a day or week to start, and see how that affects your mood, your feelings of imposter syndrome? If a complete digital detox feels unattainable, why not limit your usage daily by putting app limits on the social media apps on your phone.

- When was the last time you looked at your feed and the posts that you engage with on social media through a critical lens?
- Which posts or profiles bring up negative feelings about yourself or feelings of imposter syndrome?

Unfollow those profiles, or if need be mute them so as not to cause issues with those relationships in the real world because of an unfollow. Resist the urge to engage with those posts that make you feel worse about yourself and bring up the imposter syndrome, so that the social media algorithm can adjust to share content that actually serves you as opposed to hinders you. When you engage with social media, before posting, turn your attention to your intention.

- What is my intention for this post?
- Is it to reinforce perfectionism?
- Am I looking for vanity validation?
- Does it widen the gap between my real and ideal self?

Evolve your relationship with social media to post the rest of you and not just the best of you. And if that's not viable for you, don't attach your worth to the engagement levels of the post.

Moving on from social media, let's look at the realm of the unknown. In life, you can't be what you can't see. If you have broken through the glass ceiling as a woman, the lavender ceiling as a member of the LGBTQIA+ community, the concrete ceiling as a person of colour or several other ceilings, and you are the first person to do so in your field, you are likely to have no comparisons or role models to help guide and mentor you. There are three ways you can support yourself through this:

1. Reflection
2. Projection
3. Direction

Reflection

Support comes in many shapes and forms, none more so than in a community that you identify with. Who can reflect back to you who you are, so that you can be who you see in the mirror with confidence? Support groups are available in all different subsets based on gender, sexuality, ethnicity, physicality and more, both within your career field and beyond. Why not seek out these groups, to get support, insights and different perspectives, to navigate the problems and challenges you face.

Projection

Is there someone out there who has already paved the same or a similar path to the one you are walking that you can forge a relationship with and be mentored by? To help when your imposter syndrome arises. To alleviate any fears or concerns, and support your journey. If you can identify someone you would like to be, in one, three, five years' time, why not reach out to them for support and guidance?

Direction

If you are a pioneer in your field, the first of your kind, and the previous options aren't available to you, tap into support by utilising a coach or therapist to help unlock the answers you already have inside to the problems or challenges you face. If you struggle to ask for help, because of a long-held core belief that no one will help you based on what happened in your formative years, work through that with a therapist. Find a space, a place to counter that narrative and build an environment where you are able to gain the help you need.

If you identified with Claire's story at the start of the chapter as being a gifted child where things came effortlessly to you, evolve your relationship to your gift. I noticed a recurring theme during my two decades working for major record labels in the music industry. It was never the artists that were the most talented that became the most successful. It was the artists who combined their talents with a continued focus and commitment to work on their talents and the other areas required to be an artist who became the most successful. The same is true of each individual and their gift/s. If you don't take the time to nurture your gift, time will take it from you. Regular nurturing of the gift is the ideal approach. Like I shared earlier, too much challenge and we give up, so challenging yourself by an amount just outside your comfort zone.

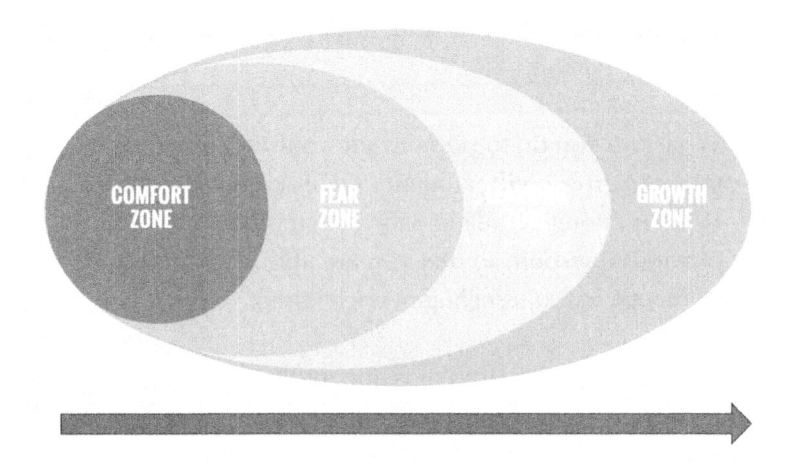

Figure 9.2 - The Four Zones of Growth.

There are four zones within which we grow through life, as can be seen in Figure 9.2. For the gifted child, they are often found in the comfort with their gift because it comes effortlessly. They have never had to work hard on their gift. If challenged by their gift, the fear zone keeps the gifted child stuck in their comfort zone. This is often through fear of being found out that the gift is not as effortless as it once was, and they will be exposed as a fraud. So, rather than pushing through the fear zone to learn more about how to harness their gift and then grow, they remain stuck. When this is repeatedly done by the gifted child, it can stifle growth, they often plateau and, in some cases, regress. If instead the gifted child continually steps outside their comfort zone, into the fear zone, where the challenge is manageable and not too overwhelming, then learning and growth will occur. This, in turn, will increase the size of the comfort zone, as the work continues to be put in to harness the gift that emerged from an early age. This will help your gift continue to grow, and the challenge will not feel too insurmountable. Also, don't be afraid to ask for help. It can often be the case that gifted children grow up to resent help, as the belief is held that help shouldn't be needed, because my gift comes naturally. Yet no man is an island. We all need help in some way, shape, or form as we grow through life. Find someone who can help support, nurture and evolve your natural gifts, who can challenge you and help you challenge yourself to become a better person.

- What can you do to step outside your comfort zone today to grow a gift, a talent, a skill set that you have?
- What is enough challenge for you in relation to the previous question, so that you are able to rise to the challenge without feeling overwhelmed?

As a society where technology now infiltrates every area of our lives and we have access to everything at the click of a device, our attention spans, and our patience levels for what we want have significantly dropped. In an era of instant gratification, where we expect everything to happen immediately, the imposter syndrome is likely to show up when we don't achieve something in an unrealistic time frame. Slow and steady wins the race as the tortoise taught us, in the race between the hare and the tortoise. Some things can come quickly, but other things take time to develop, to be embedded. For me, when I wrote my first book, I grossly under-estimated how long it would take me to write each chapter, and subsequently had to double the time frame within which it took me to complete it. As I now write this my second book, I have learnt from that perspective, and now realise that invariably things always take longer than we think. And so, I now account for that, which takes the pressure and the expectation I placed on myself off me, and as a result, doesn't give fuel to the imposter syndrome. Take the time to assess how long something is going to take and be realistic with the expectation on yourself. If ever in doubt about how long something will take, double it.

If your imposter syndrome shows up in the form of being a soloist, superhuman, or the expert, learning how to embrace support is key. No one can know everything or do everything. Relinquishing that narrative and allowing yourself to be vulnerable enough to acknowledge this will facilitate your ability to continually evolve. As humans, we don't go through life; we grow through life. Delegating to others as someone who identifies as superhuman or a soloist can both ease your load and free up more time to focus on areas that need more attention. Make peace with the fact that someone you delegate to may not be as skilled as you with the task you are giving to them as you are. Given time and training, they will, and by investing in that, you invest in yourself to progress further, by freeing up more time in the long run, to focus on other things, that will further your life and/or career. If you identify with the expert imposter syndrome, acknowledge that there will always be more to learn and know. There is often always something new to learn that can expand our knowledge, and it is good to invest in your professional and/or personal development, but that should not negate your current expertise in your specific field. Every expert was once a beginner, and every expert has more they could learn. Become comfortable knowing that in the majority of environments, you are the expert in the room. There will always be a room where you are the least experienced, but that provides a great growth opportunity, and not something that you should shy away from but embraced. Seek those spaces to increase your knowledge. Identify individuals that can support and mentor you to enhance your expertise in your field.

If you identify with the superhuman sub-group of imposter syndrome, there is an increased likelihood that you may experience burnout. A number of tell-tale signs that you are on the pathway to burnout include:

- Neglecting your own needs
- Ignoring your problems in your professional and/or personal life.
- Compromising on your own values
- Denial of new problems when they arise
- Withdrawal from others
- Impacts on your personal relationships
- Inner emptiness
- Depression

Whilst we will look at this theme more in the next chapter, I Don't Want To Miss A Thing, it is important to become familiar with the signs of burnout above, to ensure you don't go too far down the burnout pathway, before it's too late to turn back. It's true all of us have 168 hours in the week. What's also true is that we all have different levels of responsibility. What one individual may be able to achieve, another tasked with the same responsibilities may not, because of other commitments in their life.

- Do you resonate with any of the tell-tale signs of burnout?
- How much time do you set aside in your week to look after yourself?
- What activities do you do that energize/re-energize you and fill you up?

Most people will schedule in their work appointments and personal commitments, but neglect to schedule in time for themselves. If you already schedule in time for yourself, then that's great. If not, why not start today, by looking at the next month and scheduling in time for yourself to do things that fill you up, before your diary gets filled with other commitments, and make these schedule entries a non-negotiable.

Don't let your imposter syndrome cause you to stagnate, to burn out, to be crippled with fear and anxiety, to create an idealised version of yourself that is impossible to live up to or sustain.

SUMMARY

Imposter syndrome affects roughly 70% of the global population. The term was coined by Pauline Clance and Dr. Suzanne Imes in 1978, when they published their research on 'The Imposter in High-Achieving Women', finding that there appeared to be an internal experience of intellectual phoniness that was prevalent amongst a sample of high-achieving women. As time has prevailed, it has been shown that imposter syndrome affects all genders, all ages, and all backgrounds.

Dr Valerie Young (2011) identified five sub-groups that struggled with imposter syndrome. The gifted child, the perfectionist, the superhuman, the soloist and the expert. Amongst each of these, Dr Sandi Mann (2016) identified three areas that are likely to underpin an individual's imposter syndrome: low self-confidence, low self-belief, and low self-esteem. This is likely to lead to an individual suffering from negativity bias, where an individual struggles with their outlook on their life, their career, their skill set or wherever the imposter syndrome shows up. They view things as permanent (it will always be like this), pervasive (it impacts all areas of my life) and personal (it only affects me and no one else).

Imposter syndrome can leave individuals feeling stuck, in a constant state of stress and anxiety about being found out, being perceived as a failure. Overcoming imposter syndrome requires many individuals learning how to relinquish control. To be able to ask for help and support, and admitting to not being able to do everything or know everything. To take the foot off the accelerator from time to time, to avoid burnout. If viewed as the gifted child, it is about taking the opportunity to apply oneself, and nurture the talent, continuously. To not expect the talent to always be there, as the well often runs dry, unless it is replenished. Find the perfect amount of challenge, so that it isn't too much that you give up, but not too little that you get bored.

Changing one's relationship to perfectionism can help close the gap between the true self and the idealised version of oneself. Perfectionism is unsustainable in the long run. It leads to pressure, which increases stress and anxiety, which leads to a decrease in creativity and productivity, which leads to an increase in mistakes/failure. The mistakes or failure that a perfectionist is trying to avoid, is actually being created. Learning that failure is part of the process of growth and change, and adapting your relationship to failure, will relinquish the need to always be perfect. The most successful people aren't the people who haven't failed. They are often the people who have failed the most, but have taken the lessons from each time they've failed and put them into practice to help them grow.

10

I DON'T WANT TO MISS A THING

Attaining

As Jay rolled over in the bed reaching over for his wife Melissa, he was met with a cold and empty space. Opening his eyes, he saw the clock on the bedside table that read 5:52am and, surprised by the time, headed downstairs to the kitchen, where Melissa was filling her coffee up and preparing to leave the house. Having woken at 4am, Melissa had already been for a 5-mile run, showered, got ready for work, prepared their daughters lunchbox for kindergarten, and had time to review her calendar for the day, ahead of what was sure to be another busy schedule. Slightly surprised by Jay's arrival, she greeted him in a loving embrace. Grabbing her car keys off the side, their daughter Ellie sleepily stumbled into the kitchen. Melissa picked up Ellie, giving her the biggest hug, saying, 'Mummy is so proud of you. I can't wait to come and see your play later.' Passing Ellie to Jay, Melissa gave them both a kiss and as she reached the door, Jay said to Ellie, 'What do we say to mummy?' Without missing a bit Ellie replied, 'Another day…' and Melissa responded, 'Another slay.'

Arriving at the office just before 7am, Melissa had a big day of meetings lined up. Her ride or die friend Justina, who had become her first employee when she founded the cosmetics company fifteen years earlier, met her in the boardroom and would be alongside her on the start of this next chapter for the business. Going through the various decks of the major cosmetic brands that expressed interest in acquiring the company, they familiarized themselves with the intricacies of each corporation's structure. Their respective backgrounds in working with a cosmetic line for black women, and the CIA level job that Melissa's EA Joanne had done on getting background information on each of the people she would meet that day. One after the other, over the space of the day, Melissa and her team met with the likes of MAC, Bobbi Brown, Estee Lauder, Clinique to hear about how they envisioned taking Melissa's company to the next level.

Melissa didn't suffer fools lightly. She intentionally left her agenda in clear view of each of her meeting attendee's so they could see the other companies she was meeting with. As each representative from their respective company launched into their well-polished PR spiel in an attempt to woo Melissa in choosing their company for the acquisition, Melissa remained stoic in her approach. A poker face that gave nothing away, she asked the right questions, gathered the responses from each and politely shared that her legal team would be in touch, once they reviewed the various offers they had received. With the last meeting wrapped up, Melissa, Justina, and the legal team discussed the various options that had opened up to them. Joanne, the ever-caring executive assistant, came in delivering a late lunch for all in the room, a kind gesture that Melissa hadn't asked for, but was eternally grateful for, even if she did only pick at the food.

Though Joanne had been with the company for two years, it felt to Melissa like she'd known Joanne her entire lifetime. Helping Melissa, with everything from scheduling her life, to ensuring the little things didn't go a miss, like the two birthday cards she'd brought in with the lunch for Melissa to sign for her father and brother. As the meeting ended, Joanne grabbed five minutes with

Melissa to run through the rest of the week's schedule, that seemed even more overwhelming to Joanne than Melissa's usual demanding work schedule. Looking at where any changes could be made, Melissa was reluctant to outsource any of her meetings or commitments, that she felt obligated to do. Melissa noted that this was just a busy time in her life, and that she needed to make some sacrifices here and there in order to get the deal across the line. The trade-offs were often hard for Melissa. Her workload had almost doubled over the past year, as sales for the company soared following an endorsement from Oprah. This meant she could no longer do the school run in the mornings, leaving Jay to adjust his own work schedule to make things work. Other commitments were either shortened or had to be missed, too.

Not wanting to miss her twenty-five-year high school reunion, she attended, even though she could only be there for fifteen minutes. Even her date nights with Jay, that had been important to her, had fallen by the wayside, having been reduced from weekly to monthly. Melissa's company had been her baby until her own baby, Ellie, had come along. She had poured her heart and soul into building the company up from scratch and turning it into a nine-figure company. Jay had been supportive and by her side throughout, putting his own career ambitions on hold to help further Melissa's. They had talked about having another child, so that Ellie wouldn't be an only child, but a miscarriage two years earlier, and with Melissa now being forty-two, time wasn't on her side.

Melissa slid into the back hall, towards the end of her daughter's performance in the play. Though she had missed Ellie's solo performance, she was able to see the last song, catching her daughter's eye, which produced a massive smile on Ellie's face, melting Melissa's heart. All the running around like a headless chicken was worth it for that smile. As they made their way to Melissa's car, she started feeling faint and then vomited, before collapsing onto the car. Jay, scared senseless, having lost his own mother unexpectedly, quickly got Melissa into the car and rushed her to the hospital, despite

Melissa's attempts to brush it off, as just feeling slightly overwhelmed. As the doctor returned having run various tests, with Jay and Ellie by their mum's bedside, Melissa was informed that despite some dehydration, there was nothing wrong with her. Jay, confused, having seen how poorly Melissa looked at the doctor and asked, 'Are you sure, doctor?' 'Yes,' he responded, 'in fact, there's actually some good news, especially for this little girl right here… You're going to become a big sister.' Ellie jumped for joy, and relief came over Jay's face, as Melissa was not ill, but in fact pregnant. Melissa was somewhat confused. The timing of this pregnancy was far from ideal, and she also knew getting pregnant in your forties carried more risk, but she also knew that each year would bring her closer to menopause and the inability to have another child.

The next day, Melissa was due to go to work, but had overslept and was awoken by Ellie, who was excited to get to spend the morning with her mother. Melissa in a panic, made her excuses to go to the toilet, where she quickly called Joanne, to let her know her predicament, and was confused, when she could hear Joanne's voice coming from downstairs, where Jay, Justina and Joanne were all gathered around the kitchen table. Making her way to the table, Ellie pulled a chair out for her mum, and brought over some pancakes that she'd help to make with Jay. Melissa, still confused, looked at the clock and shared, 'We really need to leave now if we're to make the 9am meeting.' Justina and Joanne looked at each other with a knowing look and braced themselves, as Justina shared that the meetings for the day had been rescheduled in light of recent developments. Melissa was confused. What recent developments? Had she missed an email? Had all the offers fallen through? She wondered what was going on. Then it dawned on her. The recent development was her pregnancy. But how did they know? Melissa looked at Jay furiously. 'Don't blame me. I was going to let you tell them, but Ellie beat you to it.' She couldn't be mad at her daughter for telling Justina and Joanne her news, especially seeing the excitement on her face at becoming a big sister.

As the women talked over breakfast, whilst Jay helped Ellie get ready for school, Joanne told Melissa of the plan that would help lighten Melissa's schedule. They would play the cosmetic brands off against each other, saying to each that meetings would need to be rescheduled, causing paranoia between them all. Justina had offered to help lighten some of the workload that Melissa had been carrying. Despite Melissa's reluctance at not being involved with every aspect of the company, she trusted Justina and would attempt to relinquish some control, to create more space in her schedule, to navigate the pregnancy. 'We know how much the company means to you, but becoming a mother again, and giving Ellie a younger sibling, is something we know you and Jay want, and so we want to ensure we are supporting you the best that we can.'

Over the following months, Melissa's workload relaxed a little bit, allowing her to reintroduce her weekly date nights with Jay and do the kindergarten drop off twice a week, bringing her closer to her family again. The tactic of rescheduling the meetings worked, and a battle between the cosmetic companies to acquire Melissa's company went into overdrive, increasing the purchase price by an additional $50 million more than the high-end estimates they forecast. When the acquisition closed and the deal went through, a weight was lifted from Melissa's shoulders. She had negotiated to stay on for eighteen-months in an advisory position, with an acknowledgement that Justina would stay on as well to help oversee the transition, whilst Melissa was on maternity leave. It had been a long road to get to the point where Melissa had built the company up to one of the leading cosmetic brands in the US, and to become a wife and mother of two adorable children, but the various sacrifices she had made along the way, had been worth it, so that she could now reap the benefits.

THE MYTH OF HAVING IT ALL

A common myth that we often hear in society is that we can have it all. Whilst sometimes this may be true for people, 'having it all' comes with sacrifices, where achieving the perfect balance in life is near on impossible to reach. As we saw in Melissa's story, her drive to have it all meant that in some places she spread herself too thin, like going to her reunion for fifteen minutes, through to sacrificing her weekly date nights, in order to further the acquisition of her company. Every choice we make comes with a sacrifice. One problem often lies in the fact that we are unaware of the level of sacrifice that comes as a result of the choices we make until we've made them. The choice to have children will come at the sacrifice of your personal time, a portion of your income, that those without children don't have to sacrifice. The choice to prioritise your career can come at the sacrifice of your personal relationships, and your romantic life. In life, we all have to make choices, and as we grow through life, most of humanity gains more responsibilities. From accommodation payments through to the responsibility of dependents, an accumulation of factors can restrict an individual's ability to do things and increase the level of sacrifices that come into consideration when having to weigh up choices. Further problems can arise when an important sacrifice that has been made becomes a bigger issue, or a more prolonged one. The deterioration of your health, losing your wealth, the breakdown of your relationships, challenges to your career and more.

We are sold a myth, portrayed in the media and social media, that we can have everything all at once, but as Shonda Rhimes (2014), creator of TV shows including Grey's Anatomy, Scandal and How To Get Away With Murder, shares, the image and the truth are often two very different realities. 'Whenever you see me somewhere succeeding in one area of my life, that almost certainly means I am failing in another area of my life. … That is the trade-off. That is the Faustian bargain one makes with the devil that comes with being a powerful working woman who is also a powerful mother. You never feel 100 percent okay.' Demystifying the myth that we can have it all at the same time frees individuals up to evaluate where they focus their attention, time, and energy. To look at the trade-offs, and to not spread oneself too thin.

SELF REFLECTION TIME

As we covered in the last chapter, attempting to do everything all at the same time can occur as a result of imposter syndrome; and, more specifically, in the sub-group of the superhuman. In this chapter, however, we are looking more at how attempting to do everything all at once can create problems for you:

- Have you experienced problems in your life through choices you've made in your professional or personal life that have come at the sacrifice of something else?
- When making choices, did you foresee or take into consideration what sacrifices would come because of the choice you made?
- Do you view things you have to sacrifice as a short-term sacrifice for a long-term gain, a short-term expense for a longer-term investment?

If you don't sacrifice for what you want, then what you want becomes the sacrifice. When you go into decision making, a clear understanding of what is at stake and the end goal (which we will cover more in Chapter 12, All I Do Is Win,) is important to gain clarity about what is needed from yourself. To achieve the end goal, it is important to look at the two different types of goals. Combined, it is these two goals that will ultimately help you achieve what you want:

1. Results goals
2. Process goals

Results goals - These goals give you direction. They determine where you are heading to. The overarching objective. Your result goal might be to secure a promotion, to write a book, to own a house. Once this is clear, you need to then look at the second type of goals, process goals.

Process goals - The goals highlight what to focus on daily. They provide you with a map of how to reach your destination. They break down the steps you need to take to secure that promotion, write the chapters of the book, secure what you need to make an offer on the house. Process goals help you focus on the things needed to achieve the goal, and help determine the time needed to achieve the goal. This will enable you to carve out the time in each 168-hour week, to turn the goals into a plan, a plan into action and action into results. Before we look at your own goals and problems that may occur along the way, let's look at another story that helps to highlight this further.

STARTING FROM EXPERIENCE

Paul walked into my therapy office for the first time feeling like a broken man. He had just declared bankruptcy on a business he'd spent his whole adult life working on. His partner of seven years had broken up with him, and he had had to move out of the apartment they lived in. Due to his lack of income and limited savings, he moved into a shared apartment. At thirty-four, he was seeing his friends all around him gain momentum in their professional and personal lives. Climbing corporate ladders, getting married to partners, and starting families. Paul, by comparison, felt like a failure. He felt like he regressed back to being a teenager, especially because he depended on his family to help support him financially, something he never previously had to do.

During the first three months of our therapy sessions, Paul took the time to process the impact of what had unfolded in the previous six months. Feeling a sense of hopelessness and a loss of direction in his life, existential questions about what he would do with his future continued to arise. A turning point in the therapeutic relationship came in month four, when I asked Paul what he felt his purpose was, his calling in life. Paul deliberated on this for a long time, working out what was important to him, his values, and his beliefs. He reconnected with his passions and interests and discovered that he had neglected one of his true loves growing up, cycling. When Paul was younger, he used to play a lot on his BMX his parents bought him. He spent hours in the family garage tinkering away at the bike, making improvements and enhancements, to give him a competitive edge over others when he would race on BMX tracks.

Wanting to reconnect with his passion for cycling, Paul was still overwhelmed with the feeling of hopelessness. Paul shared, 'At thirty-four, I don't want to have to start from scratch again.' Challenging Paul, I noted, 'But this time Paul, you aren't starting from scratch. You're starting from experience. What knowledge and skills can you take from your previous business experience and what you learnt about BMX bikes growing up and apply it to this new idea you have for a business opportunity?' This opened up a different part of Paul's brain, allowing him to see things from a different perspective, and fresh approaches to the way he could create a BMX prototype became clearer.

Over the next six months, Paul asked if we could switch to a coaching format in our sessions to help him navigate the challenges of starting a new business and build a prototype of his BMX bike idea. Paul began by mapping out what he would need to make the prototype, the time, investment, and resources. As the beginning of this new business venture would be started by Paul alone, everything would fall on him. Knowing this, Paul made a range of decisions, looking at what sacrifices he would need to make to move the business forward. The first two problems were finances and space. Talking with his parents, he decided to move back home. They had kindly said that he could move in rent free, whilst he built up his new business venture and use the garage to build the prototype. This solved two issues for Paul. He no longer was spending £1,000 a month on rent, which could be reinvested in the prototype, and he now had a space within which he could work on it.

Another problem for Paul was his social life. Paul loved hanging out with his friends during the evenings and at weekends, even more so since his partner left him, but he realised that to make his new business venture a success, he would need to cut down on his social life. This would help to better manage his financial outgoings and ensure he had a clearer mind than he would often experience, the morning after a night out with his mates, or after a football match of his beloved Chelsea FC. By being able to sell his season ticket for each home game, he could also generate additional income to invest in his bike, whilst catching the games that were broadcast at home on TV. Paul knew all these sacrifices needed to be made so that he could invest in a better future for himself and his career.

A further few months passed, and despite a couple of setbacks, with technical issues around the design and implementation phases, Paul had created a prototype that could be showcased. Excited at finally achieving the first phase of his business venture, Paul was feeling stuck with how to take the prototype to the next level. He felt like the easiest option would be to take his design to one of the leading BMX brands like Diamondback and Mongoose, but he didn't have the connections or relationships. There was also a part of him that actually wanted to create his own brand and build a new BMX company that catered to a different type of BMX biker. I asked Paul a series of questions, including 'Who is your ideal client for this product? What do they do? Where do they go? Where do they spend a lot of their time? How did you generate interest in your previous business? What methods connected the best?'

Paul got to work envisioning his ideal client. He created content in video format, enlisting a couple of teenagers at a local BMX track and developed a captivating story that spoke to the values and ethos of the brand that Paul had created. Paul wanted to turn the prototype into a business, creating replica and bespoke BMX bikes for a consumer base. To do this, he needed the content and story he created to help him generate an income. Initially, Paul went to the bank to set up the business and secure a loan, to invest in the growth of the new company, but owing to his bankruptcy, he found himself ineligible to secure the kind of financing he needed. Paul felt heartbroken. He had come so far, but he could not convince financiers to help back his new business venture. His parents were unable to provide the investment Paul needed, and so he came to the next session heartbroken.

Unpacking this with Paul, I asked, 'Is there anyone in your network that can help support you from a financial investment perspective? Are there any other investors, businesses or platforms that can help you raise the money?' It came to Paul that he could launch a crowd-funding page online to help procure the investment needed. Initially donations were slow, but then it dawned on Paul that his social media presence was lacking, but that he knew people in his network with bigger reaches and connections in the media world that could spread the fundraising message further. Various BMX clubs got on board, a local newspaper shared the message, and then one day Paul was invited on BBC Breakfast to talk about his fundraising campaign to bring a new BMX bike to the world.

Paul smashed through his fundraising target, reaching over £1 million in backing. With a significant number of orders for his BMX design, Paul felt overwhelmed with the response. A fresh problem arose when Paul realised it would take him years to personally get through all the orders that came from pledges, and he realised he would need to bring in additional people to help him deliver on the campaign's pledges. To do this, Paul would need to invest in a bigger space, more machinery and hiring two people that could make the custom designed BMX bikes. Looking at his cash-flow, he realised to do this, he would have to forgo paying himself a salary, to make things work. Acknowledging that this was a sacrifice worth making, to ensure he could deliver on all the pledges he had made, he went to work, pulling in what he needed to get the job done.

A year later, Paul was presented with an interesting opportunity. An up-and-coming BMX rider, who showed great potential, had heard of Paul's new BMX company and approached Paul about getting one of his bikes. Paul was still at the point in his business, where margins were very tight. Every penny counted, and Paul felt like he couldn't afford to gift a bike to this talented new rider. Paul's dad happened to be there when Paul got the message, and he reminded Paul of the joy he had felt that day as a child when the customisations he'd made to his own bike saw him win the BMX race at his local track. Convinced to gift this teenager a bike, on the proviso that the rider would wear a branded t-shirt with the company logo on, over his racing attire, and a sticker of the company logo on his helmet, Paul quickly got to ordering some stickers and t-shirts, giving the teenager the items, as he went down to watch the BMX race.

The teenager flew around the course, wiping out his competitors and winning the race, which had Paul and his father jumping for joy. All the pictures afterwards had Paul's company logo on display, and interviews the teenager carried out after the race and with trade magazines, all nodded to the competitive advantage Paul's bike had given him. Sales of the BMX skyrocketed after that, and one day Paul got a call from an investor, who had expressed providing a significant investment in exchange for a stake in the company. As Paul came in to update me on the story and explore the decision, we took a moment to reflect on how far he'd come. The choices he'd taken, the sacrifices he had made, all in pursuit of the dream he had long forgotten about as a teenager. Eighteen-months of sacrifice had got him to this stage, and now this opportunity in front of him, would help him expand the business further, as well as allow him to move out of his parents, pay himself a salary and see more of his friends again.

Six months on, in our last session together, Paul was radiating. Business was going from strength to strength following the decision to bring the investor on board. His social life was back, after going pretty much into hibernation, and he had recently started dating again. Though he was fearful about a second business he built going bankrupt, Paul had taken the time to reflect on what had happened before, evaluating where problems arose and made sure to implement the lessons in his new business, to pre-empt and plan so that the same mistakes wouldn't happen again. Another year on, and from afar, it has been encouraging to see Paul's business grow from strength to strength and know that all the sacrifice and hard work that Paul put in continues to pay off for him.

Sacrifice is one component of achieving what you want to achieve in life. The next component is discipline. Discipline to continue to show up for whatever you want to achieve, despite the distractions, the obstacles, the problems that arise along the way.

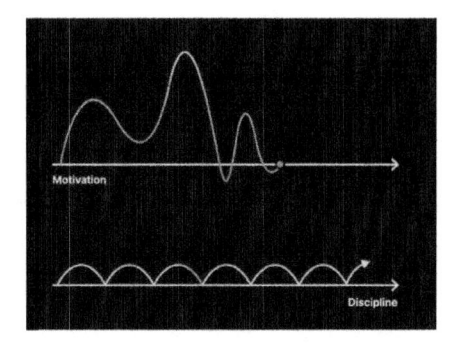

Figure 10.1 - Discipline vs Motivation.

Discipline as can be seen in Figure 10.1, is continuing to show up day after day with the same energy. Compared to your discipline, your motivation to show up will fluctuate over time. It is likely to be high at the start, then quickly taper off, fluctuating whenever a problem arises. It's too wet/cold outside to run, so I won't. It's too hard to keep getting rejected so I'll give up. Tough times don't last and neither do motivated people in the long run, but disciplined people do. Discipline is showing up when you don't want to, so that what you want shows up for you.

People often compare themselves to others looking at their successes and believing the grass is greener on the other side. The reality is the grass is the greenest where you water it. For success actually happens in the darkness. It is victory that is seen in the light. In Paul's story, his hard work happened over long days and nights for several months, before any success was achieved. It is during a season of loneliness that the caterpillar gets its wings. If you can continually sow seeds (put in the work) in the spring season (the start of the journey), nurture them through the summer season (the ongoing part of the journey), with attention, focus and discipline, adapting to any variation changes that come your way, then in the fall season, you will be able to reap the rewards of all the hard work you put in.

SELF REFLECTION TIME

Think about your discipline and sacrifice toward something you want to achieve. Ask yourself:

Are you willing to accept a 10% decrease in X (time with my friends and family, income, food intake etc) to increase the probability of Y being achieved (investment to move my business idea forward, to achieve my ideal weight)?

Podcaster Steven Bartlett (2023) notes, 'The height of your success is going to be gauged by your self-mastery through discipline and sacrifice. The depth of your failure will be gauged by your self-abandonment.' It is worth remembering that anything is possible, but most things are unlikely. They are unlikely unless you have the conviction and determination to persevere against the odds. For your dreams are free, but the hustle is sold desperately. Remember this:

- An idea without a plan is merely a dream.
- A plan without steps is merely a goal.
- A plan backed by steps and action will make your dreams come true.

My dear friend Mandy Plumb once said to me, in relation to an artist we'd both worked on, 'Excuses. They don't give me thrills and they don't pay my bills.' These words have stuck with me ever since. When I hear people give excuses or reasons for not pursuing something, I chalk it up to either a fear response or a lack of commitment. When people say they don't have time or they're too busy, I respond, 'No one is too busy. It's just a matter of priorities.' A mentor of mine, psychotherapist, and author of 'Fragile Power' (2019) Paul Hokemeyer, builds on this sharing, 'Excuses actually end up taking up more of our psychic energy than we realize. For starters, we need to spend intellectual and emotional capital coming up with reasons why we need to avoid taking action. Then the guilt and shame of having made the excuses further depletes our psychic energy. A much better investment is to just take some sort of action. Even an imperfect (gasp!) action is a great use of our psychic capital.'

Distractions can be another reason that we don't make time for the things we need to do. Author Tim Ferris (2017) highlighted this when talking to many of the busiest people on the planet. He carried out a study that showed over 80% of successful people have incorporated some form of daily mindfulness or meditation practice into their lives. The reason for this practice? Mindfulness at the start of the day helps you in practicing focus when it doesn't matter, so that you focus better later when it matters. By practicing meditation daily, and learning how to harness the power of focusing, you aren't as easily distracted by intrusive thoughts, or by tasks that take you away from what you need to be doing.

- Do you practice meditation or have a mindfulness practice?
- If not, will you commit to 10 minutes of mindfulness practice a day to improve your focus?

There is no excuse not to do 10 minutes of mindfulness in a day.

If you don't have 10 minutes, you need to look more deeply within at the problems you have with your time management skills.

- Where are you making excuses in your life?

'I don't have time to make a to do list.' 'I don't have time to work out.' 'I don't have time to practice mindfulness.' It's not that you don't have time, we all have time. One hundred and sixty-eight hours each week. It's that you don't make time. Here are some questions to ask yourself:

- What would happen if you made time for the things you aren't making time for?
- What would you have to sacrifice in another area of your life to prioritise the thing you are currently avoiding?
- Would it mean getting thirty minutes less sleep a day?
- Would it require you to spend an hour less on your phone each evening scrolling aimlessly through social media?
- What changes do you need to make?

A good exercise to introduce into your morning routine is to explore how you are going to show up in different areas of your life. Create a journal entry and ask yourself each morning to complete the following statements:

Today, I'm going to show up for myself by…
Today, I'm going to show up for my health by…
Today, I'm going to show up for my career by…
Today, I'm going to show up for my relationships by…
Today, I'm going to show up for my personal development by…

Add any other areas that you think are important to show up for. This exercise will help you in gaining focus on what is important, and work to help hold you to account so that you show up in these areas. It's about being effective with your approach to your life and your time. As Peter Drucker (2017) says, 'Efficiency is doing things right. Effectiveness is doing the right things.' But sometimes we don't always know the right things we should be doing or focusing on. Let's look at another story, and how, when faced with problems, you can become more effective in your approach to them.

ALL IN THE NICK OF TIME

Caitlin was making last-minute preparations for her forthcoming wedding to Anthony, when she received a call from the venue that was hosting both the wedding and reception. A fire had broken out in the building overnight, destroying the building, rendering the place unusable for Caitlin's wedding in 72-hours' time. Though Caitlin felt bad for the owner of the venue, she also was met with a crisis. Her whole wedding was now thrown into question, with no venue to get married in, and no reception space to hold the guests in.

Caitlin, in her professional job, was used to navigating problems and crises on the regular. Working with challenging people was part of her day job in entertainment. Being blindsided by an issue at 10am on a Friday morning, that required her to drop everything else she was working on and focus in on that issue, was an occurrence that happened more regularly than she would like. With this skill set, she felt like the character Olivia Pope in Scandal, able to handle any problem as and when it arose. Except this time, it was in her personal life, rather than professional life, and it was on one of the biggest milestones of her life to date.

Caitlin was quick to assemble those closest to her, including her mother Anna-Maria, her bridesmaids Rebecca and Dana, and an unwelcomed helping hand in the form of her future mother-in-law Janet. With the deposit already paid on the venue, and the likelihood of seeing that come back quite slim, the budget Caitlin had to work with to find a venue in NYC on such short notice proved tricky. This was the number one priority for her, and she tasked herself and her mother with locating and securing a venue at the last minute. Calls were coming in to Caitlin left, right and centre about minor details that needed decisions to be made, but with her focus on procuring a venue taking up her bandwidth, she needed to delay these decisions until the venue was secured. Caitlin's bridesmaids Rebecca and Dana asked what they could take off Caitlin's hands to help support her. Caitlin took five minutes out from ringing around venues, to go through her to do list, delegating all the items she could to them. From the wedding party dresses, through to the delivery of the wedding cake that would need to be redirected once the venue was locked in, the women set about getting all the things Caitlin needed to get done, but no longer had the time for.

Caitlin's future mother-in-law, Janet, was all a fluster when she heard the news about the wedding venue. Spiralling into a state of anxiety, Janet kept uttering thoughts out loud, including 'Oh God, what are we going to do about the venue?' 'Are we going to have to call the whole wedding off?' 'Who's going to tell all the guests before they come to NYC for the wedding?' Her anxiety was palpable, and she was causing more problems than creating solutions. Caitlin has the patience of a saint, but it tested even Caitlin when dealing with Janet. With interruption after interruption deterring Caitlin from resolving the problem she was faced with, she snapped 'Not now, Janet!' Wounded, Janet went off and sulked in the corner, and Caitlin got on the phone to Anthony. Without acknowledging him, Caitlin launched straight into what she needed. 'I don't know what you're doing right now and, to be honest, I don't care. What I need from you right now is to come to the apartment and take your mother out, before she is thrown out of our fourteenth-floor window and you find her splattered on the ground.'

Anthony knew not to mess with Caitlin when she was in this mindset. He willingly obliged, knowing that his mother could be challenging at the best of times, and took her out for the rest of the afternoon and evening. By nightfall, through sheer hard work, determination and pulling in several favours from various relationships she had made with artist relation teams in entertainment companies, she was able to secure a hotel off Central Park and its ballroom for the wedding and reception, at a 50% discounted rate. Though there was still a lot to organise and sort, the main issue had been resolved. Over the next twenty-four hours and with a lot of caffeine consumed, including a few espresso martini's, Caitlin, her mother and her bridesmaids, were able to get through all the last minute plans and changes, update all the wedding guests on the new location for the wedding, and still have time to go to the spa her bridesmaids had planned the night before her big day, to relax and unwind.

On the big day, the wedding went off without a hitch. Through Caitlin's adaptability and resourcefulness, she was able to confront the problem head on and meet the moment with strength and conviction. Utilising her skill set, Caitlin was able to do the thing that needed to be done, delay the things that could wait, delegate items on her to do list and delete things that she didn't need to focus on, or would cause more problems, like Janet. As the reception got into the swing of things, it dawned on Caitlin that she had forgotten to notify the DJ for the reception about the change in plans. Her old colleague that had flown in from London to attend the wedding could see the shock on her face and as he went over to her, she filled him in. Wanting to alleviate Caitlin of any pressure, he said, 'Leave it with me.' Within half an hour, and slightly later than initially anticipated, her friend had called up an associate Adam who owed him a favour. He was in town with a band he managed and convinced him to get his band, The Chainsmokers, to come and be the music entertainment for Caitlin's reception.

As Anthony and Caitlin took to the floor for their first dance, the couple were both radiant, lighting up the room. Their two dogs, Gus and Winnie, had even been brought to the wedding, circling around the couple as they moved across the dancefloor. Then, as the song ended, The Chainsmokers arrived, laptop in hand, and set themselves up with the help of the hotel staff, as the wedding guests partied the night away. Despite the last-minute curveball to the wedding plans, the couple couldn't have dreamed for a better day, though the next morning, as they woke up in a state of disarray having slept through their alarm, they frantically rushed to pack, realising they had ninety minutes to get to the airport to make the flight for their honeymoon to the Caribbean. Much laughter was had between Caitlin and Anthony as they got into the taxi on the way to the airport, and they made it to the desk, just in time to check-in their bags, make it through departures and board the plane, where the next chapter of their love story would begin.

Caitlin had years of experience being resourceful in what she needed to do when faced with the problem that arose with her wedding venue. This enabled her to pull in all the resources she had available to her and access some that she didn't to address the problem head on. Her time-management skill set that she had deployed frequently throughout her life could be put to good use, ensuring that she remained focused on the most important stuff and not get distracted by things or people that kept her busy or moved her further away from what was important.

SELF DEVELOPMENT TIME

In your own life, you are likely to face many distractions that impede you from achieving what you want to achieve. For example, your inbox is essentially someone else's to do list. If you continually answer emails as and when they come in, you are giving permission for further emails to come back. Of course, there will be certain correspondence that is time sensitive, but the large majority of correspondence that sits within your inbox can wait. This is where it is important to look at the time management matrix, to help you decipher where and what you should be doing with your time.

I DON'T WANT TO MISS A THING

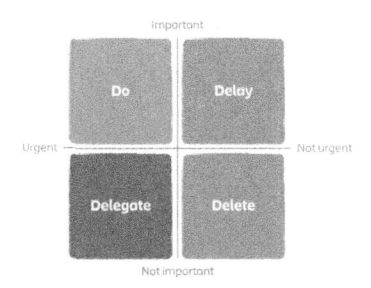

Figure 10.2 - The Eisenhower Matrix.

As seen in Figure 10.2, there are four quadrants in The Eisenhower Matrix that range from important to not important and urgent to not urgent. In Caitlin's story, the do (urgent and important) was to find an alternative wedding venue. The delay (important but not urgent) was pushing back calls on decisions that could wait to be made. The delegate (urgent but not important) picking up the wedding party dresses, sorting out some of the smaller items on Caitlin's to do list, were delegated to her bridesmaids. The delete (not important and not urgent) was Janet, who was deleted from the situation, as her contribution was not important and her views not helping with the urgency in which the situation needed to be resolved. Let's turn our attention to you.

- With a problem you face in your professional or personal life, are you able to use the time management matrix to enable you to be focused and disciplined in addressing the issue? To help you identify resources you need and to get everything done in a timely manner?
- Do you spend far too much time in one quadrant at the expense of the other?
- How much of your time is spent creating the life you want vs managing the life that you have?
- Do you struggle to delegate stuff that, if you did, could free up time, so that you can focus on more important issues/matters?

- Are there things or people that are causing you problems that could be benefited from being deleted from your time?

According to Italian economist Vilfredo Pareto (1906), 80% of your outcomes, comes from 20% of causes. Known as the Pareto Principle, in business, that could be that 80% of your business comes from 20% of your clients, or 80% of your problems come from 20% of clients. In your personal life, it could be that 80% of your happiness comes from 20% of your social circle, or 80% of your problems come from 20% of your social circle.

- Have you taken the time to reflect upon your professional life and your personal life, to see where you are spending most of your time and if that is positively or negatively affecting your health, your finances, your ability to grow?
- What would happen if you were to shift your focus? Is there room to focus more on the 20% than generates the most business or brings you the most joy and happiness?

The other component, of Caitlin's story, that stands out is her resourcefulness to overcome the problem she faces. Through utilising her network, she was able to rely upon them as a resource to delegate items on her to do list to. Her vast network of contacts acted as a great resource in helping her procure a wedding venue at late notice, and at a 50% discount too. Think about yourself for a moment:

- What resources are at your disposal that can help you with a problem you are facing?
- Is the problem easily solved by outsourcing the problem and/or paying someone to do it?

As a coach once said to me, 'If you can cut a cheque for a problem, you don't have that problem.' But not all of us have money to throw at problems to solve them. One friend of mine who began managing an artist nearly ten years ago was working on a tight budget. They needed to master a track that they were going to release as the first single for the artist. The big studios were charging hundreds of pounds to master a track, and my friend just didn't have the budget to do this. He was, however, resourceful, and through research, found someone on the freelance creative platform Fiverr to master the track for £5. The track went on to be released, and as of today, the same track with the same £5 mastering has accumulated over one billion streams on Spotify alone.

It's important to remember that the most successful people in life aren't always the ones who have access to the most resources, though that definitely gives them an advantage. It is often the ones who are the most resourceful with the resources they have at their disposal.

- What resources do you have at your disposal to help you with a problem you are currently facing in your life?
- Who or what can you tap into to help address the problem?
- Are there resources out there that you can tap into, to help you address the problem?
- Is there a financial commitment to gain the resource/s needed?
- Can you think differently, like Paul, with the crowdfunding platform to raise the funds, if you cannot access or provide the funding yourself?

Coach, author, and investor Tony Robbins (2017), through his research, has learned that people often over-estimate what they can achieve in a year, but underestimate what they can achieve in five years. This is true for many, but with discipline, focus and the ability to sacrifice for what you want, you are likely to achieve great things in a shorter period of time. Take a moment to think what you might do to accomplish your five-year goals in the next six months if you had a gun to your head. With that level of pressure, causing you to focus and gain clarity on what the most important things are to achieve your goals, and then putting them into action, it will astound you at what you can set your mind to and achieve.

It is important to note here that focus and discipline in certain areas, such as attention, doesn't always come easy to everyone. Those who are neurodiverse and have been diagnosed with ADHD or another diagnosis, may not always be able to focus for extensive periods, but they can harness their neuro-divergence by creating short 20-minute focus periods. To work with their brains strengths rather than against them. Most of the successful people you know have flaws, but have learned to maximise one or two strengths, and outsource their weaknesses, or as I like to call them, areas of development. Many individuals who identify as neurodiverse are extremely creative. This is a great resource that can be tapped into. As we discussed in Chapter 5, Mad World, if you are in the wrong environment, it can stunt your ability to evolve as a human and cause problems.

- Is the problem that your resource isn't being utilised because it's in the wrong environment?
- What would happen if your strongest resource within you had the ability to thrive?

A bottle of water costs £1 in a supermarket, £2 at a bar and £4 on a flight. The bottle of water is exactly the same, only the environment has changed. The value is determined not by the bottle of water, but by the environment it is in. The same is true of you. Your skill set and the resources you have within you will be valued differently in different environments.

- Are you in the right environment to thrive?
- What are the one or two strengths that, if you spent more time focused on them, you would stride toward your goal?

The quantification of success is not how much time you spend doing the things you love, but instead how little time you spend doing things you hate.

- How successful are you through the lens of this statement?
- What could you do today or this week to spend less time on the thing/s you hate?
- Can you eliminate, automate, outsource, delegate, or replace the thing/s you hate without it adversely impacting you and creating more problems?

Is your need to people please or say yes to people, affecting your ability to move forward? If something you are presented with isn't a hell yes, then it is a fuck no. Learn to embrace the power of No. It is a complete sentence. As Greg McKeown (2021) writes in Essentialism, 'Make peace with the fact that saying no means trading popularity with respect.' If you suffer from FOMO, fear of missing out, why not start evolving your perspective to JOMO instead? JOMO is the joy of missing out. Knowing that missing out on things you feel compelled or obliged to go to, or through fear that something good will have happened that you will have missed, is replaced instead at the joy of being able to focus on what you want to do, on building a better future for yourself.

When James Cameron was filming the original Avatar, the highest grossing film of all time (when not adjusted for inflation) at $2.92 billion USD, he handed out t-shirts to all the crew, which read:

Hope is not a strategy.
Luck is not a factor.
Fear is not an option.

Timing accounts for a lot, as we discovered in Chapter 6,

Talking About My Generation, but one thing is for certain: the harder you work, the luckier you seem to get.

Discipline + resourcefulness + timing = opportunity.

And it is those who have put in the work, through discipline, sacrifice, resourcefulness, and time management, that often find themselves in the right place at the right time to take advantage of the opportunity when it presents itself.

SUMMARY

In life, we all have to make choices which lead to sacrifices. From our professional lives to our personal lives, if we don't sacrifice for what we want, then what we want becomes the sacrifice. It is important when going through the decision-making process, which will be covered more in Chapter 12, All I Do Is Win, that you understand the impact the sacrifices you make will cause, both in the short-term and longer-term. Whether a sacrifice of say 10% in one area is worth the payoff in another area, you are investing that time, money or other resource for.

Focus and discipline are key factors in determining your trajectory for success. If you are starting out with something new, don't be deterred at the start, your first attempt at anything is likely to be poor, but by reviewing, gaining feedback, and building from each attempt you will become better at what you are applying yourself to. Though all of us have the same 168 hours in a week, not all of us are Beyonce and have a team of people at our beck and call to help us achieve what we are focused on achieving. Yet we are all resourceful human beings. Through the time management matrix, you can work to determine what is important from unimportant, what is urgent from not urgent, and then learn to either do what needs to be done, delay it, delegate it, or delete it.

Through your own network and financial resources, you can be resourceful in sourcing options to solve problems you face. If your skill set isn't desirable in one area, outsource it to someone or something that can do that for you, so you can focus on harnessing your strengths or putting yourself in environments where those strengths can flourish and thrive. It is important to have focus and discipline, to have good time management skills and be resourceful, not only on your way to attaining success but also in maintaining it too. In the next chapter, we'll look at what is needed to maintain your goal, so that problems don't arise and you aren't left wondering what happened when it all falls apart.

11

WHEN IT ALL FALLS APART

Sustaining

Body dysmorphia had plagued Richard for most of his life. Ever since he was a teenager and discovered he was gay; he would head to the local shop, browsing the shelves where he would bear witness to the Adonis bodies that always seemed to grace the covers of Attitude and Gay Times magazines. Held up and celebrated as the idealised version of what a male should look like, Richard, whose weight had fluctuated in childhood and throughout his teenage life, longed to look like those who graced the covers of the magazine.

And so, his quest began. To pursue a chiselled physique that Richard hoped would be the answer to all his problems. Unsure of where to start, and prior to the internet era where access to information was at his fingertips, he turned to what he knew, his mother. Richard's mother, Sandra, was overweight and had been on diets ever since he could remember. A new year's resolution would be made at the start of every year to lose weight by Sandra, but year after year, nothing seemed to change. Any weight she lost would quickly pile back on, and then some more in certain instances, and so Richard vowed to not make the same mistakes his mother had made.

Richard would try out whatever the diet of the moment would be. At first it was Slim Fast. Three milkshakes a day, to keep the weight at bay. Initially, Richard saw the weight fly off and was excited by the results. Though the six-pack wasn't appearing, the excess weight that weighed him down both physically and psychologically had meant he had shifted from overweight to slim, from a large in clothing to a small. But before long, the weight started to creep back on. Surviving on three milkshakes a day proved unsustainable for Richard and his dreams of looking like the Adonis's covering the magazines slipped further and further away.

Over the subsequent years, Richard would try whatever trend came into fashion, hoping this time, the diet-de-jour would finally produce the results he longed for. From the Atkin's diet to the Master Cleanse (popularised by Beyonce when she lost 20lbs in 2 weeks for a film role). The Keto diet to Paleo diet, Richard, tried them all. With many of the diets producing immediate results that were visible to the eye, Richard would convince himself that this time, the diet-de-jour would be the one that stuck. But time after time, he would end up reverting back to old ways.

Even trends in the fitness world could not deliver the results that Richard wanted. From digging out old home workout videos his mother had that he would watch, through to gym workouts and fitness classes. No matter what Richard tried, he would find himself yo-yo-ing up and down the weight scale. Sometimes Richard would get close to what resembled a six-pack appearing before it slipped away again, even faster than it would appear. Having struggled with his weight for over twenty-five years, Richard was ready to concede defeat. Acknowledging to himself that the Adonis bodies covering the magazines he would read and fill his social media feeds were not meant to be, Richard swore to himself he would never attempt another diet or get caught up in another fitness craze again.

Richard had never been in a long-term relationship and was caught by surprise when he found himself in one in his late thirties, and after dating for a few months, Richard and his partner John decided to move in together. John, though not having the body of a Greek Adonis, had a physique that Richard could only dream of. One evening, when the couple got into an argument, as all couples do, John did something completely different from what Richard had done. John said, 'I need some space. I'm going for a run', and left the flat. Richard, however, reverted to what he always did when confronted with a wave of uncomfortable emotions. He reached for the cupboard and pulled out a bar of chocolate.

Having modelled what his mother did, he swallowed down his emotions by seeking solace in food. His relationship to food had always been complicated, but it was in this moment, seeing how both he and his partner had different reactions to the same stimuli (an argument), that a light bulb went off in his head. All this time, Richard had been focusing on diets, trying to gain an ideal physique, and sometimes coming close. Yet, Richard could not maintain the results because his relationship with food (and exercise) hadn't been explored on a deeper level. His relationship with food was complex. A form of pleasure and comfort when triggered. A form of punishment when on a diet.

Over the following months, Richard evolved his outlook. He became aware of his triggers and, instead of reaching for the latest sugary snack to ease the emotional discomfort he felt, he found healthier ways to process his emotions. Talking them through, finding healthier snacks, going for runs. Having already sworn off diets, Richard continued to evolve his relationship to food. No longer did he deprive himself of carbs this month, fatty foods the next month and so on, but instead made lifestyle changes, looking at moderation and allowing himself treats. Working out became a collaborative endeavour with his partner. They would often go to the gym together, sometimes training side by side, other times doing different classes. What had once been something Richard felt he had to do, he now looked forward to.

That Christmas, Richard and John set off to the Caribbean, and for the first time, Richard was no longer body conscious around the pool or at the beach. For twenty-five years, he had always had a complicated relationship with his body, hiding it away through both shame and fear of judgment. But here he was, happy with his body and though not having the six-pack he once strived for, Richard had a toned physique with a four-pack visible.

Richard is not alone in his struggle with his body image. According to a study, shared by Todd (2016), that was carried out by National Eating Disorder Association, 42% of gay males have an eating disorder, a significantly higher percentage than straight females, lesbians, and straight males (the study didn't account for other groups to cross compare). Idealised versions of what the perfect physique for different genders and sexualities that feed into this are played out in public forums. From the Greek Adonis heralded as the ideal physique in the gay community, through to heroin chic at one point being heralded for females with a focus on being size zero (or double-zero), individuals striving to achieve these often-unrealistic expectations, can lead to, at the least body dysmorphia, and on to the more extreme end, an eating disorder that can cause hospitalisation and even death.

With the advent of social media and an ongoing need for many to curate a perfect image of themselves, physicality has moved further to the forefront, where the statistics outlined by NEDA in the previous paragraph are constantly growing. Body dysmorphia and eating disorders that were once more heavily associated with one or two groups are now more evenly distributed across the board. This has been reflected in a change in consumer habits, with leading UK travel agency Thomas Cook, in 2018, closing their 18-30 holiday packages. A rite of passage in the UK for teenagers and young adults, 18-30 holiday packages comprised a cheap flight and hotel to a party location somewhere in Europe, where you would save as much money of your holiday budget as possible, to spend on boozy nights out in bars and clubs, repeating this for the duration of the holiday, without a digital footprint that could be shared for all to see.

In the image conscious world, we currently find ourselves in, as a result of social media, people want to look good for the 'gram or the 'Tok. Short haul holidays have been replaced for far-flung exotic destinations that look picture perfect to post on socials. With idealised bodies receiving higher engagement rates than the 'average' human body (which will vary from culture to culture), people are evolving their consumption habits and physicality to fit into this mould. A study carried out by Drink Aware (2023) found that over 20% of people under 25 don't drink alcohol. Though it may seem encouraging that more people are turning away from alcohol, if you dig a little deeper, you'll find that many questioned were motivated to do so not because of the negative affects alcohol can have on your health or relationships, but primarily from an aesthetic point of view, of wanting to have the ideal look. A report by the American Academy of Facial Plastic and Reconstructive Surgery (2020) found that 72% of surgeons reported seeing patients who sought surgery to look better in their selfies, driven by what has become known as vanity validation.

This continued evolution of our relationship to our bodies shows no signs of slowing down. As technology continues to infiltrate every area of our daily lives, new ways and additional pressures of gaining the perfect look, the perfect physique, will emerge. My job here in this book, and especially in this chapter, is not to pass judgment, but to help you turn your attention to your intention. To allow you to reflect on your patterns of behaviour and what may lead you to gain but not maintain your ideal body weight, shape, physique, if this is a problem area in your life. The cost financially, physically and psychology in maintaining physical alterations to your body.

Going back to Richard's story, studies show that up to 97% of diets fail, and that dieters regain all of the weight they lost within three years. The main reason for this, as I've mentioned before, is that it takes one thing to gain or attain the ideal weight, but it takes a completely different thing to maintain it. Attaining the goal is a short-term target or objective. Maintaining that goal is a long-term target or objective. Attaining, comparatively speaking, is the simple part. Maintaining is the hard part. For maintaining requires you to consistently show up again and again over a long period of time, through the good times and the hard times. The road to success, as they say, is filled with potholes. Those potholes with Richard would show up in triggers that saw him seek comfort and solace in food when emotionally activated, for you it may be something else, if in relationship to your body. You may grow comfortable and complacent once you reach your ideal weight, taking your foot off the pedal. One-pound creeps on and then another, and before you know it, you're tumbling back to the weight you started at before the diet, because of comfort and complacency. Comfort and complacency are two of the main causes of a loss in maintaining that which you have attained. Let's next turn our attention to Paula and Stefan to see how this plays out in relationships.

THE IMPERFECT COUPLE

Paula and Stefan met for the first time at their friends Aleksy and Saskia's wedding. Their eyes met across the church, and it was love or, more likely, lust and infatuation, at first sight. As the day carried on, the pair finally got talking when they found themselves sat at the same table during the wedding reception. The chemistry between them was electric and by the end of the night on the dancefloor, the pair were locked in a display of public affection. Paula was keen to take it slowly, as she had been swept up in a relationship once before that burnt bright but faded fast. Stefan understood and was patient. He continued to show up and speak in

Paula's love language, quality time, with Paula being able to reciprocate speaking in Stefan's love language, physical touch.

The dating period went on for a couple of months before Paula and Stefan made their relationship official. Still very much in the honeymoon period, the couple were infatuated with each other. When they met up with Aleksy and Saskia a few months into their relationship, the newlyweds couldn't help but glow with pride, sharing that they both knew if they got the couple in the same room, that each of them would find in the other their respective soul mate. The relationship continued to blossom over the following months, and a year into the relationship, Stefan popped the question to Paula. Over the moon, Paula instantly said yes, and the couple got to planning their wedding.

The wedding would fall on the second anniversary of the night they met, a date in the calendar that held special meaning to them. Everyone at the wedding looked on at the newlyweds, many shedding a tear at what they viewed as the perfect couple. Stefan was forever attentive to Paula's every word, Paula physically affectionate to Stefan. They were the couple that everyone aspired to be. In quick succession, Paula and Stefan had two children, and though the children were all-consuming, the couple continued to show up for themselves and each other. Yet somewhere along the way, something slowly started to shift. As Stefan secured a promotion into a senior leadership role, he became less present both physically at home because of the demands of the role, but also when he was at home, he was often distracted by emails and calls constantly coming in both during the evening and at weekends. This caused Paula to withdraw. The usual hugs to greet her husband when he returned home became more and more infrequent. A gentle grab of the shoulder or pinch of the bum slowly disappeared. The sofa they used to occupy cuddled up together after the children had gone to bed, whilst watching their favourite TV shows and unwinding after a long day, had been replaced by them sitting on separate couches, disengaged from each other. Their attention either locked onto their phones or on the TV.

The sexual intimacy had drifted away too. Once having a healthy and frequent sexual relationship, they were now averaging sex once every fortnight. Both had chalked it down to what they believed was the post marriage, post children phase, where sex became less frequent and they had both resided to a new way of sexual intimacy. This pattern continued over the following months and year, and as the chasm between them continued to grow, the once revered and idolised couple had become strangers in their own relationship. Concerned that their relationship was heading in the same direction as her parents; divorce, Paula and Stefan agreed to couples therapy, to rebuild, repair and restore their relationship and I found them sitting in my office, both keen to save their marriage but unsure exactly where or when it started to go wrong.

Over the course of their time in couple's therapy, Stefan and Paula were able to acknowledge and take ownership of the parts each of them played in the slow deterioration of their relationship. Stefan's pre-occupation with his work and career affected the quality time he spent with Paula. Paula, hurt by her love language not being spoken to her by Stefan, slowly withdrew her physical touch. Stefan, as a result, though not initially noticing the withdrawal, quickly picked up on it. But rather than addressing it, he felt hurt that his love language was not being spoken to, and withdrew further, too. Over time, they had become caught in a cycle, with each person's inability to communicate the others' love language, causing them to withdraw further.

I noted it is not conflict that ends relationships, but neglect. The neglect of meeting the other person's needs. To show up and support the other person. To operate as a team, rather than two individuals. Whilst through their relationship, as with any relationship, situations and circumstances evolve, a job promotion for Stefan, the introduction of two dependents in their children that took up more time in their week than before, they also still had their needs to be factored in. Yet in Paula and Stefan's case, their needs, as often is the case for many married couples, had been neglected as the demands on them evolved. Through couples' therapy, both Stefan and Paula got to understand their partner's love language. They learned how to communicate more effectively with and to each other. They made a recommitment to themselves and the relationship, to ensure they continued to show up to each other, no matter the other demands placed on them. To communicate the need for support and understanding, if they were struggling to keep up their side of their commitment to the other, and to avoid resentment and neglect from creeping back in.

A few months after completing couple's therapy with Stefan and Paula, I received a letter to my office and was surprised and honoured to find they had invited me to a vowel renewal ceremony. Ethically as a therapist, it is a grey area on forming any type of relationship other than therapist and client with individuals you work with, but in this instance, I decided to attend and was happy to see the couple continue to practice what they had worked hard on in couples therapy, returning to the relationship they had at the beginning of their union, with a renewed sense of commitment to each other.

With over half of all marriages ending in divorce today, the likelihood is that if you have been, currently are, or are going to be married, you no longer hold the vowel 'Till death do us part' but instead, subconsciously opt for the vowel, 'Till neglect drives us apart'. Marriage holds different values in different cultures, continues to evolve over generations, and has moved away in several cultures from the ownership of another in the traditional sense of man and woman, to a more collaborative and symbolic gesture. Yet divorce rates continue to rise, with irreconcilable differences being given as the main filing cause. Further research confirms that it was neglect that is the leading cause of divorce. Neglect to meet one another's needs, that one or both parties withdraw, and in many cases, finding something or someone else to meet that unfulfilled need.

SELF REFLECTION TIME

Zooming out of marriage specifically, and onto relationships more broadly, if you've been unable to sustain relationships in your life, have you looked at your contribution to the breakdown of the relationship? Granted, there are a percentage of relationships that naturally run their course. As the saying goes, 'People come into our lives in three fundamental ways:

1. **For a reason** - To teach us something.
2. **For a season** - To get us through something, or
3. **For a lifetime** - To be with us through the good times and the hard times.

This chapter is not looking at those first two relationships, but those relationships that you believed were due to last a lifetime. Think about a current or former relationship, where problems are driving/or drove you apart and ask yourself the following questions:

- At the end of the relationship, were/are you putting in the same amount of effort and energy as you did at the beginning of the relationship?
- Were you speaking to the other in their love language? The five love languages are; quality time, physical touch, words of affirmation, gifts, and acts of service.
- If not, when did this shift?
- Did your partner reduce communicating to you in your love language?
- What did this bring up for you, and how did this impact your relationship?
- Are you willing or able to reinvest the energy you put in at the start of the relationship?

- Can you make a small step today to increase your use of their love language?

A common myth, I find when individuals or couples come to my practice, is they want the other person to change. I always remind these clients that we cannot make another person change, especially against their will. What we can do is change ourselves, which will, as a by-product, change the way the other person interacts with you.

- If you are having problems in any of your relationships that you wish to salvage, where can you take ownership and accountability today to turn the tide on that relationship for the better?

Body image and relationships are two recurring themes that come through my private practice with clients. Another client group whom I work with that applies to this chapter are those who struggle with addiction and recovery.

THE ROAD TO RECOVERY IS LONG AND ARDUOUS

As I opened the door to the office I worked out of at a rehabilitation facility, I was met by a 32-year-old man named Ashley. Recently admitted to the rehab, he had been referred to me by my case manager, following a 2-week detoxification period, where Ashley was supported as they weaned him off his addiction to crystal meth to help him through the withdrawal symptoms he was experiencing. This wasn't Ashley's first rodeo. He had been in rehab two previous times before, but in each case hadn't been able to stay the course and relapsed back to using drugs once more.

Determined to do things differently this time, Ashley showed up and was an active participant in all the group sessions at the rehab, that were run similarly to that of a fellowship meeting. Working individually with Ashley to complement the group work, we peeled back the layers slowly but surely, to uncover what was lying beneath the addiction. My dear friend and mentor Adrianna Irvine always says, 'It wasn't the tip of the iceberg that sank the titanic, it was what was lying underneath'. Emotional dysregulation is often common amongst those who struggle with addiction, and the addiction of choice, be it alcohol, drugs, sex, gambling, porn, money, work, food or a number of other vices, is an attempt to cope with what is coming up, by numbing, avoiding or suppressing that which is too uncomfortable to deal with.

Ashley was showing positive signs of engagement at the rehab, and upon discharge from the facility continued to come back for outpatient treatment in our one-to-one sessions, but as we delved deeper into Ashley's past, tell-tale signs appeared that a lapse and potential relapse was likely to occur. Ashley had entered rehab not only with an addiction to crystal meth, but a cross addiction (where an individual can have two or more addictive behaviours).

Alongside drugs, Ashley was addicted to sex and porn, having become a male escort in his teenage years, following being sexually abused as a child. Though Ashley hadn't lapsed back into these addictions, he displayed addictive tendencies to sugary drinks, snacks and shopping. These new vices for him helped to alleviate the overwhelming feelings he was left with during therapy. Despite working with Ashley to help him regulate his emotions, through breathwork, mindfulness, and a host of other techniques, Ashley was struggling to navigate what was coming up for him.

Additional support was provided to Ashley through daily fellowship meetings and a sponsor external to the rehab, but despite everyone's best efforts to help support Ashley, he relapsed 6 months into his recovery. Though the period within which Ashley remained in recovery had been six times longer than either previous attempt, his ability to stay in recovery, at least on the third attempt, proved not possible for Ashley.

SELF DEVELOPMENT TIME

Recovery from an addiction is often primarily focused on the cycle of change in a person's behaviour, but this equally applies to any area of your life you are looking to change, from your relationships as with Paula and Stefan, to Richard's relationship with his body.

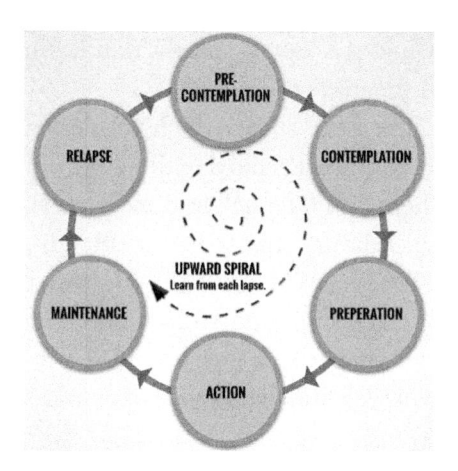

Figure 11.1 - The Cycle Of Change

As seen in Figure 11.1 the Cycle of Change diagram above, there are six stages to the cycle:

1. **Pre-contemplation** - The first stage is pre-contemplation, and this is usually a period of denial, defeat or even a lack of awareness of a problem, where there is no intention of changing behaviour.
2. **Contemplation** - The next stage, contemplation, is where you are or become consciously aware of the problem, but have yet to commit to take steps to address the problem.
3. **Preparation** - Following this is preparation, where you look to make a plan of action to address the problem.
4. **Action** - After preparation is action, where you put in place the plan of action in the attempt and hope to

address the problem and change the behaviour or outcome.
5. **Maintenance** - The fifth step is maintenance. As we've explored throughout this chapter, maintenance can often be the hardest of the six stages to navigate, because it takes an ongoing commitment to show up for oneself, to create a lifestyle change, to put in the work consistently beyond the initial result or success that has been obtained in the cycle of change.
6. **Relapse** - The sixth stage, which happened with Ashley and his addiction or Richard with his various diets, is relapse. Where you fall back into old patterns of behaviour or relating, and the cycle often repeats again and again. Yet the cycle is not like a hamster wheel, where you keep going round and round, getting nowhere. It is more like a tornado or hurricane, where each time you continue to elevate upwards.

For relapses, often can be presented as opportunities to learn and grow from. In my book, The Shitty Committee, I write about a technique I used called Here Comes AFGO (Another Fucking Growth Opportunity) that can be used during relapse or a perceived failure, to help you bounce back and continue moving forward, allowing you to learn from the situation and to do better the next time. With Here Comes AFGO, there are three questions to ask yourself and reflect upon when relapsing into old behaviours:

1. What went well?
2. What did I learn?
3. What can I do differently moving forward?

This period of self-reflection provides an opportunity to focus on the positive parts that happened with the cycle of change.

Using the three stories in this chapter as examples, answers to question one could include:

- I managed to stay sober for 6 months.
- I was able to reach my ideal weight.
- I was able to speak my partner's love language more frequently.

Answers to question two could include:

- I get overwhelmed when revisiting my past sexual abuse and develop strong cravings.
- When I have arguments with my partner, I reach for junk food.
- When I get stressed with work, I neglect speaking my partner's love language.

Answers to the last question could include:

- I can learn to regulate my emotions more, lean into my sponsor, and attend more meetings.
- I can replace junk food snacks with healthier options or find another way to process my feelings after an argument.
- I could find a better way to manage my stress, so that it doesn't spill into my relationship with my partner and lead to a continuing decline in our relationship.

Lapses or relapses in behaviour and reverting to old patterns of relating, when trying to create lasting change, are more than likely to occur. According The National Library of Medicine (2019), the average number of relapses that occur before someone remains in recovery from addiction to drugs or alcohol is 5.35 attempts. Knowing this statistic may be scary for some, but it can also be reassuring. For as the Aaliyah song goes, 'If at first you don't succeed, dust yourself off and try again.' Whilst there isn't as much research in other areas about maintenance and recovery, as previously shared, 97% of diets fail, primarily because the maintenance part isn't present in diets. Diets are more of a band-aid over a bullet wound, a quick fix rather than a long-term solution.

Another area we can look at where changes often occur is the most popular time of the year, New Year's Day. Roughly 80% of New Year's Resolutions end up failing by mid-February according to a study conducted by the US News and World Report (2023). But why is it so hard to maintain a change in behaviour, outlook, lifestyle? Research has shown that it takes on average 21 days to form a habit and around 90 days to embed it into your subconscious, so that your new way of being becomes second nature. Some lasting changes can take shorter, and some longer, but most adaptations take several weeks to a few months of consistent stimuli, daily practice and a continual showing up for oneself and the new behaviour, for a new neural pathway in the brain to be created, to replace/over-ride/counter a previous behaviour or narrative that you were operating from.

If you went to the doctor for an infection, and they gave you anti-biotics to take once a day for two weeks to get rid of the infection, but you stopped taking them after three days, it is unlikely that the infection will shift by itself. If you will listen to the doctor to get better by following the guidelines and change the current health situation you are in, then what is stopping you from doing the same in other areas of your life? In short, as we covered in the last chapter, I Don't Want To Miss A Thing, it's probably a lack of discipline and accountability to yourself.

Maintenance to see a lasting change in your behaviours takes an ongoing commitment to yourself. When embarking on a pathway of change, many people set out to create that change on their own, hoping or expecting to rely on will-power alone. Yet, if we look at the previous statistics around diets, new year's resolutions, and the relapse rate in general, many of these occur as a result of a lack of ongoing discipline and will-power to maintain the new behaviour that they are adapting to. Varying studies show that between 27% - 54% of people find that a lack of will power is the most significant barrier to lasting change. If there is an area of your life, you are looking to create lasting change in answer the following questions:

- What can you do to help ensure you remain on the pathway to change?
- Is there anything in your past that you have successfully been able to change that you can pull upon and implement into this new area of change?

Let's look at three main areas that you can focus on, to help address any problems you may have around maintenance and relapse, to help increase your odds of maintaining a new way of being.

ACCOUNTABILITY

Let's start first with accountability. According to a study carried out by the American Society of Training and Development (2022), you are up to 95% more likely to succeed by simply directing your accountability to a third party to help hold you to account. Committing the goal to someone else will lead to a 65% increase in likelihood of you sticking with the goal. Holding consistent check-ins on a minimum weekly basis is likely to increase that percentage to up to 95%. Even holding yourself to account, through maintenance lists to reward charts (I used gold stars to mark off the completion of each chapter in this book) can increase your success rate by up to 40%.

- How can you hold yourself to account during this period of change to not only gain but maintain that which you are looking to achieve or change?

- Is there a partner, friend, family member, colleague, sponsor, personal trainer, coach, therapist that you can call upon?

Identify at least two and reach out to them. Don't be disheartened if someone is unable to be an accountability partner. There is more than likely someone out there to help hold you to account. Should there be no one in your network available to you, there are platforms online that you can tap into that offer accountability partners in a whole host of different areas that a quick google search will be able to help you with.

- Could a complementary self-accountability document (a diary tracker, a wall chart) help compound your commitment to maintaining change?

For some, it can add unnecessary pressure and have the adverse effect. In recovery, many focus on one day at a time, rather than overwhelming oneself with the bigger picture. Whilst some celebrate milestones of their recovery with chips in fellowship meetings, others don't like to track their progress, instead wishing to remain focused on the here and now. There is no right or wrong way, merely your own preferred way that works for you. For me, as mentioned, I used gold stars to help me maintain my progress. What would work for you? You can even make small changes to your everyday routine to aid your progress. Why not change your morning alarm, from whatever sound you currently have to the sound of clapping. That way, every morning, you begin the day by celebrating waking up. Not a bad way to start a day, right?

LANGUAGE

Next up is language. Words are one of the most powerful determinants in maintaining change.

- Have you observed the language you use when embarking on change?
- Is your language positively reinforcing this new behaviour or is it negatively reinforcing it?

A common phrase I pick up on in my private practice when working with people on change, is 'I have to…' or 'I had to…' This is a tell-tale sign to me that a lapse or relapse to old behaviour is lurking, ready to strike at any moment. For resentment towards the change is showing up in their language. In this instance, I ask my clients to replace the words 'have to do', to 'get to do', and ask them to see if that makes a difference. For example, 'I have to go to the gym' turns into 'I get to go to the gym.' 'I have to spend quality time with my colleagues' turns into 'I get to spend quality time with my colleagues.' Even evolving the words you use to describe things can make all the difference. Instead of using the words diet and exercise, replace them with words with eat and train. Small differences in the language you use can lead to big results.

The language we use is a pre-cursor and a tell-tale sign to whether we are progressing towards maintaining that new behaviour or regressing back to old behaviours. Monitor your language, review which words evoke negative connotations, and identify the opposite or an alternative positive word that can replace it to improve your chances of maintaining that change.

THE BIGGER PICTURE

Finally, a commitment to lasting change requires seeing the bigger picture. Play the long-term game rather than constantly looking for quick fixes or instant gratification. Continually show up and putting in the work. It will often require you to evolve your perspective from what you want to happen and what you need to happen to what has to happen. You may want the weight to magically drop off or need your partner to express your love language to you, but what has to happen is you have to show up and put in the work.

It is important to celebrate the milestones and wins as you go along, but as Joe De Sena (2017) co-founder of Death Race, Spartan Race shared when someone said, 'To stop and smell the roses.' (a famous expression to celebrate the success or savour the moment), he responded, 'Who is maintaining the roses?' If we get too caught up celebrating the milestones, we take our eye away from the goal and objective and that's when progression can lead to regression.

- What can you do, not only today, but each day moving forward, to ensure you keep your eye on the bigger picture and continue to progress in the maintenance of what you wanted to achieve?

Keeping one eye on the bigger picture will help to ensure you don't lose sight of the over-riding goal/objective. It will give you the focus and clarity needed to help ensure you continue to maintain and sustain what you have attained, as we will explore more in the next chapter, All I Do Is Win.

SUMMARY

Archilochus once famously said, 'We do not rise to the level of our expectations, we fall to the level of our training.' Maintenance is about training our minds, our bodies, our perspectives continuously. Expecting things to stay the same once we've achieved them will only lead to disappointment. When you achieve the desired outcome, then what? Have you planned for that? Or are you like the dog, who, when catching up with the car after chasing it, doesn't know what to do? You have to continue to put in the work on a regular and consistent basis. Hold yourself to account and, ideally, find an accountability partner who can help hold you to account.

The pathway to success is full of potholes. Lapses and relapses are a common part of the process of change. Very few people can make a lasting change on willpower alone. If you can prepare for relapses and use the model Here Comes AFGO to learn and grow from a relapse, your bounce-back rate to maintaining a new way of being is one step closer to being achieved. Be conscious of the language you use. Positive reinforcement and reframing of words will increase your likelihood of maintaining lasting change. By keeping one eye firmly placed on the bigger picture, you will continually remind yourself of the ongoing objective.

12

ALL I DO IS WIN

Future Proofing

It was the forty-second birthday of twins, Marwa and Omar, who were celebrating their joint birthday at a restaurant local to where their mother Dot lived in South-East London. Gone were the party days of yesteryear, where drinks would flow, absinth shots would be drunk, and memories would be lost. The night was a more subdued affair with friends Saga, Chris, their younger sister Alana and a few other close friends and family members joining the celebrations. The bond between the two siblings had always been close. Though Marwa was now based in NYC as a captain for Delta airlines, and Omar, a leading surgeon in St Thomas' hospital, which meant their time together, because of proximity and workload, didn't allow them to get to see each other as much as they did growing up.

As the restaurant manager, who'd kindly kept the restaurant open late for the celebration, came over to the table to let the group know he would now have to close the restaurant as it was 1am, the group were surprised where the time had gone, having arrived six hours earlier. They said their goodbyes, and as Marwa and Omar embraced, sharing a long hug, they sensed something different this time, the twin telepathy still strong between the two. Before they would spend the early hours at their mum's house having a nightcap and talking, but with Marwa piloting a plane back to NYC first thing in the morning and Omar having four patient operations, they returned to their hotel and home, respectively.

The following morning was Christmas eve, and the air was filled with Christmas cheer. Marwa's co-pilot and flying crew had got her a belated birthday present to celebrate, and though she was tired, she was excited to be heading back to NYC to be with her partner and his family for the holidays. Omar, at the same time, was preparing for the operations he would be part of and over-seeing that day. Going through the various procedures with the team, many of whom he was working with for the first time, Omar looked at the list of patients one more time whilst putting on his scrubs. Everything began smoothly as the flight took off and the first operation started. Cruising altitude was reached, and the route seemed smooth, with little to no turbulence across the Atlantic forecast. Back at St Thomas', the first operation had gone without a hitch, and the patient was returned to the ward to wake up from the anaesthesia and recover.

Around six hours into the flight, Marwa began getting a weird feeling something wasn't right. At the same time, Omar was walking into his third operation of the day, feeling the same thing. Omar had done this operating procedure over a hundred times before, so was almost on autopilot, but he couldn't shake the feeling. Then, suddenly, things started to take a turn. The crew could hear a colossal bang in the cockpit, and the plane jolted. A vulture had somehow flown into the path of one engine and being caught in it had rendered the engine useless. Marwa and the team quickly turned the plane's autopilot off, to manually operate the plane, and got to work to solve the problem. Omar, meanwhile, was dealing with a similar crisis of his own. His patient had gone into cardiac arrest, whilst following a standard operating procedure. It was extremely rare for an operation of this type to result in a patient going into cardiac arrest, but the team assembled to try to save the patient, who seemed to be flatlining.

Marwa was able to steady the plane with the help of her crew, for they had been trained on what to do should a bird impact an engine. Though this was a rarity to happen at 35,000 feet, rather than between the ground and 10,000 – 15,000 feet where most bird impacts occur, the crew worked together clearly, calmly, and effectively, to address the situation. Unfortunately, this wasn't to be the only problem they would occur, when twenty minutes later, the other engine failed. Having run through all the various options available to them, from attempting to restart the engine, to needing to make an emergency landing, Marwa contacted Boston's air traffic control, to notify them that the plane had experienced engine failure and would need to make an emergency landing at the airport. Communication and clarification remained clear and concise between everyone in the cockpit. The cabin crew were informed of the situation, and passengers on board were notified that the plane would be diverted to Boston to make an emergency landing. Despite the change in plans, and a few passengers who were understandably concerned, everyone else stayed calm, and as the plane came into Boston Logan airport, with fire trucks and emergency units on standby, Marwa and her co-pilot safely landed the plane, where the on-ground team were waiting on hand, to help navigate the aftermath of what unfolded.

Omar's team seemed to be blindsided by the cardiac arrest. Communication wasn't effective between the team as they attempted to save the patient's life. The surgeon's assistant was struggling to remain level-headed, his reaction time to command slower than required, losing valuable seconds in an attempt to save the patient. As the patient continued to flatline, the first two attempts with the defibrillator to bring the patient back were unsuccessful. It became clear to Omar, that they were losing the patient. After a third attempt with the defibrillator to bring back the patient, they pronounced the patient dead.

As both Marwa and Omar, respectively, completed paperwork to review what had unfolded, leading to the respective problems they had experienced, the outcomes showed a very different approach. For Marwa, her and the team had communicated clearly and effectively, worked through all the various reasons for the problem, understood all the options to choose from to resolve the problem, and executed their decisions with clarity and efficiency. For Omar, it became clear with hindsight that several minor problems had occurred during the procedure. This led to the patient going into cardiac arrest, which was compounded by the team's inability to communicate clearly and effectively during their attempts to save the patient. Marwa was able to return to NYC that evening, relieved that she landed the plane safely, avert disaster and save everyone onboard's life, including her own. Omar, by contrast, returned home deflated, losing the last patient of the day before he was off for Christmas day. He struggled to wrap his head around what went wrong. The twins messaged each other that night to wish each other Merry Christmas, and with Omar still awake, he rang his sister. Telling her what unfolded, Marwa was slightly shocked, but somewhat unsurprised that her brother had experienced something, as she felt the same feeling she always felt, when something was wrong between one of them. Omar mentioned he felt the same thing and was taken aback when Marwa shared what had happened on her flight. The two, relieved each of them were safe, said their goodnights, thinking what a difference a day makes.

Both Omar and Marwa experienced problems in their respective jobs, but as seen, the outcomes of the situations were very different. Not every flight that experiences problems on board has a successful resolution like Marwa's flight did, and not every flatline results in the death of a patient, like Omar's did. However, the motivations behind each profession when a problem occurs have very different reasons. As author Matthew Syed notes in his book Black Box Thinking (2016), 'When pilots make mistakes, it results in their own deaths. When a doctor makes a mistake, it results in the death of someone else. That is why pilots are better motivated than doctors to reduce mistakes.' This was something I witnessed on my trip to Antarctica with Lisa Nydahl, who shared details about her ongoing training over her thirty-five year career at Delta as a pilot and captain, to ensure the pilots were continually prepared for every eventuality, which was then reflected in Lisa's calm and collected manner and attention to detail. Now this is not a slight at doctors/surgeons, as they all do the best they can with the resources they have. It's just to say that the stakes are a lot higher for a pilot than a doctor or surgeon. For a pilot holds their own life in their hands when something goes wrong. A doctor/surgeon, on the other hand, holds a patient's life in their hands when something goes wrong.

This is where the importance of what psychologist Gary Klein (2007) calls a pre-mortem, or what others refer to as prospective hindsight, comes into play. A pre-mortem is the concept of imagining a future event has happened, and then analysing why. Studies have shown that through the use of a pre-mortem, it increases the ability of people to correctly identify reasons for future outcomes by thirty percent. This is a significant increase in the likelihood of not only being able to identify problems but also being able to troubleshoot these problems, to factor in what would need to be actioned should any of these problems arise. As a result, several pathways for different outcomes are mapped out, and a path of action is able to be taken effectively, should any of the pre-mortem problems come true.

Let's look at another example of where a pre-mortem could have been utilised to deal with a problem before or when it showed up, rather than when the problem blowed up and it became too late to solve.

IT'S JUST TOO LITTLE TOO LATE

In the late 1990s and early 2000s, pop-mania was reaching its peak around the world and no more so than in the United States. Off the back of the Spice Girls, who had become a global phenomenon around the world, a plethora of pop acts, were being ushered into the world. MTV had, since the early 1980s, become responsible for breaking artists, in the same way FM radio had before it. Unlike today, where music videos are available at your fingertips with a quick search on YouTube, viewers were beholden to the programming of MTV, as to when the video of their favourite artist would be aired. This changed on September 14th, 1998, when MTV launched TRL (total request live). With interviews and performances from all the leading popstars, rock stars, R&B and hip-hop acts, premieres of music videos; whose production values went from strength to strength, and an interactive video chart, fandemonium seemed to go stratospheric. As discussed in Chapter 6, Talking About My Generation, timing can play a significant factor in the success of an individual, a project, a business. And the stars aligned perfectly for three acts in particular, all of whom were under the same record label: Jive Records.

One act on the label, Backstreet Boys, released their third album 'Millennium' in May 1999, with the album selling over 1.13 million copies in the US alone in its first week, a record at the time. The video for their second single 'Larger Than Life' which cost over $2 million, became the second most requested song in the history of MTV TRL's chart, (the first, Backstreet Boys video 'Shape Of My Heart') and lead single 'I Want It That Way' received nominations for both Song and Record of the Year at the Grammy's, a rare feat for a boyband. All of this led to the album shipping over 11 million copies in 1999 in the US alone and selling over 24 million copies worldwide, a massive win for the band, the label and the retail industry. Another boyband and Jive label mates, *NSYNC, were up next. Their sophomore album, 'No Strings Attached', preceded by the first single 'Bye Bye Bye', took the boyband and made them stratospheric in the United States. The album smashed the record set by Backstreet Boy's 'Millennium', selling 2.41 million copies in its first week. The album sold over 12 million copies in total in the US, with an initial shipment of over 9 million units, to record stores and retail outlets, providing another amazing payday for the likes of Tower Records, who were the go to record store for anything music related. Next up was label mate Britney Spears, who'd exploded out of the gate with her debut single '…Baby One More Time' and had become another MTV darling, with her MTV VMA performances going down as some of the most iconic moments in pop history. In May 2000, Britney's sophomore album broke the record for debut release week sales for a solo artist debuting with 1.3 million sales in the US and amassing over 10 million copies in the US, and 20+ million worldwide.

Over the course of those twelve months, the retail industry was eating pop mania and fandemonium up, no more so than Tower Records. In the space of twelve months, three acts had delivered a combined first week sales of nearly 5 million albums, and between the three releases, generated 30 million plus album sales in 18 months in the US alone. Tower Records couldn't get the records into the hands of the fans fast enough, making sure they always had enough supply to meet demand. There would be queues outside the record stores on release day, with fans eagerly awaiting the doors to open so they could get their hands on the new release by their favourite acts. Other big releases in 2000, by breakout acts including Eminem's 'The Marshall Mathers LP' (1.76 million albums on release week) Limp Bizkit's 'Chocolate Starfish and the Hot Dog Flavored Water' (1.05 million albums on release week) had Tower Records laughing all the way to the bank.

As we covered in Chapter 6, 'Talking About My Generation', the record industry went into freefall, following the peak of the recorded music industry in 2001. Napster and other illegal file-sharing platforms made music accessible to fans at the click of a button, and this began to significantly impact the physical sales of albums. Sales had been growing continuously for years to reach the astronomical heights that these pop, rock, R&B and hip-hop acts were posting on release week. Music industry executives were initially nonchalant about the future of music. Executives at Tower Records were blasé at the situation, believing the music industry would resolve the illegal downloading of music, and that this momentary blip affecting sales wouldn't last. One executive is claimed to have said that 'fans and music lovers will always want to come to a place where they can access and listen to music.' With endless racks, holding over 40,000 releases in the bigger stores, and listening pods, so that shoppers could listen to tracks before purchasing the release, Tower Records executives believed music lovers and shoppers would always want to come to a record store. This executive was partially right, people will always want to come to a place where they can access and listen to music. The problem for Tower Records was, they assumed it would always be a physical space and not a digital one.

Unlike Tower records, where everything in the basket needed to be profitable for them to succeed as a business, other established organisations that sold music like supermarkets, and new entrants to the market like Amazon, could offer music releases as a loss leader, making their profits from other products like food and alcohol, or from avenues like Amazon Web Services (AWS). This acted as a further disadvantage to Tower Records, who could not sell their primary product as a loss leader, as it would put them in the red. As the illegal file-sharing battles with major labels and platforms including Napster and LimeWire wore on, tech giant Apple, went about offering a solution to the problem, and in April 2003 launched the iTunes store, where fans and music lovers could legally purchase and download music. With illegal downloading still rife, and legal downloading taking off, Tower Records was really starting to get into trouble. They hadn't foreseen the turn of events, that music would move to a digital format, and that the physical format would transform from a consumption format to a collection format, being reclassified more as a merchandise or memorabilia item, than something people would actively use to listen to.

Tower Records became like a cruise ship. Moving slowly to the changes that the marketplace had introduced, it had also become weighed down by the financial costing of its offering of physical product, retail space rent and more. New entrants in the retail market, like Amazon and Apple, were like speed boats in comparison. More agile and able to quickly move to changes as the market evolved. By 2006, Tower Records filed for bankruptcy and all of the stores in the US closed. Today only one store still remains standing, in Tokyo, Japan, the second largest music market in the world that still leans heavily into consuming music physically. Virgin Megastore, another international music store, shut down all their stores in 2007.

We've seen this happen repeatedly in other business sectors, too. In 2000, John Antioco, CEO of Blockbuster Video, the home entertainment mammoth, met with Marc Randolph about the potential acquisition of the company he co-founded, Netflix, for $50 million. Antioco, deemed Netflix, whose offering at the time was an online DVD mail-order service, as a niche business, and felt that 'The dot.com hysteria is completely overblown.' Blockbuster's inability and reluctance to see the future had brought about its eventual downfall, closing all of its corporate owned stores by 2014. Netflix, on the other hand, continued to adapt, moving from a website ordering DVD business to a video-on-demand platform in 2007, and today is the leading streaming platform in the world.

In the fashion world, one of the biggest brands, Topshop, went out of business in 2021. Failure to adapt to new entrants on the market like online start-ups BooHoo and ASOS, who directly competed with the high-street brand rather than a high-end brand like Gucci, directly ate into its sales. A laisse-faire approach to the power of online shopping, combined with the impacts of the COVID-19 pandemic, put the final nail in the coffin for Topshop.

Even low-cost retail outlet Primark was caught off-guard by its reluctance to embrace change. Primark's refusal to move online meant that when the COVID-19 pandemic hit in 2020 and shops shut down, with no online sales channel, the discount clothing store was faced with total closure and burning through £100 million of cash each week. The retail powerhouse was forecast to make £1 billion of operational profit in the year to September 2020 in the UK, and ended up making less than a third of that. Whilst their business no doubt would have been affected by the pandemic, a loss of 70% of revenues could have been prevented, if adaptation to their existing model had been planned for and rolled out. It is only in 2023 that Primark has rolled out their click and collect service online, where at the time of writing, it still is unavailable in many stores nationwide, and they have announced no current plans to launch an online store.

SELF-REFLECTION TIME

Let's turn our attention for a moment to you and explore how you plan for and deal with problems in your life.

- Do you deal with problems when they show up or when they blow up?
- Are you the kind of person who buries their head in the sand like an ostrich waiting for the problem to pass?
- Do you confront problems head on?

In my book 'The Shitty Committee', I use a boat in a storm metaphor to talk about the three different approaches to problems and change, which are:

1. **The optimist** – who expects the winds to change, and so does nothing.
2. **The pessimist** – who complains about the wind, and so does nothing.

3. **The realist** – who adjusts the sails, to change direction.

When looking at the three different approaches to problems, which one do you most identify with? With Tower Records, they definitely had the optimistic perspective. Expecting the illegal downloading problem at the turn of the century to be resolved by the record labels, and then things would return to normal. It is possible that in different situations, you switch from your go to perspective to a different perspective. It's also understandable that in certain moments, an initial reaction may have you lean into one perspective. It is important to honour your thoughts and feelings in that moment before switching to another perspective. As we will see later in this chapter, the optimist perspective and pessimist perspective both have valuable contributions when it comes to decision making, but they should be used to inform decisions, not dictate decisions.

Disruption in both our professional lives and personal lives, as well as in business, often comes from the outside in. As such, an outside in approach to pre-empt problems can help navigate them should they arise down the road. The digital revolution over the last two to three decades has evolved, how businesses operate, how advertising is carried out, how we connect as humans. Whether we like it or not, the digital revolution is not going anywhere, and so we have to adapt to 'a new normal'. This was an overused term, that was banded around by politicians all over the world as countries went into lockdown and were forced to adjust to new ways of living, working, operating, but it applies here. Sometimes we have the resources to be able easily navigate these problems as they arise, or in the case of the COVID-19 pandemic, be given directions as to how to proceed. In other cases, we may not be as fortunate, and therefore the problems are likely to continue unless we utilise a way to find a solution.

Author and leadership expert Chris Fussell (2015), suggests that it is important to have and regularly review a running list of three people in your professional life, whom can be interchangeable as and when needed, that are successful in an area you wish to be or continue to be successful in, that you are always watching:

1. Someone senior to you that you want to emulate.
2. A peer who you feel is better at the job than you are.
3. A subordinate who does the job that you did better than you did.

I remember my first record label boss and ongoing mentor Hugh Goldsmith at Sony, mentioned to me a few years back, that he felt the roles had reversed in some ways and that I was a mentor to him, which not only was such a beautiful thing to hear, but took me by surprise. As I came to understand his view more, he shared I could provide insights into a new way of looking at things. That though his topline knowledge was still very strong in a lot of areas, the depth of a different generation like mine could be a resource that could be mined (in a positive way) to help gain further insight. Additionally, when driving in Los Angeles with my last record boss before becoming a therapist, former Warner chairman Christian Tattersfield, as we discussed getting older, he shared a great pearl of wisdom. 'In your forties, you are an old, young person. You can often cling to youth. But as you transition into your fifties, you become a young old person, and with your children growing up, they breathe a new lease of life into you, sharing with you what's trendy and cool, differently to the way you viewed things before.' This outlook has helped me to understand the problems of holding on to something or the past that you fear losing, as opposed to relinquishing that hold and embracing the new, which could open a whole new host of possibilities.

These two examples dispel the myth 'you can't teach an old dog new tricks', not that I view either of my mentors as old. For it is all about mindset. Your perspective on things. You can be pessimistic Pete and complain about getting old, or you can do something about it. To be proactive and equip yourself with knowledge and understanding that you can then apply.

SELF DEVELOPMENT TIME

Think about your own life for a moment.

- Is there a problem professionally or personally that you could benefit from additional help and support from one of the three different types of people mentioned on the previous page?
- Who is someone senior to you that you could emulate?
- Who is a peer in your career that you feel is better than you, whom you can learn from?
- Who is a subordinate who has a desirable skill set that you could learn from?
- If you are not already tapping into them, how can you?
- If you have direct access to them, when you will contact them to support you through the problem?
- If you have indirect access to them through a friend or associate, can an introduction be made?

A connection from a mutual friend or an acquaintance has a much higher chance of a response, comparative to an unsolicited connection, which on average is likely to only warrant a 7% response rate. If you have no way of contacting the individual, is there a way to consume their knowledge and understanding, through interviews, podcasts, social media, books, and other formats, to help you address and navigate problems, that they have an understanding of?

Success leaves cues, and two of the biggest businesses in the world, though having slightly different approaches to adaptability, have something we can all learn from and apply into both our professional and personal lives. Let's begin with Amazon, who though they have become one of the biggest companies in the world, still pride themselves in viewing Amazon as a Day 1 company.

FUTURE PROOFING

Daniel Slater (2020), the worldwide lead for culture of innovation at Amazon, shares that 'Day 1 is both a culture and an operating model that puts the customer at the centre of everything Amazon does. We strive to deeply understand customers and work backwards from their pain points to rapidly develop innovations that create meaningful solutions in their lives. Day 1 is about being constantly curious, nimble, and experimental. It means being brave enough to fail if it means that by applying lessons learnt, we can better surprise and delight customers in the future.' This is compared to a 'Day 2' mentality that a lot of businesses adopt as they grow over time, owing to their need to adjust its approach to manage the organisation as it scales. The problem is, it can slow the company down, as we saw with Tower Records becoming like a cruise ship, meaning the company becoming less agile, and further away from the customer, focused more on internal challenges and conflict, rather than external customer focus and continuing to innovate.

In his 2016 shareholder letter, Jeff Bezos, founder of Amazon, built on this further: 'Day 2 is stasis. Followed by irrelevance. Followed by excruciating, painful decline. Followed by death. And that is why it is always Day 1. To avoid Day 2 culture, a company must be hyper-vigilant, remained focused on its customers, and stave off practices that hamper its ability to rapidly innovate.' As humans, we become quick to adapt to a new normal. Bezos continued, 'Yesterday's wow quickly becomes today's ordinary. Customers can provide endless ideas and inspiration to innovate, and their needs and desires will drive you to invent on their behalf.' The problem with most businesses is they drift further away from their client needs as the organisation grows and other things get in the way, driving a rift between organisation and client, which, down the road, leads to problems occurring. The same is true in romantic relationships. For most people, the freshness of a new relationship means bringing your best self to the relationship, putting all of your effort and energy into the relationship. Yet most people move from a Day 1 relationship to a Day 2 relationship, where the honeymoon period wears off and the other partner is likely to be taken for granted. Children can further drive a wedge between the relationship, as time is taken from the relationship to focus on the needs of the children at the expense of the relationship. As previously shared in Chapter 4, 'When Two Tribes Go To War', it's not conflict that causes relationships to end, it's neglect. And by neglecting a partner or neglecting a client, they are likely to go elsewhere to get their needs met. This can lead to the relationship ending or the company going out of business, if the neglect continues.

SELF REFLECTION TIME

Here are some questions to ask yourself about your approach to life that may cause problems:

- Do you have a Day 1 approach to your life, or a Day 2 approach?

This again may be different again in different areas of your life. It may also be the case at certain periods of time, as discussed in Chapter 10, 'I Don't Want To Miss A Thing', that one part of your life needs to face some sort of sacrifice, so that another part can flourish.

- If you have areas of your life where a Day 2 approach is taken, does this cause problems for you?
- How do these problems show up?
- Are they perpetual problems that can only be solved by mutually agreeing to disagree?
- Are they situational problems that can be addressed and solved by making time for them?

- Are they problems that can't be solved, so they are being avoided through distraction or fear of confronting the inevitable?

Take some time to reflect on this, and how a Day 2 approach to certain areas of your life may cause problems. Once you have taken a moment to reflect on this, think about what you can change, to help move from a Day 2 to a Day 1 approach.

- Will you commit more time to the relationships you've neglected?
- Will you carve out more time to focus on the evolving needs of the customer?
- How will you go about doing this?

This is something Google (or Alphabet as the parent company is now known) has become renowned for in their organisation. The founders of Google implemented the 20% project into their organisation early on, whereby staff are encouraged to devote 20% of their time at work to pursuing personal projects, that could aid the growth and diversification of Google into new areas. The only stipulations were that it had to benefit Google in some way, and their ideas would become the intellectual property of the company. By creating a specific period within which creativity is encouraged and enabled, it allowed employees the space to tap into a different part of their brain, or as we learnt in Chapter 2 'Wave After Wave', a different brain frequency; Alpha or Gamma, to come up with innovative ideas. Through implementing the 20% project into Google, both Gmail, which with over 1.5 billion emails, is the most used email platform, and AdSense, the advertising platform that back in 2014 generated 22% of the company's yearly revenue, were both conceived. It's not to say that at some point, these ideas wouldn't have been conceived, but by proactively taking the time to get creative, it allowed Google to continually innovate. Not every idea created will be a success if implemented, but as the ice hockey player Wayne Gretzky famously said, 'You miss 100% of the shots you don't take.'

- How often do you make the time to think of new ideas or creative adjustments that you can make in your professional or personal life?
- When was the last time you did this?
- Did making the time to get creative help you find fresh approaches or ideas to problems you were facing?
- When will you schedule time in your diary, your week, your day to think creatively? To address a problem or challenge in your life?

Sometimes we need more than just a creative mindset or a Day 1 approach to problems in our lives and take a more holistic approach to the situation.

DECISIONS. DECISIONS. DECISIONS.

One afternoon, out of the blue, a head-hunter approached Francesca about a job they were looking to fill. Francesca who was a high-flying investment banker at one of the leading investment companies in the UK, had been happy at the company she had worked for over the past ten years, working her way up from an apprenticeship to vice president of the company. Throughout her time at the company, Francesca had been supported and nurtured in her growth, but the latest role that she'd been in for a year had been challenging due to the relationship with the SVP, who was her direct report. The head-hunter stated the new company had been familiar with Francesca's work over the years, and with a new SVP position opening up, they wanted to poach her.

Francesca was flattered by the offer, but when informed that there was a tight turn around on needing a decision, and that the company wanted to meet with her as a formality before offering her the job, she panicked. Though Francesca worked well under pressure, she struggled with the weight that this decision entailed. Her decision-making process was all over the place, with Francesca oscillating between the pros and cons of the accepting the new job, the emotions that came up with the decision and other factors. Even her usual SWOT analysis that she'd used from time to time at work to make investment decisions for her clients wasn't working for her. At the time, Francesca was working with me in a therapeutic capacity, and booked in an emergency session to help her gather her thoughts and come to an informed decision about what to do moving forward. As Francesca entered my office, she was surprised to see six baseball caps on my desk, all in different colours. 'What are these for?' Francesca asked, and I shared, 'All will be revealed in due course.'

As we worked out way through the session, I got Francesca to put on the blue hat first, to help define the parameters of the session. What were the outcomes she would like to achieve by the end of the session, and how I could help take on this role to ensure we stay on course? Once that was established, I, as the facilitator, took the blue cap and placed it on myself, and handed Francesca the white cap. Under this cap, Francesca was to focus only on the facts about the new role and her current role. Stating the salary differences, the compensation packages, the titles, the office locations and other variables. When an emotion came up, that didn't align as a fact, I, with the blue hat on, shared 'We will come to emotions with the red hat, but for now we are just focusing on the facts.' Once all the facts were laid out, we moved to the red hat to discuss the emotions around the decision between roles. Here, Francesca could focus in on her emotions and specifically the conflict between her loyalty to the company she'd worked at for ten years and the frustration she felt at her boss, whom she felt was stifling her career. After this we moved to the black hat, to establish all the negative reasons for taking the job as well as the negative reasons for staying in her current job. Once these had been outlined, we switched to the yellow hat, focusing on all the positives for both going to the new job and staying in the old job. Using the green hat, Francesca, could look at new areas she hadn't explored, which included other jobs that may also be out there for her, as she hadn't been looking for a job, but now one had landed on her lap, she might explore if other roles were also open.

As the session came to a close, I handed Francesca back the blue hat, asking her to reflect on all the various perspectives we looked at during the session and see if any conclusions could be drawn. Through the process, Francesca had realised that whilst she had loved working at the company she'd been at for over a decade, she would be staying out of a sense of loyalty to the company, whereas this new role would be a chance to continue to grow and develop in her career, an aspect that was extremely important to her. There was one caveat, she realised, through exploring ideas with the green hat. There could also be other jobs out there that she might be equally or better suited for her. And so Francesca would use that evening to explore other job options, whilst moving forward with the head-hunter for the new position.

In the next session, Francesca came in with a spring in her step. Full of gratitude, she was thankful for 'the mind-blowing' session she'd had, which helped her gain clarity on a decision she was desperately trying to grapple with on her own. In the end, she moved forward with the offer from the head-hunter, having met with the new company and getting on well with the team. I'm pleased to report that a further eight-months on, following her notice period at her old company, Francesca continues to make strides in her career, taking like a duck to water in her new role.

From time to time, many of us can struggle to make informed decisions on important issues. Emotions can cloud our judgment, resulting in us sometimes making errors in what we decide, though emotions with certain decisions can be the right pathway to follow. Information overload can lead to analysis paralysis. Former US Secretary of State Colin Powell (1998) believes that between 40%-70% of information collation is the right amount to come to a decision. With less than 40% of the information needed, you are often shooting in the dark with your decision. If you are waiting for more information beyond 70% of the information needed to make a decision, it may result in missing an opportunity, with the decision being made for you either by time itself, or by someone else beating you to the post.

Let's go back to Francesca's story as the hat approach to decision making, with a problem she faced may sound intriguing to you. Psychologist Edward De Bono (1985) had noticed in his work that when people were attempting to make decisions, be that individually or as a group, many would end up being conflicted. Some would have their emotions over-ride logic. Others would let their negativity-bias blind themselves to the positive aspects of the problem they were facing or the decision they needed to make. He also noticed, the go to decision-making approaches like SWOT (Strengths, Weaknesses, Opportunities and Threats) analysis or Cartesian Logic (a set of four questions asked to help decision making), were not covering all bases, and so De Bono set about creating his own tool, known as the six thinking hats, that helped individuals, couples, groups and businesses come to informed decisions. In Figure 12.1, I have outlined the six different hats and what each hat represents.

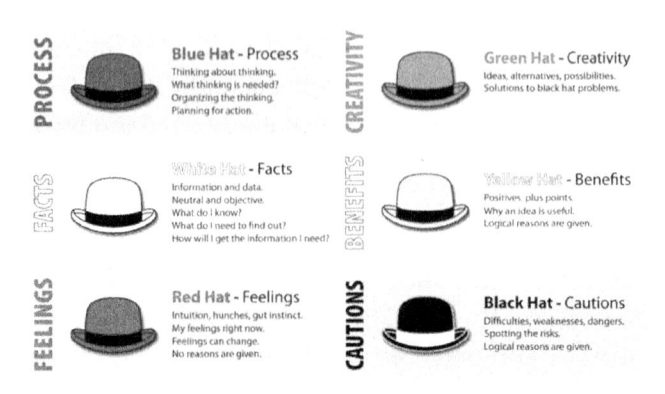

PROCESS — **Blue Hat - Process**
Thinking about thinking.
What thinking is needed?
Organizing the thinking.
Planning for action.

CREATIVITY — **Green Hat - Creativity**
Ideas, alternatives, possibilities.
Solutions to black hat problems.

FACTS — **White Hat - Facts**
Information and data.
Neutral and objective.
What do I know?
What do I need to find out?
How will I get the information I need?

BENEFITS — **Yellow Hat - Benefits**
Positives, plus points.
Why an idea is useful.
Logical reasons are given.

FEELINGS — **Red Hat - Feelings**
Intuition, hunches, gut instinct.
My feelings right now.
Feelings can change.
No reasons are given.

CAUTIONS — **Black Hat - Cautions**
Difficulties, weaknesses, dangers.
Spotting the risks.
Logical reasons are given.

Figure 12.1 - The Six Thinking Hats.

Through the decision-making process, the hats don't have to be worn in a specific order, but the following recommendation I outline is a pathway that often works when coming to an informed decision. It may help as I go through this, to pick something you need to decide on and see how the process goes for you.

BLUE HAT THINKING

To begin with, start by putting on the blue hat (you don't have to buy the colour hats, you just use them metaphorically for what they symbolise). The blue hat is for processes. Here you outline the process, what outcomes you want to achieve by the end of the process, what needs to be factored in, and if in a group setting, how the facilitator of the process will use the hat to bring the meeting back on track, if for example someone has slipped into another hat when not appropriate.

WHITE HAT THINKING

Once this has been set, it is good to then put on the white hat. The white hat is for facts. Here, all the facts are to be laid out objectively. It is important that proven facts (known as first class facts) and believed facts (known as second class facts), facts believed to be true but not yet checked but easily verified, are the only two facts to be included. Interpretations, opinions and beliefs are not for this hat. These can be laid out in other areas, as there will be something, often a belief or a feeling, behind them.

RED HAT THINKING

Next up, the red hat can often be a good hat to put on. The red hat is for emotions. Here, the emotions and feelings around a decision can be explored and understood. Feelings can change, and this is why they need to be separate to the white hat, which is based in fact alone. Feelings as previously said are a good decision driver, as we have a gut instinct, a good/bad feeling about something and these need to be understood. Understanding your feelings to the decision can help you pose more questions to come to an informed decision.

BLACK HAT THINKING

From here, moving to the black hat next often helps. The black hat focuses on cautions. Our brains have a negativity bias, so it is often quite easy for individuals and groups to highlight and focus on the problems. The risks can be spotted and highlighted and logical reasons given to the cautions. If you don't like what you must decide on, and you are turning towards a no more than a yes, make sure it can be backed up with a logical reason. If not, this needs to be under the red hat of emotion, not the black hat of caution.

YELLOW HAT THINKING

After all the cautions have been outlined, it can help next to move to the yellow hat. The yellow hat is focused on the positives and provides a good counterbalance to the black cap. This hat can suggest positive reasons for the decision that needs to be reached and also provide solutions to the black hat problems that were raised.

GREEN HAT THINKING

Once the other hats have all been worn, moving to the green hat can help to explore further ideas and alternatives to help with the decision-making process. The green hat can be useful, especially when you have a lot of experience with something, as you may have picked up blind spots and don't notice the things that are new about it.

It can be worthwhile going around each hat once more to see if anything was missed, and then use the blue hat to come to a decision. If a group decision, dependent on what culture you find yourself in, it may be a decision is reached by consensus or a decision reached by the leader. Usually through this process, the decision makes itself clear, but sometimes it doesn't and needs a vote to be cast, or the outcome could be that a decision can't be made until further work is done, and that in itself is a decision, which helps the group move forward.

By separating the different thinking processes, it can help segment out the different approaches. In a group setting, if you have got someone who is a negative Nancy that always focuses on the cautions, you can use the six-hat decision making method as a polite way of shifting her perspective. 'Nancy, I'm wondering if you could take the black hat off for a moment and put the yellow hat on to focus on the positives.' Equally, if someone is getting emotionally caught up in a hat other than the red hat, you can say, 'I see this is bringing up a lot of emotion for you right now. If I can ask you to hold on to that emotion for a moment and we will switch to the red hat, so this can be explored further.' This gives the group, and more specifically that individual an understanding, of what is required from them at each point, and it is up to the facilitator in the blue hat, to keep a track of this, so things don't veer too far off the track.

Flexibility is welcomed in this process. As I mentioned, the structure I've highlighted is a suggestion. Often you may flit back and forth between hats rather than following a specific order, which is fine. The primary goal is to separate the different approaches to thinking out, so that each has the space to be able to be worked through fully. A problem can't be solved on the same level it was created at, and so a different approach and a different way of thinking must be used. The six thinking hats method I've found to be the best approach to addressing problems or decision-making head on, to reach an outcome both efficiently and effectively.

SELF-REFLECTION TIME

- If you tried the six-thinking hats process just now, how did you get on?
- Did you come to a decision?
- Did it resolve a problem by providing an outcome and a pathway forward for you?
- What decisions can you try the six-thinking hats process on moving forward?

SUMMARY

Over the course of this chapter, we've looked at how your approach to decision making can create problems for you in your life or lead to solutions. An optimistic approach can lead to blind spots, expecting things to happen without the follow through. A pessimistic approach can lead to blame and victimhood, compounding the problem. Whereas a realistic approach will encourage adaptability and a willingness to move forward, rather than staying put.

Taking a pre-mortem approach to problems can help you fail-proof a situation ahead of time helping you to foresee any issues and come up with solutions, so there is a roadmap and a pathway through, should that problem arise. Day 1 thinking can further compound this, by insuring complacency doesn't set in, causing problems in your business or your relationships. Adopting Google's 20% project philosophy can allow you the space and the bandwidth to think differently and look at things from a more creative or objective perspective. This can create new opportunities, solutions, pathways that may have previously been unavailable to you.

When having to evaluate a problem to find a solution or go through a decision-making process to come up with an answer, using the six thinking hats method by focusing on specific areas one step at a time, can provide clarity of thought, helping the decision-making process be both efficient and effective. As humans, we don't go through life; we grow through life, and the person who makes no decisions or stays stagnant gets what's left behind when everyone else has moved on. By taking a proactive approach and implementing some of the techniques and methods in this chapter, you can increase your problem-solving skills and reduce problems from occurring in the first place.

13

A HERO LIES IN YOU

Self-Reflection

Taylor placed down her bag beside her feet as she attempted to make herself comfortable on the couch. Having arrived a few minutes late to our first session, I was intrigued by this woman sat before me, who fidgeted uncomfortably, adjusting, and readjusting her dress. A former client of mine, Freddy, who recommended that she come and see me to help her navigate through the various problems in her life, had given Taylor my details. After going through the various formalities and the therapeutic contract, I handed over to Taylor to hear from her, what brought her to therapy and what she would like to achieve by the end of our time together.

As Taylor recalled the series of events that unfolded on an eventful day, the firing from her job, the break-up from her partner Joe, the humiliation of being called out by her friends, I got a sense of where the work would take us, and I wondered how willing and able Taylor would be to put in the work. To create the changes in her values, her beliefs, her behaviour, to live a more fulfilling life, with less denial and blame, and more accountability and responsibility. Asking how I can help, Taylor shared 'Freddy was saying how much you've helped him over the past two years, and I have to agree he has changed in that time, and so I want you to fix me too.'

A common request that I often hear from clients, I broke it to Taylor that my role here was not to fix her but to help her gain awareness of what has shaped the woman sat in front of me. From there we would together in the therapeutic relationship move towards a space of acceptance, owning how she got to this place and her role in it. 'It is only when we accept ourselves as we truly are that change can come about, and that journey takes time,' I shared. 'I don't have time. I need to sort this out right now.' Taylor's frustration and impatience were palpable, and it gave me a beautiful insight into how her relationships played out beyond the therapeutic space.

In the first few sessions, Taylor was both cold and combative. Knowing that it generally takes clients roughly five to six sessions before trust is formed and the deeper work can begin, I endeavoured to create a space where all feelings were honoured, without judgment, but curiosity, to put her at ease. Taylor started to thaw around session eight, when having learned to self-soothe and regulate her breathing, allowing her to increase her window of tolerance, she wasn't activated by my curiosity about her patterns of relating.

This provided an opening to explore her family of origin, and how that had informed a lot of who she'd become. As we unpacked her mother's smothering and controlling ways, and her father's poor timekeeping because of his alcoholism, I explored what narratives this had given her. Understanding how her brain had downloaded all the information she'd received as fact, by being in the gamma brain wave state up until around seven years old, she came to see she had an anxious attachment style. That she had found herself drawn to those who would take care of her, rescuing her when problems arose, allowing her to play the damsel in distress.

Her parents' use of criticism and denial mirrored Taylor's relationship to conflict. They would often react rather than respond to one another, and they dealt with problems when they blowed up rather than when they showed up, highlighting a pattern of avoidance. Added to this, Taylor had never seen her parents model repair from the rupture in their relationship, and as a result hadn't learned how to model healthy conflict resolution. This showed up in her relationship with others, and as time passed, Taylor was able to take ownership of her contribution to conflicts that arose, practice gentle start-ups when looking to resolve a conflict, and to self-soothe and take time out when feeling flooded with emotion, so that she could address the conflict rationally and logically.

The environments and culture Taylor found herself in and drawn towards had compounded her beliefs and behaviours. Her relationship to time, modelled on her father, was acceptable in some situations, but she realised that it wasn't in others, including at the beginning of our therapeutic relationship, when she would turn up five to ten minutes late, and then expect the session to run over to make up for her late start. Taylor had been told repeatedly that she was a gifted child. Her use of the English language was unmatched by many growing up. But her lack of continued application to further develop her skills in this area, and a culture where participation trophies were handed out to make everyone feel equal, caused issues in her career. Taylor started to feel like an imposter. She knew she was good at writing but felt overly challenged by others who were equally as good. The pressure to perform would impact her relationships with others, as her frustration would spill out if mistakes were made.

This led to feelings of perfectionism, compounded by social media and wanting to look like she had the perfect life, the perfect job, the perfect partner, the perfect friendship group. Keeping up this image resulted in a splitting of her real self from her idealised self. Taylor would often spread herself too thin, run late to everything, which was already an issue for her, and leave others disappointed and Taylor frustrated. Taylor took the time to review what was important to her, and how she could evolve her perspective. She worked out where she could make sacrifices in her life and become more disciplined to help her on the new pathway she was forging, to create a better relationship with herself, with others, and with her career.

One session towards the end of our therapeutic relationship, Taylor came in feeling helpless. She had regressed to old behaviours, and it had caused a problem with one of her closest friends. Acknowledging that lapses occur, and that in the cycle of change, there can on average be six lapses before the change becomes lasting, Taylor felt less downcast about the situation. Laughing that this was yet another fucking growth opportunity and saying with all the growth she's been doing, she's surprised she's not ten-foot tall, Taylor embraced the lapse and regression. Taking the lessons from everything we'd covered in therapy, Taylor could take ownership of what she had done and was able to offer a heartfelt apology to the friend and restore their friendship.

Just over a year on from our first session together, time had come for the therapeutic relationship to end. As we sat together, reflecting on the journey Taylor had been on, the woman she was when she entered my therapy office, to the woman she'd become, Taylor became all emotional. 'I never realised how most of the problems I experienced in my life, were because of how I interacted. I was the problem in so many areas of my life, and I am forever thankful to you for helping me to see that and helping me to change.' Her heartfelt words brought a tear to my eye, as I acknowledged that though she may have been the problem, she was also the solution in so many of these cases. Through her willingness to do the hard work and her determination to not continue to make the same mistakes time and again, Taylor realised she was no longer the anti-hero, and that she had become her own superhero, because a hero lied in her.

I believe as long as there is a willingness and an ableness, anyone can bring about a change in their lives. We can all be the villains in the story of our lives, and we can also be the hero, with the two often sitting side by side. For some people, the villain is firmly in the driver's seat, with the hero locked inside the boot. Help, in this case, is often needed, and a therapist can help to free the hero. The opposite can also reign true, which can lead to a saviour complex, and sometimes the villain needs to take the wheel, to show us the low road, so that we can appreciate the high road and all the roads in between.

I see my work as a therapist as a cross between being an archaeologist helping clients to excavate their past to better understand the impact of their history, and an architect helping clients to build a better future for themselves. I come with the tools, tips, and techniques to help clients explore the terrain, excavate and build, but ultimately, I am standing alongside them as they carry out the hard work. As you have made the journey through the chapters in this book, I hope that in some way, shape or form, I have been able to do the same.

SELF DEVELOPMENT TIME

Reflecting back, as this penultimate chapter comes toward an end, it feels appropriate to review your journey across these pages by asking several questions, to understand what you have taken from this book and where you may head next. Make the time to reflect and answer these questions, whether in the book if you have a physical copy, or in a notebook, journal or diary if you are reading this as an e-book or listening to the audiobook.

What have you learned through the course of this book?

What have you uncovered about yourself?

In what areas of your life have you identified that you are the problem?

How can tapping into the different brain wave frequencies help you moving forward?

In what ways does your attachment and/or dependency style affect your relationships?

How has your relationship with conflict shaped your interactions with others?

In what ways have the environments you've grown up in, or the environments you find yourself in, contributed to the problems you have in your life? Is there an opportunity to create healthier environments for yourself in the real or digital world?

Have you been affected by the generation you were born into, and have you been able to harness the opportunities your generation affords to you over other generations?

How have feelings of shame in your life impacted your relationship with yourself and others? What beliefs did the shame create, and is that a narrative that can be let go of?

How self-aware are you? Who do you tap into to help you see your blind spots or the unknown parts of yourself? Has this increased level of self-awareness encouraged or brought about a change in your life?

In what way/s does imposter syndrome show up in your life? How does this manifest in your behaviours? What can you address this, to create a healthier relationship with yourself?

To address the problems in your life, are there sacrifices that need to be made to live a more fulfilling life? How will you ensure you remain disciplined and focused on this pathway to change?

Are there resources you need to help on your pathway to change? How easily accessible are these resources? If they are unattainable to you, are there other options or work arounds?

When change comes, how will you ensure you sustain what you have gained?

If a lapse occurs, how can you learn and grow from it, to prevent further lapses or a reversion back to your problematic ways?

How adaptable are you to change? What would help make you more adaptable?

How do you approach decision-making to problems or pathways you face? Will engaging in a pre-mortem to reverse engineer what will happen, to then create a plan, reduce or remove the likelihood of a problem arising? Will using the six-hat technique to help you view the decision-making process from a variety of different perspectives to come to an informed decision help?

Are you able to see that the solutions to many of your problems lies within, through evolving your values, your beliefs and your behaviours?

Are there any other areas or problems in your life that you want to look at which have not been covered in this book?

My hope for you, is that through reading this book, exploring and answering the questions in this chapter, and reflecting on what you've read across the pages of this book, that you have gained a better understanding of yourself, your psyche and how to navigate and work through the problems in your life. Maybe you're the problem, maybe you're not, but in nearly every case, you will be the solution.

14

CAN I GET AN ENCORE

Further Resources

Congratulations. You've made it to the end of the book, and hopefully in one piece. My goal for you as a reader, as you have navigated your way through each of these chapters, is that this book has provided you with a deeper level of insight and understanding about yourself. Where the various problems lie in your life. How to take ownership by being accountable and responsible for your role in these problems, and what you will do to overcome them. It will probably have been uncomfortable in places when reflecting upon yourself. For some, you may have come away with more questions than answers. You may have realised at the end of this book that there are further problems in other areas of your life that weren't covered in the various chapters of this book.

The purpose of 'Maybe You're The Problem,' is to offer a broad overview of a dozen key themes that I continually see showing up in my private practice, that are likely to also show up for you. The hope is that the knowledge, wisdom, and understanding I have gained through my training, my own life experience and through my clients, and that I have then shared in these pages, will be of service to you. By balancing both the stories and the theoretical underpinnings to help you understand how problems may arise in different areas of your life, along with practical and thought-provoking questions and action points, the goal is to help you realise where maybe you're the problem in certain areas of your life and provide you with solutions.

For a large percentage of you who bought or potentially reluctantly received this book as a hint, what I have enclosed within this book will be sufficient to help you move forward. No further support is needed at this time. For others who are on a continual journey of growth, you may want to continue looking at where you can make more changes in your life. To be equipped with further knowledge and understanding about yourself. To gain more tools and techniques to navigate your way through problems as they arise in your life. If you identify with this, then I have additional ways in which I, the author, can offer further support to you beyond 'Maybe You're The Problem' across the next few pages.

SIGN UP TO THE
'STEP INTO YOUR SPOTLIGHT' COURSE.

'Step Into Your Spotlight' is a course created specifically to help individuals who feel stuck in their pursuit to achieve their goals, dreams, and aspirations in life. Designed as a ten-week live online programme, the weekly modules will take individuals on a journey by helping them become unstuck and allow them to stride with pride as they make their way towards their spotlight. The course, divided into three parts, begins by helping individuals to define and align with what their specific spotlight is professionally and/or personally. The next part of the course will help individuals to establish the pathway towards their spotlight, by identifying all the challenges and opportunities along the way, learning how to navigate them as they arise. The tail end of the course will prepare individuals as they move towards, step into, and bask in the spotlight.

There are two cohorts over the course of each year, beginning in January and September, respectively. The course runs on Mondays from 6pm – 8pm UK time and made up of twelve individuals. Two free scholarship spaces are available in each cohort, with applications open two months before, to enable individuals from all different backgrounds and all different walks of life, the opportunity to benefit from the course. If this sounds like the perfect course for you, scan the QR code below to gain further information on the course and to register your interest.

GRAB A COPY OF MY DEBUT BOOK
'The Shitty Committee'.

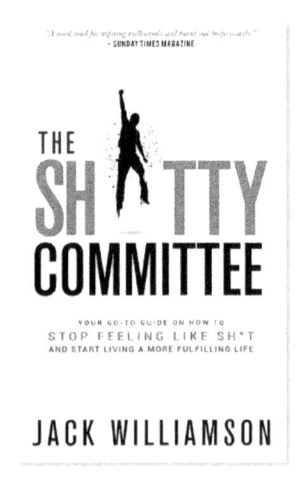

Heralded by The Sun as 'A book full of wisdom' and The Sunday Times as 'A must read', if you haven't already checked out my No.1 international best-selling book The Shitty Committee, you can read the synopsis for the book, and scan the QR code to get yourself a copy today.

The Shitty Committee is a no-punches-pulled, generation-defining go-to guide for anyone who is ready to stop feeling like shit and start living a more fulfilling life. Both incredibly powerful and refreshingly entertaining, The Shitty Committee will take you on a journey of self-discovery, served up in 15 bite-sized chapters across three sections, full of inspiring stories, profound advice and easy to do exercises. This book has been designed to:

- Introduce readers to the three types of The Shitty Committee: Internal, External, and Consumable.
- Help readers identify, evaluate, and eradicate the thoughts, people, or things from their lives that make them feel like shit.

- Assist readers in creating a more fulfilling life, leading them along the pathway to achieve their full potential.
- Guide readers as they step into their spotlight, to gain, maintain and sustain the life their heart desires.

By the end of The Shitty Committee, the various tools, techniques, and methods readers will learn in this book, from how to weather any storm through to why we should all become gynaecologists, will ensure they have everything they need to define, design and align with the life they've always dreamed of.

WORK ONE-ON-ONE WITH ME.

For those of you who benefit from working individually to process and work through problems, issues or challenges you are facing in your life, I have a limited number of one-on-one slots in my private practice available. If you are interested in working with me in a one-on-one setting, drop me an email at hello@musicandyou.co.uk where we can explore and understand what you are looking for, and work out if I am the right fit for you.

SIGN UP TO MY MAILING LIST
FOLLOW ME ON SOCIAL MEDIA

If you would like to access more regular updates from me in video or visual format, head over to Instagram and TikTok to follow my profiles. On both profiles, I share tips, tools, and techniques across a whole range of issues. I also provide theoretical knowledge and insights into the areas of mental health and psychology to help followers gain a better understanding of the human psyche.

Additionally, you can sign up to my weekly newsletter, where you can be the first to know about new offerings, books, courses I am running, as well as gain access to free resources. Either search **@JackCDWilliamson** on TikTok & Instagram or scan the QR code below to follow me and sign up to my newsletter.

ACKNOWLEDGMENTS

First and foremost I would like to thank Mandy Plumb, for unknowingly getting me out of a funk and inspiring me through your own work, to write this book. Without you, this book would not have been made. To my mentors, Hugh Goldsmith, Adrianna Irvine, Lou Lebentz and Paul Hokemeyer and Christian Tattersfield, thank you for continuing to help me look within and become a better person. Emily Lewis, thank you for editing this book, and for all the fun things we've done over the years around the world. Will Hooson, thank you for helping with the recording of the audiobook, there's probably enough bloopers to make a second audiobook. Your patience and understanding is eternally appreciated. Joe Lever and Amy Hancock, thank you for all your creativity in designing the artwork and all the accompanying pieces.

Kelly Thatcher, thank you for being such a source of joy and making my working days more enjoyable, with your humour, wisdom and always delivering the tea. Nirvana, thank you for always being there and providing me with a sounding board, to share my thoughts with. Kate Foster-Berry, I can't wait to see Kate At The Tate, and thank you for continuing to have me be your muse. Stephen Woods, what can I say. The adventures we've had and will continue to have. Thank you for being you. Anthony Hurd, I'm so proud of you starting your own business and I can't wait to see what Level 4 brings. Caitlin Geehan, for being my sister from another mister. For always making me laugh with the tea, and our go to expressions 'Well Shit' and ' Don't you be putting that trauma all up in my head.'

Justina Parry and Jo Joslin, you two beautiful ladies, brighten up my darkest days. Wayne Russell 'D'ya know what…' the tea is always piping hot with you, and I love you for it. Jevan Levy, thank you for being my soul brother and for the best hugs a human can give. Mel Redmond, for being able to put to words how I feel, without saying a word. June Allen, my therapist and business sister from another mister, thank you for always inspiring me to be the best version of myself. David Palmstrom, I always look forward to our brunches and seeing how our careers evovle. Sarita Tamber and Liana Bullard, thank you for your humour and for being the best studying partners one could ask for. Rose for always keeping it real.

To my mum, for putting up with me for 40 years, I definitely am the problem, but I continue to try and work on that. Maria Williams, I've loved getting to know you and Lily these past few years, it's a shame it took losing my dad to do so, but every cloud has a silver lining.

Sharon Eccles, I've never laughed so much in my life as I have with you. You and Halima, have been the gift that will forever keep giving. Lizzie Townsend, thank you for your creative genius and bringing my website to life. Leah Stockford, thank you for always being with me on this writing journey, it's such a solo journey, so it comforts me to know you are there alongside me. Stefan Demetriou, thank you for friendship and guidance, as I begin to carve my way into the world of TV.

Sarah Hall, you my dear are a comedic genius. I can't wait for the sitcom. Kelly Betts aka Pocket Rocket Princess aka K-T-B, you are the sister I never had, and Reggie the son I never wanted haha-haha. Frank and Ivanna Borin, I am so grateful to have you in my life, here's to many more adventures with you both. Tanu and Nikita, it's been an honour getting to know you. Ellie Rapaport thank you for being a beacon of light in this dark world, for standing up and speaking out when others won't. Sam Tewari, thank you for making me a better person.

Ginger, Madillac, Courtney, Reggie, Killian, Lisa, Robert, Francis, Cyndie, Mandy, Danielle, Dame Judy Davis and all the extended relations, thank you for accepting me into your family, and for being my American family when I am away from home. Jason, thank you for all your insights, I'm excited for the next chapter of your life, after WeHo.

To the TrekFit community, including John, Richard, Richard Burke, Trevor, Typhoon, thank you for creating a space for me to switch off and reconnect with nature. To the Until community including Masterpiece Rhys, Brad the Grad, Blue Tick Nick, Breathwork Sam, Lauren Double-Nose Ring, thank you for making a working environment so enjoyable.

And last but by no means least, Jin Jin. Thank you for being my guardian angel. Your kindness, compassion and genuine support for other people, are just three of the thousands of amazing qualities you have. I will forever be indebted to you.

BIBLIOGRAPHY

CHAPTER 1

Coffey, D. (2022) Does The Human Body Replace Itself Every Seven Years? Available at: Live Science

Psychology Today (2011) How Often Do People Lie In Their Daily Lives. Available at: Psychology Today

CHAPTER 2

Anderson Live. (2012) Hypnotised Woman Forgets The Number 7. Available at: YouTube

Abhang, P. (2016) Introduction to EEF and Speech-Based Emotion Recognition. Science Direct. Academic Press. London.

Peterson, C. (2021) What is your earliest memory? It depends. *Memory*.

Rai, J. (2022) If you have a brain you have a bias. But why? Robert Walkers Group. Available At: Website

Erikson, E. (1998) The Life Cycle Completed. W.W Norton & Company. London.

Melinosky, C. (2023) What To Know About Gamma Brain Waves. WebMD. Available at: WebMD

Coogan, M. (2001) The New Oxford Anotated Bible; New Revised Standard Edition (Luke 23:34).

Dilts, R (2018) NLP II: The Next Generation. Dilts Strategy Group. London.

Hale, K. (2019) 10 Of The Worlds Greatest Achievements To Come Out Of The Bathroom. Available at: Mira Showers

CHAPTER 3

Bowlby, J. (1969) Attachment and Loss. Pimlico. London.

Heller, R. Et al. (2011) Attached. Bluebird. NYC.

Dumitru, O. (2023) What Do Americans Say About Their Attachment Styles. Available at: YouGov

Guy-Evans, O. (2023) Repetition Compulsion. Why Do We Repeat The Past. Available At: Simple Psychology

Ayala, D. (2022) The Four Types Of Dependency In Relationships. Available At: Psych To Go

Beattie, M. (1997) Codependency No More. Bluebird. NYC.

West, C. (2020) The Karpman Drama Triangle Explained.

CHAPTER 4

Carter, T. (2021) The True Failure Rate Of Small Businesses. Available at: Entrepreneur

Robbins, A. (2001) Awaken The Giant Within. Simon & Schuster. UK.
Gottman, J. (2023) The Seven Principles For Making A Marriage Work. Orion Spring. NYC.
CBS (2016) US Presidential Debate. Available at: CBS News
Trump, M. (2020) Too Much And Never Enough. Simon & Schuster. UK.
Saad, L. (2016) Trump and Clinton Finish With Historically Poor Images. Available at: Gallup
Gladwell, M. (2002) The Tipping Point. Abacus. NYC.
Turnauer, M. (2019) Where's My Roy Cohn. Sony Pictures Classics.
Robbins, M. (2017) The Five Second Rule. Post Hill Press. NYC.
Perel, E. (2023) Where Shall We Begin. Esther Perel Global Media. Available at: Where Shall We Begin
Sifers, S.(2006) Abnormal Psychology. Collins College Outlines. NYC.

CHAPTER 5

Manku, M (2021) Critical Caste Theory: The Caste System In Indian Hindus. Amazon. UK.
O'Brien, V. (2023) Unpacking Takk Poppy Syndrome ANd Australias Love-Hate Relationship With Success. Available at: Refinery 29
Sandemose, A. (1933) A Futitive Crosses His Tracks. Themis Forlag. Sweden.
Ferriss, T. (2017) Tribe Of Mentors. Vermillion. NYC.
Japan (1947) The Constitution Of Japan. Available at: Japan Government
Meyer, E. (2016) The Culture Map. Public Affairs. NYC.
Pack, S (2022) The Truth About American Tourists. Available at: Telegraph
Hertz, N. (2020) The Lonely Century. Sceptre. UK.
Wylie, C. (2019) Mindf*ck. Cambridge Analytica and the Plot to break America. Random House. UK

CHAPTER 6

Twenge, J. (2023) Generations. Simon & Schuster. NYC.
William Strauss et al (1992) Generations: The History Of Americas Future, 1584 to 2069. William Morrow & Co. NYC.
Life Course Associates (2014) Generational Archetypes. Available at: Life Course
Mannheim (2013) Ideology and Utopia. Routledge. London.
Ortega, J. Et al (1931) The Revolt Of The Masses. Routledge. London.
Mill, J. (2004) The autobiography of John Stuart Mill. Neeland Media. NYC.

Life Course Associates (2011) The Generational Diagonal. Life Course
Carlsson, S. Et al. (2021) The Spotify Play. Diversion Books. UK.
IFPI (2023) Global Music Report. Available at: Music Industry Stats
Gladwell, M. (2009) Outliers. Penguin. UK.
Forbes (2024) Real Time Billionaire List. Available at: Forbes
Watson, S. (2022) The History Of HIV treatment. Available at: WebMD

CHAPTER 7

Burgo, J. (2018) Shame. Watkins Publishing. UK.
Bradshaw, J (2006) Healing The Shame That Binds You. Health Communications. UK.
Lebentz, L. (2023) The Voyage. Available At: Voyage Academy
Lancer, D (2019) Individual and Marital Therapy with Narcissists. Available at Psychology Today
Low, A (2000) Intellectualisation. Available at: Recovery Inc

CHAPTER 8

Luft, J. (1969) Of Human Interaction. Mayfield Publishing. UK.
Famakinwa, j. (2012) Is The Unexamined Life Worth Living? Cambridge Press. UK.

CHAPTER 9

Thom, S (2019) Why Do I Feel Like an Imposter. Vibrance Press. London.
Pauline Clance et al (1972) The Imposter Phenomenon In High Achieving Women. Available at: Article
Eruteya, K (2022) You're Not An Imposter, You're Pretty Amazing. Available at: HBR
Young, V. (2011) The Secret Thoughts Of Successful Women. Crown Currency. London.
MacNaught, S (2022) Imposter Syndrome: The Numbers. Available at: Article
Dixon, S (2023) Daily Social Media Usage Worldwide. Available at: Statista
Mann, S. (2016) The Science Of Boredom. Robinson. UK
Seligman, M. (2018) Learned Optimism. Nicholas Brealey
Rogers, C. (1977) On Becoming A Person. Robinson. UK.
Sandberg, S. (2015) Lean In. WH Allen. San Fransisco.
Tom Hanks
Schultz, H. (2012) Onward. Rodale Incorporated. Seattle.
Landy, M (2014) Social Media Users Feel Jealous. Available at: Scope
Wilding, M. (2022) The Five Different Types Of Imposter Syndrome. Available at: The Muse

CHAPTER 10

Dicker, N. (2014) Does Success In One Area Mean Failure In Another. Available at: Medium

Ferriss, T. (2016) Tools Of Titans. Vermillion. NYC.

Rhimes, S. (2014) Dartmouth University Commencment Speech. Available at: Dartmouth

Drucker, P. (2007) The Effective Executive. Routledge. UK.

Koch, R. (2022) The 80/20 Principle. Nicholas Brealey Publishing. UK.

Robbins, T. (2017) Unleash The Power Within. Available at: UTPW

McKeown, G (2021) Essentialism. Virgin Books. NYC.

Hokemeyer, P. (2019) Fragile Power, Why Having Everything Is Never Enough. Hazelden Publishing. NYC.

Pareto, V. (1906) Pareto Principle. Available at: Pareto

CHAPTER 11

Feldman, M. Et al. (2007) Eating Disorders in Diverse Lesbian, Gay and Bisexual Populations. Available at National Library of Medicine

Drink Aware (2023) The Sober Myth. Available at: Drink Aware

American Academy Of Facial Plastic and Reconstructive Surgery (2020) The Selfie Endures and Is Stronger Than Ever. Available at: AAFPRS

Orbach, S. (2023) Weight Watchers wins when our diets fail. Available at: Guardian

Kelly, J. Et al. (2019) How Many Recovery Attempts Does It Take To Successfully Resolve An Alcohol or Drug Problem? Available at National Library Of Medicine

Howley, E. (2023) Why Most New Years Resolutions Fail. Available at: US News

APA (2012) What You Need To Know About Will Power. Available at: American Psychological Association

ASTD (2022) You'll Be 95% More Successful With This One Leadership Trick. Available at: ASTD

Abdal, A. (2016) Expectations/Hopes vs Training. Available at: Archilochus

Todd, M. (2016) Straight Jacket. Penguin. UK.

CHAPTER 12

Syed, M. (2016) Black Box Thinking. John Murray. NYC.

Klein, G. (2017) Seeing What Others Don't. Nicholas Brealey Publishing. NYC

Tannenbaum, R. Et al. (2012) I Want My MTV. Penguin. NYC.

Dailey, H (2023) Million Selling Albums. Available at: Billboard

Oppelaar, J. (2001) Jive Jumps In 2000. Available at: Variety

Hanks, C (2015) All Things Must Pass - The Rise and Fall Of Tower Records. Gravitas Ventures. NYC.

Seckler, C. (2019) Major Corporate files have more in common than you'd think. Available at: Conversation

BIBLIOGRAPHY

Randolph, M. (2019) That Will Never Work. Endeavour. LA.

TFR (2021) The Rise and Fall of Top Shop. Available at: TFR

Eley, J. (2023) Primark Resists Move Online Despite Pandemic Shock. Available at: Financial Times

Fussell, C. Et al. (2015) Team Of Teams. Penguin. NYC.

Campaign Monitor (2022) What Is The Average Open Rate On Emails. Available at: Campaign Monitor

Slater, D. (2020) Elements Of Amazon's Day 1 Culture. Available at: Amazon

D'Onfro, J. (2015) The Truth About Google's Famous '20% Time' Policy. Available at: Business Insider

De Bono, E. (1999) Six Thinking Hats. Little Brown. Boston.

Printed in Great Britain
by Amazon